£7.95
34

Advanced Machine Code Techniques for the BBC Micro

Also by A. P. Stephenson

Discovering BBC Micro Machine Code
0 246 12160 2

Other Granada books for BBC Micro users

Introducing the BBC Micro
Ian Sinclair
0 246 12146 7

The BBC Micro: An Expert Guide
Mike James
0 246 12014 2

Word Processing for Beginners
Susan Curran
0 246 12353 2

BBC Micro Graphics and Sound
Steve Money
0 246 12156 4

6502 Machine Code for Humans
Alan Toothill and David Barrow
0 246 12076 2

Practical Programs for the BBC Micro
Owen and Audrey Bishop
0 246 12405 9

21 Games for the BBC Micro
Mike James, S. M. Gee and Kay Ewbank
0 246 12103 3

Disk Systems for the BBC Micro
Ian Sinclair
0 246 12325 7

Advanced Machine Code Techniques for The BBC Micro

A. P. Stephenson
and D. J. Stephenson

GRANADA
London Toronto Sydney New York

Granada Technical Books
Granada Publishing Ltd
8 Grafton Street, London W1X 3LA

First Published in Great Britain by
Granada Publishing 1984

Copyright © 1984 A. P. Stephenson and D. J. Stephenson

British Library Cataloguing in Publication Data
Stephenson, A. P.
　Advanced machine code techniques for the BBC micro.
　1. BBC Microcomputer—Programming
　I. Title　II. Stephenson, D. J.
　001.64′25　　QA76.8.B3/

ISBN 0-246-12227-7

Typeset by V & M Graphics Ltd, Aylesbury, Bucks
Printed and bound in Great Britain by
Mackays of Chatham, Kent

All rights reserved. No part of this publication may
be reproduced, stored in a retrieval system or
transmitted, in any form, or by any means, electronic,
mechanical, photocopying, recording or otherwise,
without the prior permission of the publishers.

Contents

	Preface	vii
1	Architecture of the BBC Machine	1
2	The 6502 Microprocessor	33
3	The 6502 Instructions and Addressing Modes	52
4	Handling the Resident Assembler	77
5	Multi-byte Loops	101
6	Sort Routines	113
7	Using Subroutines, Macros and Look-up Tables	157
8	Direct Screen Addressing and Hardware Scrolling	173
9	Interrupt Techniques and the User Port	193
	Appendix A: Binary and Logic	215
	Appendix B: Operating System Calls	234
	Appendix C: 6502 Complete Instruction Set	235
	Appendix D: Glossary of Terms	249
	Answers to Self Test Questions	254
	Index	257

Preface

This is the second of two books on machine code for the BBC Micro. Because the first, *Discovering BBC Micro Machine Code*, assumed only minimal prior knowledge of the subject, no attempt was made to delve into the more difficult (but powerful) addressing modes offered by the 6502 assembler. Neither was it considered prudent to devote space to hardware, even those aspects which directly influence application software such as the user port, the Tube and the 1 MHz bus.

For continuity reasons, this book, besides repairing some of the omissions mentioned above, treats many of the relevant subjects again but in more detail and, as the title suggests, from a more advanced viewpoint. The word 'advanced' should be interpreted in the relative sense – relative, that is, to the level maintained in the first book.

The elements of binary have been relegated to an appendix to prevent polluting the main text yet again. Binary, to machine code enthusiasts, is rather like the repeal of the corn laws to students of history – lacking in glamour but necessary for continuity. Many microcomputer enthusiasts have come from the ranks of the electronic hobbyist and will have an interest in computer control of electronic gadgets. However, not all readers would share their enthusiasm so, like binary, the treatment of TTL logic devices is given in an appendix also.

The self-test questions may help those who may not be too sure whether they have understood what they have read ... a situation quite common when reading any 'explanation' of microprocessor behaviour patterns.

Numerous machine code routines are included which should help readers to understand the more difficult parts of the text. Some of the lengthy programs will be found to have direct practical value, in business, educational or leisure fields. However, because it is impossible to anticipate bizarre applications, they have been written in a way which should encourage individual tailoring.

The sensible way to employ machine code in the BBC machine is to use it in segments within a BASIC program. It would be pointless, and certainly masochistic, to write entire programs in machine code. The BASIC in the BBC machine is good but there are times when the demands of speed and memory economy justify a temporary leap into machine code and back. The programs in this book, which have been well-tested, are primarily designed to be used in this way. They are indeed, no more than machine code segments. However, in order for them to RUN and to encourage experimentation, they have been spliced into an outer BASIC framework. As for the choice of programs, no apologies are made for the almost total absence of arithmetical routines. Although it is traditional to include routines for multiplication, division, etc., it is doubtful whether they are of much interest to microcomputer users.

An entire chapter, however, is devoted to sort routines because this is one of the areas where the advantage of machine code over BASIC becomes most impressive.

With regard to graphics, the reader is presented with two options, one using the resident service routines and the other using direct screen addressing. The latter option is recognised as being contrary to establishment guidance but, if there are some beneficial results to justify the risk, who cares?

A. P. and D. J. Stephenson

Chapter One
Architecture of the BBC Machine

Background material

Although not strictly essential, the would-be machine code programmer will find it helpful to take some interest in the hardware layout of the computer and the historical events which led up to the present design. Such interest need not extend to detailed electronics because it is possible to gain a fair understanding of the overall system without it.

The hardware of any microcomputer can be described as a collection of integrated circuits (chips) and a few separate (discrete) components such as resistors, capacitors and transistors stuck on a printed circuit board (the pcb). Communication with the outside world (peripherals) is via an assortment of plugs or sockets accessible from the back. Some computers may have more memory than others, may have more plugs and sockets and perhaps a few more chips than others but it would be difficult to pinpoint any profound differences in the hardware design.

von Neumann's influence

A computer, whether it is one of the mainframe giants or a small one designed for home use, will in all probability be a 'von Neumann machine' (discussed in Chapter 3). That is to say, it will be designed in accordance with fundamental principles laid down by the eminent mathematician of that name. Although it has always been fashionable to credit Charles Babbage with the 'discovery' of the computer, it is questionable whether his contraption of cogwheels and levers had any real effect on the evolution of the modern computer. It was left to von Neumann to set out the first 'block schematic', suggest the main data flow paths and the timing sequences required to build a practical automatic digital computer. Because of his contribution to computer science, John von Neumann (1903–1957) is affectionately known in many quarters as the 'father of the computer' although, like all leaders of a team, he probably received a disproportionate share of the credit.

It is sad that all great men eventually have their greatness disputed. In recent years, poor old von Neumann, or rather his principle, has been attacked. It is said by some that computing progress has been stifled by slavish adherence to his original concepts of *sequential* data flow. They argue that in spite of the enormous improvements in computer power which have taken place over the last four decades, these have been due mainly to improvements in computing *components* rather than developments in computing science. To some extent, this is true. In the case of internal memory, for instance, there is no fundamental difference between the old magnetic core memory with its thousands of ferrite rings wire-knitted together and the modern semiconductor RAM chip. Similar comparisons can be made between the central processor of the earlier machines and the modern variety. The valves gave way to discrete transistors which in turn gave way to boards full of logic chips. Eventually, the central processor, particularly in the case of the minicomputer and microcomputer, became available as the single-chip 'microprocessor'. In spite of all this it would be true to say that apart from enormous reductions in cost and size, most modern computers are not profoundly different in principle to their World War II ancestors; they are still von Neumann machines.

The computer generations
Some attempt has been made to classify computers into so-called 'generations'. The early machines which used valves belonged to the First Generation, those which used discrete transistors became the Second Generation. When integrated circuits replaced discretes the Third Generation was born (in the mid-sixties). The first integrated circuits contained between four to ten simple logic gates per chip which, at the time, was heralded as an exciting breakthrough in technology. The most famous chip in that era was the 7400 quad NAND gate, manufactured by Texas Instruments, and one of a family of chips known as the 'TTL logic series'. It is still going strong at the time of writing. Before the marvel of TTL had time to be digested, Silicon Valley in California produced its next bombshell – 'Large Scale Integration' or LSI which earned the name of the Fourth Generation. LSI chips were first produced as semiconductor read/write memories. They were in fact 'dynamic RAMs' and were directly responsible for the virtual death of the traditional core memory.

The microprocessor
In 1971, Intel launched the first *microprocessor* which, quite unexpectedly, changed the entire nature of computing. It was unexpected in the sense that the device was never intended to be used in any other way than as a *control element* in digital-operated machinery. Instead, the 4004 sparked off a full scale development spree as engineers began to appreciate the enormous potential of such a device. Silicon Valley became split into fragments, with new firms each rushing to improve on the success of the 4004. The first improvement was Intel's 8080, closely followed by Motorola's 6800 and the

Zilog Z80. The microprocessor used in the BBC machine is the 6502 which, as we shall see later, may be considered as a modified 6800. Apart from the original 4004, which was a four-bit microprocessor, the others mentioned above are eight bits wide or, to use technical language, they have a 'word length' of eight-bits. This means that all data transfers into or out of the microprocessor take place in bunches of eight binary bits. In relation to the more traditional computers, a word length of eight bits is embarrassingly small and places a heavy responsibility on the designer of the software operating system. It is complicated process to handle data efficiently, particularly when the data is in the form of 'large' numbers greater than 255 decimal. The only way it can be done is to handle numbers by eight-bit instalments which is time-consuming and therefore reduces computing power.

16-bit microprocessors
Over the last few years, a number of 16-bit microprocessors have appeared on the market although they have yet to enjoy the low prices resulting from mass marketing. Owners of the BBC machine will be aware of the Second Processor options, one of which is boasting the presence of a 16-bit microprocessor, the 16032. Not only is the 16032 a true 16-bit chip, some of the internal registers can handle 32 bits at a time. The resulting power of the BBC machine will then be equivalent to a minicomputer, rather than a microcomputer. When considering the cost of the 16-bit second processor (which admittedly is rather high) it should be remembered that the computing power available will be out of this world – at least the microcomputing world. Those who are considering the purchase of the Second Processor option would be advised to think carefully before buying the 'cheaper' 8-bit versions. They will be using either another 6502 or a Z80. Of course, there will be a great improvement, apart from the extra 64K of memory but the improvement will not be revolutionary. The 16-bit version will cost more than twice as much but will elevate the system to an entirely new dimension. From the viewpoint of the machine code programmer, the advantages will be even more apparent. It is dangerous to prophesy future market tendencies but it is quite probable that there will be an astonishing demand for the 16-bit processor. In fact, it may be a case of history repeating itself. The original miscalculation was the false estimate of the relative popularities of the Model A and the Model B. In spite of the £100 extra in price, the demand for the Model B was much higher than for the Model A, and was one of the factors which contributed to the chaos during the launching year of the BBC system.

Software development
Improvements in software have not kept pace with hardware improvements. It is unlikely that they ever will. Machines are being built with frightening power and it is becoming increasingly difficult to produce

software of sufficient complexity to exploit fully the hardware available. The computing world is currently obsessed with the new breed of computers being designed, alleged to have built-in *intelligence*. These will represent the *Fifth Generation*. Already we are subjected to a new crop of buzzwords relating to 'artificial intelligence' or AI. Whether or not it is sensible to credit a computer (even a fifth generation species) with intelligence before even humans have agreed on a definition of their own intelligence is questionable. In any case, what is exactly meant by 'artificial'? Perhaps we shall soon have artificial plastic!

Hardware of the BBC Micro

Although the User Guide and the advertisement brochures list all the various input/output facilities available, it will do no harm to repeat some of it here with some extra details aimed at the machine code programmer. When programming in BASIC, or indeed any high level language, it is not necessary, perhaps not even advisable, to worry much about the mysteries under the bonnet. In the case of machine code programming you cannot afford to be totally ignorant of the machine itself. Although the resident assembler provides some protection from the harsh realities of life beneath the keyboard it is still very much a game of battling directly with a primitive machine.

Removing the top cover

Even if you have no experience with electronic equipment you should not hesitate to remove the top cover of the machine and have a good look at what lies beneath. It is an easy task if carried out as follows, although it should be pointed out that technically the guarantee would be invalidated – so be very careful!

(1) Switch off at the wall and *remove* the three-pin plug from the socket.
(2) Wait for half a minute to allow stored charges to decay.
(3) Locate the two fixing screws at the back of the case (probably marked FIX) and remove them.
(4) Locate the two fixing screws underneath the case at the front, beneath the keyboard (probably marked FIX), and remove them.
(5) Carefully lift away the top case, exposing the circuit board beneath.

When ready to replace the cover again, take care that you don't bend or damage the three tiny red lights at the left of the space-bar. They are supported only by their own connecting wires and it is easy to trap them beneath the cover.

Locating the components

The dominant sight, when first exposing the interior, is the shiny

Architecture of the BBC Machine 5

aluminium (or perhaps steel) box which occupies a large area at the left. This is the 'power pack' which converts the dangerously high (230-240 volts) mains supply into low voltages supplying power to the various components on the circuit board. The supplies are +5V at 3.75A,-5V at 0.1A, +12V at 1.25A. All these voltages are with respect to ground (zero volts). Such low voltages are not dangerous so all areas of the board outside the metal cased power pack offer no electric shock hazards to the human finger. In spite of this, it is unwise to poke around too much because your fingers could cause damage to some of the delicate components on the board. Some of the chips, particularly the large ones, are very susceptible to static charges which can accumulate on the fingers although, theoretically, they are immune once they are secured in the circuit board.

At the top right-hand corner is a small metal box marked with the manufacturer's trade mark ASTEC. This is the UHF modulator which, if you are relying on a TV as the screen output device, modulates the logic voltages from the board onto an ultra high frequency signal, which is interpreted by the TV as a bona fide aerial signal. The output is via a coaxial cable outlet at the back marked UHF OUT. If you are using a purpose-built monitor rather than a TV, there are two alternative outputs. One of these is a 'composite video' marked VIDEO OUT and is intended to accommodate some makes of black and white monitors. The interface components include one of the few discrete transistors used. According to the circuit details on page 504 of the User Guide it appears impossible to obtain colour output unless a small modification is made. The remaining screen output is the RGB (Red Green Blue) interface and is the most efficient method of energising a colour monitor, providing a direct and uncluttered signal. The Microvitec colour monitor would use the RGB output.

Sending characters to screen output

As far as machine code programming is concerned, irrespective of the particular output in use, characters can be sent direct to a screen address by use of an STA instruction or, preferably, by OSWRCH. It is appreciated that these code words will have little meaning to those who are entirely new to machine code. STA in machine code is similar to POKE and OSWRCH is a resident operating system subroutine, standing for Operating System WRite CHaracter. Our reason for prematurely introducing these machine code terms is to emphasise a golden guideline of the BBC machine:

> Always use the official operating system subroutines to send or receive data to peripherals.

This means avoiding absolute addressing of peripherals (no poking). Note carefully that this is a guideline and not a rule. The reason behind it is tied up with the second processor – should you ever buy one. Any software you write using absolute and addressing of peripherals may not work when the second processor is connected. It should be mentioned that direct access to screen addresses will produce faster responses than using OSWRCH.

The ROM chips

Once the top case has been removed, as previously described, the keyboard can be lifted off by undoing the two exposed nuts. If the removal is merely to examine the components beneath, it is not essential to unplug the keyboard. In fact it is unwise to plug and unplug any microcomputer connections more frequently than necessary. Beneath the keyboard to the right and near the bottom are five sockets for ROM chips. Except for the few thousand early models, only two of these sockets will be inhabited. The socket at the extreme left houses a 16-pin ROM which is the BASIC language interpreter. Next to this is the Operating System ROM. You should ensure that this ROM is the 'latest Series 1' model because some of the earlier types had a slightly suspect operating system called 'Version 0.1'. It is easy to find out which operating system you have by entering *HELP followed by RETURN. The response should be:

OS 1.20

A response such as OS 0.1 indicates that the old ROM is resident.

Bank-switching

The remaining three sockets are left blank for additional ROMs. There are many firms which supply special ROMs which can be plugged into the vacant sockets: for example, Acorn's word processor called 'View' or the other popular word processor called 'Wordwise' marketed by Computer Concepts. There are also several language ROMs available and many application ROMs. The total direct addressing space available on the 6502 microprocessor is 64K. The operating system takes 16K, the BASIC language ROM occupies another 16K and the remaining 32K on the Model B machine is devoted to RAM. This means there is no direct addressing space left for any additional ROMs. The method employed to escape from the impasse is a technique known as bank-switching. This allows the resident BASIC language ROM to be 'switched out' and replaced by one of the special ROMs. Thus it is an 'A or B but not both' situation. Bank-switching is software-controlled which normally defaults to BASIC under power-up conditions. However, if additional ROMs are in place, the operating system will be aware of it (or them) and the new default condition on power-up is to the ROM in the right-most position. For example, if Wordwise is plugged into any one of the vacant sockets, the default condition on power-up will be Wordwise instead of BASIC. To switch over to BASIC it will be necessary to enter *BASIC or the abbreviated form *B.

The response to the BASIC command *HELP will now be modified as follows:

WORDWISE

OS 1.20

The response indicates that Wordwise has priority over BASIC on power-up because it is displayed first. If the relative priorities are found in practice to be irksome the situation can easily be changed by swopping over the two ROMs so that the BASIC ROM is right-most. The unprecedented popularity of the BBC machine has stimulated professional programmers with the result that many other high-level languages are available in ROM form including PASCAL, FORTH and LISP.

PROM programmers
An alternative use for the spare sockets is to enable you to insert your own EPROMs. They can be bought in blank form; that is to say, they have no programs 'firmed' in. With the aid of special kits called EPROM programmers, it is possible to transfer a machine code program from RAM to the EPROM which can then be plugged into one of the spare sockets. There is one small snag, however. Make sure that all bugs are removed before you transfer it to EPROM because you cannot change parts of the program. It is an all or nothing process. If there is a bug in the EPROM, it is necessary to erase the entire contents and start again. The erasure process requires the chip to be exposed for a certain time in a special box containing an ultra-violet lamp. A fully erased EPROM contains '1's in every bit position so all the addressed locations contain FF (hex). A discussion on hex notation appears in Chapter 3.

The user port

The BBC machine has standard interfaces for printers, disk, cassette etc. and also caters for individual needs by means of the *user port*. This is a multipin socket outlet accessible from the underside of the case. It is completely undedicated and is therefore free to activate any device you choose – providing you know how to make the correct connections and are able to write suitable software.

Although the port behaves as an independent set of outlets, it is actually one half of a complex input/output chip called a Versatile Interface Adaptor (VIA for short) bearing the type number 6522. The two halves of the VIA are reffered to as the 'A' and 'B' sides. The B side is dedicated to the parallel printer interface and the A side is the user port. The port is essentially a ten-wire interface between the computer and the world outside. Eight of the wires are used for data and two for controlling the data. Any one of the data wires can be programmed to behave as either an input or an output, which obviously adds to the versatility. It is worth examining some of the possibilities:

(1) Assuming a device could be switched ON or OFF by simple logic, we could independently control eight of them. They would all be programmed initially as *outputs*.
(2) Any one of eight devices could send a logic signal back to the computer. They would all require initial programming as *inputs*.
(3) Three devices could be controlled by the computer and five could send signals back.
(4) By employing simple decoding chips, it would be possible to control any one of 256 output devices. Conversely, any one of 256 devices could send a signal to the computer.
(5) Two devices each requiring four inputs could be driven in parallel.

With regard to the two control wires mentioned above, one is always an input but the other can be programmed as an input or output. The input control wire can be used to initiate an *interrupt* sequence. That is to say, an input signal can cause the present program to be interrupted and a jump made to an entirely different program. (Interrupts are discussed in Chapter 2.) The use of interrupts can be a hazardous exercise because the entire operating system is already controlled by interrupts. For example, when the computer is switched on and a flashing cursor is displayed, the machine appears docile and in a resting state. This is far from true. In fact there is a furious battle going on in the operating system. Every few milliseconds, the display system rudely interrupts whatever is going on (most probably waiting for a key to be pressed) to repaint the screen picture. The screen display only appears stationary to the eye because every single dot, which makes up the 'picture', is repainted many times per second. Due to the persistence of normal vision, a screen picture need only be repainted every few milliseconds so there is ample time in between for the computer to carry out your orders in a series of interrupted instalments.

Interrupt requests

If the order involves the use of a peripheral, such as a cassette tape recorder or a printer, it is probable that the operating system will handle them by yet another interrupt sequence. The question of relative priorities then arises. For example, what should happen if the printer sends a signal to interrupt while the system is already in an interrupt condition, such as repainting the screen?

In real life, the needs of certain people have priority claims over the needs of others in order to maintain a well-ordered, stable society. A similar arrangement has been found to work well in computing systems. Certain interrupts must be considered to have higher precedence than others and permission to interrupt must be granted first rather than allowing a disorganised free-for-all. The 6502 microprocessor is fitted with *interrupt-request* logic which, in conjunction with appropriate software, can maintain tranquillity. When an interrupt request signal from a peripheral appears on a control input line, it is passed, via the VIA, to the microprocessor. A certain bit in the processor (called the 'interrupt mask bit') is examined. If the mask bit is a '0', the interrupt is allowed. If, however, the bit is in the '1' state the request is noted but activation is delayed until such time as the mask bit is reset to zero. The actual setting or resetting of the mask bit is, of course, the responsibility of the programmer. We shall see later that the 6502 microprocessor has two instructions for defining the state of the mask bit. To set the mask to '1', the instruction is SEI (SEt I bit). To reset the mask to '0', the instruction is CLI (CLear I bit). The mask is referred to as the 'I bit' in 6502 language.

Serial and parallel interfaces

Most computers, including the BBC model, use the ASCII code to represent characters. Each character requires one byte (a byte is eight binary bits). There are two ways of sending these characters along wires to, say, a printer some distance away:

(a) *Parallel transmission*, in which eight wires are used to send every bit of the code simultaneously.
(b) *Serial transmission*, in which the eight bits are sent, one behind the other, along a single wire.

It is worth examining the relative merits of the two systems because the BBC machine provides provisions for both serial and parallel feeding of peripherals. Superficially, it would appear that parallel transmission would be much faster, eight times faster than serial. This is true but in most cases, particularly where printers are concerned, the difference is seldom of any interest because the weakest link in the chain is the printer rather than the transmission delay along the wires. Thus, if we run the same printer by serial transmission and then change to parallel (assuming the printer allows either option) we will find no difference in printing speed. The cogs and levers still take up more than 99% of the printing time. Traditionally, serial transmission dominated the scene, particularly for feeding the now almost obsolete Teletype, a two-way device which combined a sending keyboard, a paper tape reader/punch and a printer. It was Centronics, a company which specialises in printers, which contributed to the popularity of the parallel transmission. In fact, their design for allocating the various control functions has been copied and virtually standardised by what is known as the Centronics interface. The BBC has a parallel Centronics interface although it is simply labelled above the socket as the 'Printer'.

The RS423 interface

The BBC Micro also has provisions for a serial interface via the socket labelled 'RS423' which now deserves some explanation. As stated above, the Teletype was the standard peripheral in earlier days and the serial interface was known as the '20mA current loop' because it demanded a current of 20 milliamps from the computer to drive the printer relays. This was in the days when computers were massive things and 20 milliamps was a negligible drain on the relatively enormous power supplies of the time. When logic chips arrived on the scene, operating on almost negligible current, 20 milliamps just to drive the printer started to become almost absurd. One of the results was the formation of a new serial 'standard' called the RS232 interface which demanded only a small current drive. In fact it would be better to consider it as a voltage rather than a current-driven system. The RS423 interface is almost identical (in fact compatible) with the RS232 but in many respects it is superior. There is always an upper limit on the length of wires between the sending and receiving end of a serial transmission line. The RS423 allows a longer length than the RS232.

Although the printer has featured in the above discussion on the RS423, it is a general purpose *interrupt driven* interface, capable of linking any device which requires a serial interface. For example, it can be used to connect two BBC machines together so they can mutually converse with each other. Figure 1.1 shows the interconnections required between the two sockets. In addition to the wiring shown, small software routine is necessary before the two machines can talk to each other.

The serial nature of RS423 data requires some rather complex logic operations. One difficulty, inherent in all serial transmissions, is the method of establishing some form of marker signal to indicate the three distinct parts of the message – for example, the quiescent state in between characters, the start of a character and its end. This is handled by the 'start' and 'stop' bits at either end of the 8-bit character string. For some time now, manufacturers of microprocessors have always supplied ready-made

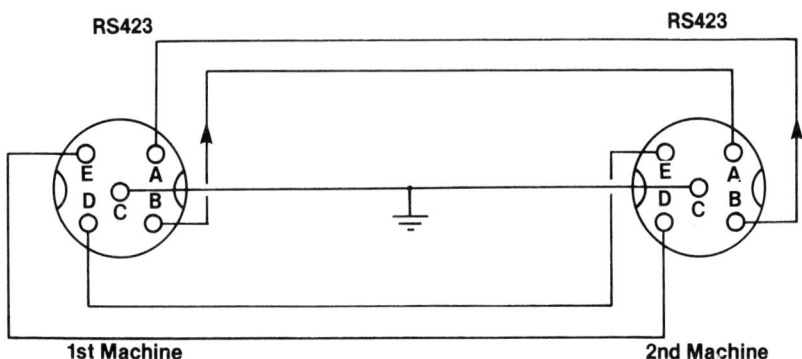

Fig. 1.1. Connecting two BBC machines together.

solutions to such problems in the shape of specialised chips. The common name for the class of chip which handles the serial transmission of data is 'Asynchronous Serial Interface Adaptor' (ASIA for short). The particular species in the BBC machine is the 6850. This chip converts the 8-bit parallel output from the computer data bus into serial form. It also generates the start and stop bits, together with the correct timing circuitry. The 6850 is to serial interfacing as the 6522 is to parallel; that is to say, the ASIA and the VIA are serial and parallel interfaces respectively.

Analogue to digital conversion

Digital computers are designed to operate in a restricted, but nevertheless predictable, *two-state* environment. Voltages are either in the '1' state (about +5 volts) or in the '0' state (about 0 volts). Conditions in the world outside have no such restrictions. Physical variables, such as wind, temperature, pressure, electrical voltages etc., can assume a wide range of values. A voltage which somehow is made proportional to a particular physical quantity is called a *voltage analogue* of that quantity. Thus, if a wind velocity over the range 0 to 100 miles per hour were represented by a voltage between 0 and 10, the scaling factor would be 10 miles per volt. The particular gadget which converted the wind speed to voltage would be termed a *transducer* and, in its most simple form, could be an electrical generator with the shaft driven by wind blades. Linearity of the scale would obviously depend on a strictly proportional relationship between shaft speed and output voltage. However, a program could easily be written to account for non-linearity in any transducer.

The BBC machine has a special analogue to digital input socket marked 'Analogue In'. It enables any one of four analogue input channels to be converted to a digital number. Unfortunately, this facility, if some of the popular computing magazines are to be believed, appears to be used almost entirely for waggling games paddles. This is a pity because the interface is suitable for a wide range of applications. Figure 1.2 shows how to wire up a simple circuit in order to experiment with the converter.

The top diagram, Fig. 1.2(a), shows the connections between a 10K potentiometer (known in electronic circles as a 'pot') and the 15-pin Analogue-In socket at the rear of the machine. It enables any voltage between 0 volts and a nominal 1.8 volts to be applied to the analogue-to-digital input by twiddling the knob on the pot. A word of warning is not out of place here. The wiring from the pot should never be soldered directly to the pins on the computer socket. Always use a plug and socket connection. There are many firms that supply the correct socket already attached to a ribbon cable. Soldering direct to the machine's Analogue-In socket is crude and unprofessional. In fact this warning applies to all external connections because there is always a danger of the leads shorting together by wisps of solder. The output from the pot is

12 Advanced Machine Code Techniques for The BBC Micro

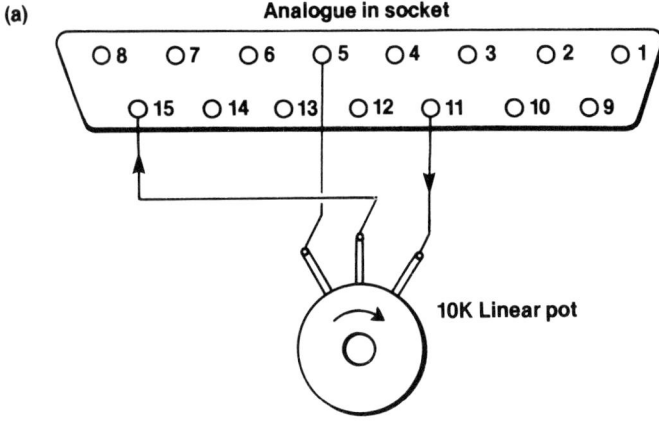

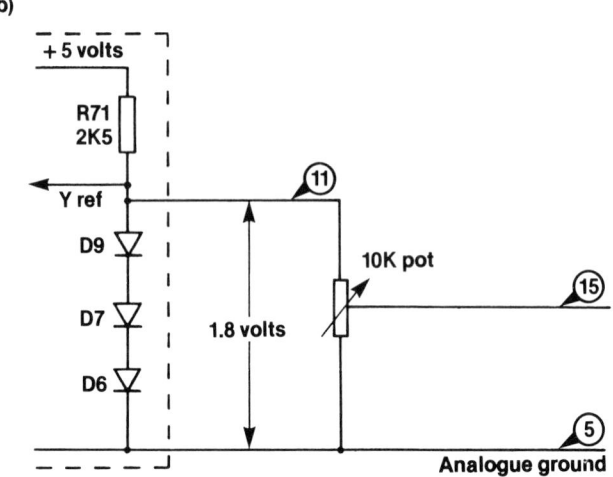

Fig. 1.2. Analogue to digital hook-up.

connected to pin 15 which is Channel 0 although there is no reason why any of the other three possible channels could not be used.

Figure 1.2(b) is for the benefit of those who feel happier if they know what they are doing. The circuitry to the left of the dotted line is within the computer. The 1.8 voltage reference line is obtained internally from a divider chain across the +5 volt supply to ground. The three silicon diodes are in series with each other, providing a total forward voltage drop of about 1.8 volts. Silicon diodes have the useful property of dropping about 0.6 volts when in forward conduction and within reason, irrespective of the current through them. However, it would be unreasonable to expect *exactly* 1.8 volts output to the pot.

The wiring can be tested out with a simple few lines in BASIC as described under the keyword ADVAL on pages 202-204 in the User Guide. (Machine code versions appear later.)

Using the four channels

The chip performing the analogue conversion to digital is an interrupt-driven D7002: a standard, but nevertheless sophisticated, component. It converts the analogue input voltage into a 12-bit binary number so each additional bit increases the number by an increment of 1/4096. It allows any one of four input voltage channels to be measured. Figure 1.3 shows how to experiment with four controlling pots.

The four pots are in parallel across the reference supply (pin 11 and 5) with sliders connected to the channel input, pins 15, 7, 12 and 4. If 10K pots are used, the total load of 2.5K is a little on the heavy side. The current limiting resistance, R71, shown previously in Fig. 1.2, causes the voltage to

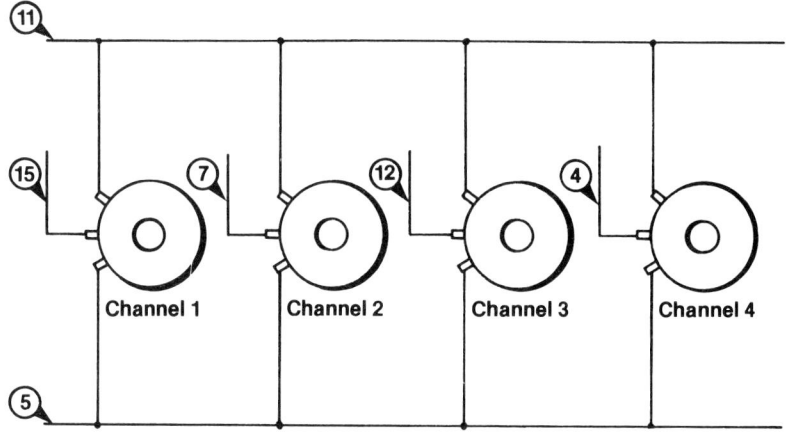

Fig. 1.3 Four-channel control.

the stabilising diodes to be pulled down to a rather low value of 2.5 volts. The next highest preferred value of pot would be a reasonable compromise. The four controls can be tested immediately by the following simple BASIC lines:

```
10 MODE 7:Channel=1
20 REPEAT
30 Analogue=ADVAL(Channel)
40 PRINT TAB(5,10+Channel)"Channel nu
mber ";Channel,Analogue
50 K=INKEY(100)
60 Channel=Channel+1
70 IF Channel>4 THEN Channel=1
80 UNTIL 2=3
```

The program will continuously display all four channel readings in the form of 5-digit decimal numbers, the readings changing as the pots are varied. Line 50 is to slow up the changes to prevent blurring. It is interesting to try out the above even if you have not wired anything to the Analogue-In socket. The display will show four numbers, varying in the region of 50000. The reason for this is the open-circuit condition of the input channels causing an indeterminate 'floating-to-high' state. As the User Guide explains (page 202), the internal operating system has allowed for possible replacement of the D7002 by a higher resolution version, so the digitised range appears as 0 to 65520 instead of 0 to 4095. As a result, the readings go up in increments of 16 rather than 1.

Floppy disk controller

Floppy disks pose a greater interfacing problem to both the hardware and software engineer than the relatively simple cassette tape backing store. A special disk controller chip, the 8271, is responsible for the primary hardware interface. The repertoire of extra commands required to make full use of the disk filing system is buried in a special ROM, known as the DOS (Disk Operating System) or the DFS (Disk Filing System). The necessary power to drive the disk motor and the disk electronics is supplied from a 40-pin socket beneath the keyboard.

Memory mapping and page numbers

The peripheral devices so far discussed are standard to the model B, with the exception of the disk interface components which are optional extras. All peripherals are memory-mapped, meaning they are all accessed as if they were normal memory locations rather than responding to special machine code instructions. Thus, the floppy disk controller chip 'resides' at the five memory locations &FE80, &FE81, &FE82, &FE83 and &FE84. The '&' prefix indicates that the numbers are in *hexadecimal* rather than decimal. The hexadecimal (hex for short) counting system is widely used in machine code work, particularly when referring to machine addresses. If hex is unfamiliar to you, see page 71 of the User Guide or skip to Appendix A of this book. A complete hexadecimal address consists of four hex digits. The first two digits are best thought of as the *page number* and the second two digits as the *position on the page*. Referring back to the five addresses occupied by the floppy disk controller, we could say they are all on page &FE of the memory map.

Sheila addresses

The machine addresses for all the peripheral interface chips so far discussed are on page &FE. This particular page has been given the rather charming name of Sheila. Thus the Sheila address band is between &FE00 to &FEFF. The positions on the page are allocated as follows:

6845 CRT controller: &FE00 to &FE01

In BASIC, this is accessed by the VDU 23 command. For example, VDU 23; R, V; 0; 0; 0 places the value V into register R of the CRT controller.

6845 ASIA: &FE08 to &FE09

This is where the parallel/serial conversion is carried out when accessing the cassette tape or the RS423.

Serial ULA: &FE10

ULA stands for 'Uncommitted Logic Array' which would imply it can be used for anything! It is one of the new breed of 'miracle' chips, containing the groundwork necessary to build a logic system of any desired form. In the initial stages of manufacture, it is rightly named an uncommitted logic array. However, before it leaves the factory the customer supplies further information which turns the previously uncommitted array into a conglomerate of committed functions. Thus, although the name ULA sticks, those in the BBC machine are certainly committed arrays. This particular ULA helps in the organisation of serial peripheral devices.

Video ULA : &FE20 to &FE21

The logic buried in this chip is responsible for much of the superb graphic and colour facilities available.

Paged ROM controller : &FE30

This is a simple *decoder* chip (74LS161) used to switch over the paged ROMs referred to earlier.

The internal VIA : &FE40 to &FE4F

There are two 6522 VIAs in the machine. This one is designated 'internal' because it is used for several purposes, indirectly concerned with the control of input and output.

The external VIA : &FE60 to &FE6F

This 6522 is dedicated to the parallel printer interface (Centronics) and the user port. The 6522 VIA consists of two, almost identical, halves. The 'A' side is committed to the printer and the 'B' side to the user port. As can be seen from the address range, the 6522 requires sixteen machine addresses in order to make full use of it. One function carried out on the 'A' side is the interrupt-driven clock used in the TIME keyword when in BASIC. The timers on the 'B' side are available for users' programs.

The floppy disk controller : &FE80 to &FE84

This is the home of the 8271 chip mentioned earlier.

Data link controller : &FEA0 to &FEA3

This is an advanced chip containing much of the logic required to control the Econet communications interface. It is part of the optional extras offered.

Analogue to digital converter : &FEC0 to &FEC2
This is the D7002 chip previously discussed.

At this point, it is worth repeating the earlier warning regarding the dangers of directly addressing any of these machine locations. However, the warning was in the nature of advice rather than a rule. There is nothing illegal in direct accessing the peripheral devices although, apart from the user port, it is unlikely that you will ever find the need to circumvent the resident operating system subroutines. The above information and addresses were primarily intended as background information. However, there will always be a few of the more intrepid readers who may feel a desire to 'improve' on the operating system, even at the risk of crashing or jeopardising the smooth running of a future second-processor.

Fred addresses and the 1 MHz Bus

Sheila addresses are concerned with what may be broadly described as standard peripherals. The BBC machine, however, caters for more ambitious schemes, such as Teletext, Prestel, dealer's test kits, etc. There is a multipin socket beneath the machine known as the '1 MHz Bus' which caters for these optional additions to the system. These are allotted addresses in the band &FC00 to &FCFF. This band (page &FC) is named Fred, a less charming name than Sheila but still quite novel. The individual allocations within Fred are as follows:

Dealer's test equipment : &FC00 to &FC0F
Testing and fault diagnosis of the BBC machine is rendered easier for dealers by a special box of tricks known as PET (no connection with Commodore's famous family of micros). PET stands for Progressive Establishment Tester and occupies sixteen locations within Fred's band.

Teletext : &FC10 to &FC13
Most readers will know that a Teletext adapter can be bought, enabling a range of free software to be down-loaded directly into the RAM locations from BBC transmissions. It is also possible to call up and incorporate any of the standard Teletext pages in your own programs. An updated list of the software available currently appears on page 701 of Teletext.

Prestel : &FC14 to &FC1F
Prestel is the Rolls Royce version of Teletext, providing access to an enormous, and still growing, storehouse of information. The information comes via the normal telephone system so it requires a *modem* (*mo*dulator and *dem*odulator). A modem provides the necessary conversion from computer logic signals to audio tones, suitable for passing down a telephone line. The coupling is acoustical, rather than wired, in order to circumvent the rules relating to unauthorised interference with telephone

Architecture of the BBC Machine 17

equipment. Prestel is two-way in action, meaning you can also send your own messages back to Prestel. There is one snag of course – you have to pay for telephone calls and also an extra charge on top for certain of the Prestel pages.

Test equipment : &FC80 to &FC8F

Some more allocations for testing purposes.

Reserved for user's applications : &FCC0 to &FCFE

There is an ever-growing range of hardware available designed to plug into the 1 MHz bus. As can be seen from above, a generous range of addresses are left vacant for the purpose, sixty-three in fact.

ROM paging register : &FCFF

This is a single byte address used for paging different ROMs. (See JIM address band.)

JIM addresses and the 1 MHz bus

The address band &FD00 to &FDFF is called JIM and is primarily designed for connecting up alternative memory chips (up to 64K of RAM or ROM) via the 1 MHz bus. Note that the word 'alternative' is used rather than 'extra' because the full 64K can only be page-accessed in competition with the resident 64K. Connecting up the memory is not a task you should attempt unless you feel confident or, preferably, have gained some experience with decoding logic (some general information on logic can be found in Appendix A). In the meantime, it is worth mentioning that the solitary address &FCFF, called the 'paging register' in the Fred band, will be found to have important significance to the decoding network.

Wiring details of the 1 MHz bus

Page 503 of the User Guide gives a diagram of the connections to the 1 MHz bus. However, a scaled down version is shown in Fig. 1.4 which tends to emphasise the decoding problem.

There are several abbreviations in the diagram which may demand translation. One of the more depressing features of computer hardware is the proliferation of abbreviations which designers use. To the designer, the letter groups may be 'plain English' because of familiarisation. To the non-expert, they present a fearsome obstacle to progress, made worse by the lack of standardisation.

The 1 MHz socket pins are labelled the same as on page 503 of the User Guide but make no attempt to show the correct orientation of the corresponding pin numbers. You must refer to the original diagram in the User Guide if you intend to use the bus. The position of the 6502 microprocessor has been included in order to gain an overall perspective of the bus. Discussion of the wiring can be treated under three headings, the *address bus*, the *data bus* and finally the *control lines*.

18 *Advanced Machine Code Techniques for The BBC Micro*

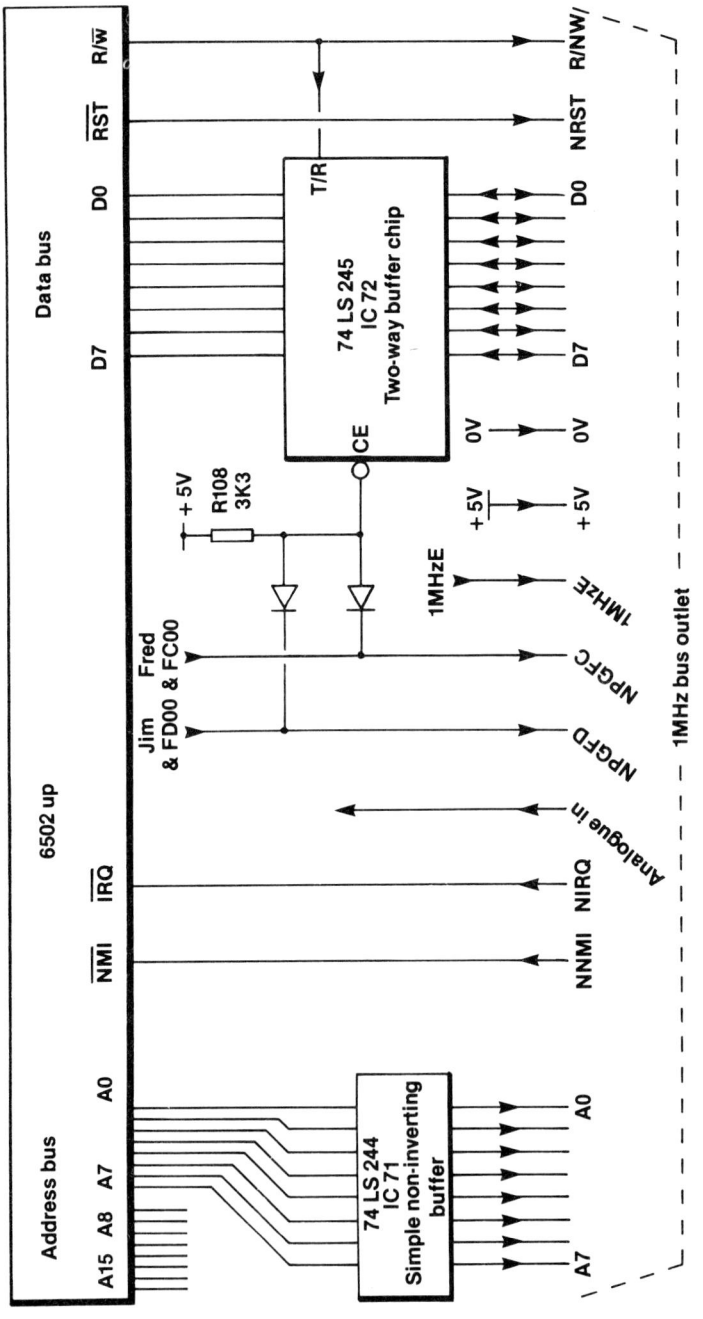

Fig. 1.4 Simplified drawing of the 1 MHz bus.

Architecture of the BBC Machine 19

The address bus
There are 16 wires on the address bus of the 6502 microprocessor, labelled A0 to A15. Only the 8 lower order wires, however, A0 to A7 are brought out to the 1 MHz bus. In order to provide the bus with high current drive, a 74LS244 non-inverting buffer (IC71) is used. The chip has no logic function but the wires are electrically stronger when they emerge. The address bus is *one-way* only. That is to say, signals can only pass from the microprocessor.

The data bus
The 8 wires, D0 to D7, from the microprocessor pass the 1 MHz bus via a *two-way* non-inverting buffer (IC72). This is a 74LS245, a more complicated buffer than the one used on the address bus because it must allow signals to pass to and from the microprocessor. Obviously, it cannot pass signals both ways at once so it must be controlled to either READ (pass data to the microprocessor) or WRITE (pass data from the microprocessor). The control terminal on the chip is labelled T/R which means 'Transmit/Receive'. Why wasn't it labelled R/W to make it tie up with READ and WRITE? The answer is due to the general purpose nature of logic chip design. A bidirectional buffer could have many uses apart from reading and writing to and from memory so it uses the wider terms 'transmit/receive'. Another control on the buffer is labelled CE which stands for 'Chip Enable'. This allows the entire chip to be switched ON/OFF or, using established jargon, *enabled* or *disabled*. Thus, the buffer can be placed in any one of three states, the READ state, the WRITE state or completely OFF altogether. When in the OFF state, the microprocessor data bus is completely unaware of its existence. It is said to be 'floating'.

The control lines
The address and data buses are well-defined entities. By comparison, the control lines of any computer system always seem an unruly mess. Odd-looking single lines carrying funny labels appear to wander around different parts of the microcomputer in an undisciplined manner. The sheer complexity of the complete microcomputer wiring means that only parts of it can be shown at once. This means that some of the control lines appear to end abruptly, only to appear again on another diagram, apparently starting from nowhere! To assist bewilderment, some of the address wires may be used to 'control' and data wires may even be used for addressing purposes. There are no short-cuts to understanding, it's merely a case of methodical plodding through each control and gradually becoming accustomed to the strange-looking abbreviations. Referring to Fig. 1.4 again and dealing with the easier parts first:

The power lines
The bus supplies a +5V and a 0V line for your external use although it is

not to be treated as an inexhaustible source of power. However, it should be ample for running extra memory and/or a reasonable collection of logic chips.

Reset line (labelled NRST)

It is important that all parts of the computer and any equipment you may add on to the 1 MHz bus begin in step with each other. The microprocessor sends out a master reset signal which, in 6502 data sheets, is labelled RST. The bar over the top is a well-standardised method of indicating reverse logic, the bar standing for the word 'not', indicating that reset action will occur on a logic 0 rather than a logic 1 (for further details on logic, see Appendix A). For some obscure reason, the 1 MHz bus uses the prefix 'N' instead of the bar, to indicate reverse logic. So the line which starts off from the microprocessor as RST, emerges out of the bus as NRST (the N meaning 'not').

Read/write control (labelled R/NW)

The 6502 microprocessor labels the line R/W. This indicates that a logic 1 on the line cause a READ and a logic 0 causes a WRITE. Note it is used to control the T/R terminal of the two-way buffer as well as providing an external line to the 1 MHz bus.

The 1 MHz clock (labelled 1 MHzE)

The source of the oscillator, known as the 'clock', is not shown. It may be required for external projects which require timing synchronisation with the resident clock system. It is worth mentioning at this point that the resident 'master clock' is 2 MHz, so external projects run at half speed. This is not a bad thing because the lower the frequency, the less critical you need be on the choice of components.

Analogue in

This allows an additional signal to be picked up and fed to the audio circuits of the computer. Any signal here is superimposed on any other audio signals. It is not an extra channel. The rms signal voltage must not exceed *3 millivolts* or distortion and possibly damage may occur.

Interrupt request (labelled NIRQ)

This caters for external projects which rely on interrupt procedures, such as an extra 6522 VIA, or perhaps the more simple 6520 PIA. It enters the microprocessor under the label $\overline{IRQ}$ which means Interrupt ReQuest. As the bar over the top shows, it recognises only a logic 0. Although not shown on the diagram, there are several other contenders for interrupt. Because there is only a single line available, the various interrupt inputs are normally wire-ored (see Appendix A).

Non-maskable interrupt (labelled as NNMI)

This is brought out for external use but using it is fraught with danger of a crash. A signal on this line could endanger the operating system which expects to have exclusive rights to it. You are strongly advised to forget that it even exists!

Fred and JIM (labelled as NPGFC and NPGFD respectively)
NPGFD stands for Not PaGE FD, indicating that it is logic 0 active. Earlier discussions on FRED and JIM described them as particular pages (&FC and &FD) in memory. It now seems odd that single wires should have similar names. The answer is that the data lines D0 to D7 on the 1 MHz bus must only be activated when either of these pages are addressed – that is to say, only when the higher order pair of the hex digit addresses are FC or FD. Figure 1.4 gives no indication of the source of the FRED and JIM wires, but it is evident that they must somehow be fed from a decoder which senses when the higher order address lines (A8 to A15) carry the binary code corresponding to &FC or &FD. Full technical drawings of the BBC machine are difficult to obtain, so Fig. 1.5 is offered as one way the decoding might have been arranged.

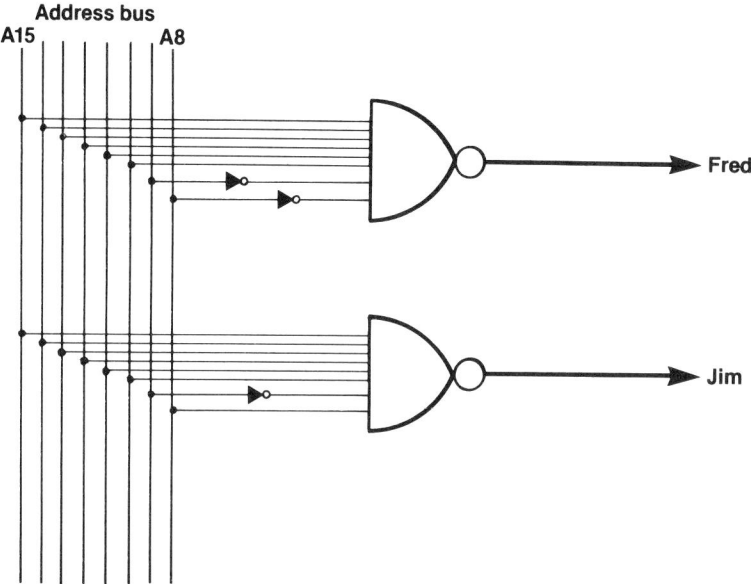

Fig. 1.5. Decoder for producing Fred and Jim.

The decoding uses NAND gates which deliver a logic 0 only when all inputs are at logic 1. The binary pattern for &FC is 1111 1100 so two logic inverters are necessary from lines A8 and A9. The binary pattern for &FD is 1111 1101 so only one logic inverter is required from address line A9.

Referring back to Fig. 1.4, the Jim and Fred lines are fed, via two diodes, to the chip enable (CE) pin on the two-way data buffer. Note that this pin has a tiny 'bubble' at the input which is a standard symbol indicating that reverse logic is required. (This explains why a NAND instead of an AND gate was used in Fig. 1.5.) Thus, the data bus is only routed to the 1 MHz bus when the chip is enabled by prior selection of Fred or Jim.

A few words of explanation may be needed with regard to the two diodes. In conjunction with the 3.3K resistor (R108), they form an OR gate for reverse logic. The register normally pulls CE high to +5 V, disabling the buffer chip. When a logic 0 from either Fred or Jim appears at the cathodes, the appropriate diode conducts and pulls the CE pin down towards 0 volts which enables it.

Suggestions for 1 MHz bus projects

The previous explanation of the bus will be interesting only to those who use, or have a yearning to construct their own extension systems. It is surprising how newcomers to machine code often become more interested in hardware projects even if they have previously showed little curiosity. This is because machine code programming probably creates more interest in computing theory and logic systems than BASIC or most high level languages. The 1 MHz bus is beautifully designed for expanding the capabilities of the machine and experimenting. It would be a shame if your socket is always left vacant and collecting dust. Assuming you have never before tackled logic design or construction, the following advice may get you started:

(1) Obtain a copy of *Application Note 1: The 1 MHz Bus* from Acorn. This gives a well detailed description of the bus although you may find it a little heavy-going in parts.

(2) Scan through magazines which cater for both hardware and software. *Electronics and Computing* is a good example, and it is usually refreshingly free from articles by games fanatics.

(3) Study Appendix A of this book and supplement it with one of the many books available on logic theory. Ian Sinclair's *Beginner's Guide to Digital Electronics* is excellent.

(4) Get a friend, or become friendly with someone, who is knowledgeable in the field of electronics. There are usually one or two of these types lurking around your local computer club. However clever you become at logic design, you may require some expertise in electrical matters, if only to avoid damage to the equipment. Soldering plugs, sockets and IC pins is not quite the simple exercise we are sometimes led to believe.

Almost any device can be switched ON or OFF by computer instructions providing it is controlled by a logic 1 or a logic 0. The device can be a simple lamp, the jib or winding gear of a crane, the points on a model railway or even one of the many chips available in the '74' series described in Appendix A. From now on, it will be assumed that the term 'device' is *logic controlled* so it is unnecessary to burden the mind with its particular function.

Address decoding

If there are several different devices, each one must have an associated code acting as an *identifier*. This code will be the device 'address'. The 1 MHz bus is equipped with address wires A0 to A7 which can be tapped for supplying the *two least significant* hex digits of the address. The *two most significant* hex digits have already been decided for us since the 1 MHz bus is restricted to page FC for device control. As explained previously, the line marked NPGFC is available on the bus to enforce this page. There are 256 different address codes possible on one page according to the binary pattern set up on A0 to A7. That is to say, the address range of our page FC extends in theory from &FC00 to &FCFF. However, we should restrict the coding of our special devices to the small band set aside for User Applications, &FCC0 to &FCFE. It is comforting to know that decoding A0 to A7 is easily achieved by special decoder chips available in the 74 series. These decoders are general purpose but skilfully designed for slipping neatly into a variety of systems. Figure 1.6 shows a possible hook up for driving any one of eight devices.

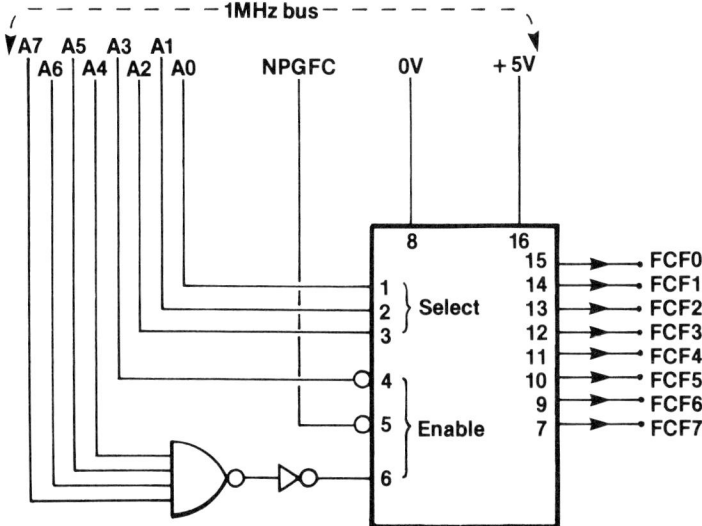

Fig. 1.6. Selecting any one of eight devices.

The 74LS138 is a well-known decoder chip. It has eight individual output lines, only one of which can be 'activated' at any one time. The output chosen to be active depends on the binary pattern applied to the three *select* lines. However, whatever the select pattern applied, the chip will still not be functional until all three *enable* lines are correctly driven. The combination of selection and enabling can be used to provide unique address decoding for each of the outputs. Working out address decoding is an art which is essential for those who intend to design their own add-on boards, so the following step-by-step explanation of Fig. 1.6 is worth studying carefully. The explanation is limited to one of the outputs (pin 15) labelled as address FCF0:

- The line NPGFC, already supplied from the 1 MHz bus, is passed directly to pin 5, pulling it down to 0 V and, because this pin has a 'bubble', is correctly enabled. Thus, apart from anything else, the chip only comes alive when the *first two* hex digits of the address are FC (Fred in other words).
- The address lines A4, A5, A6 and A7 provide the inputs to a NAND gate. This only gives logic 0 out if all four inputs are logic 1. But pin 6 requires a logic 1 to enable it (no bubble at input) so the NAND gate output is inverted in order to correctly enable pin 6. So we conclude that the *third* hex digit of the address must be F (because 1111 is F) to ensure that pin 6 is enabled. We have now established the first three hex digits of the address FCF0.
- If the last hex digit is 0, the *four* address wires A0, A1, A2 and A3 must all be logic 0. Note that A3 is connected to pin 4 which is a bubble input and enabled only by a logic 0. The remaining three address lines are connected to the select pins. The internal design of the 74LS138 is such that logic 0 on all three select pins activitates only pin 15 and is therefore correctly labelled FCF0.

Thus, to switch ON any device connected to pin 15 of the decoder chip, all we have to do is to specify address &FCF0.

If all this appears difficult, it may help if you pencilled in the binary pattern for F0 on the eight address lines as follows:

```
A7 A6 A5 A4 A3 A2 A1 A0
 1  1  1  1  0  0  0  0
```

Tracing the '1's and '0's back to the decoding chip will confirm that the chip is fully enabled (with pin 15 activated) only by the address &FCF0.

What about the other seven outputs? The only difference will be the pattern on the three select lines driven from A0, A1 and A2. The internal design of the decoder chip ensures the following behaviour:

A2	A1	A0	Output selected	(hex address)
0	0	0	pin 15	FCF0
0	0	1	pin 14	FCF1
0	1	0	pin 13	FCF2
0	1	1	pin 12	FCF3
1	0	0	pin 11	FCF4
1	0	1	pin 10	FCF5
1	1	0	pin 9	FCF6
1	1	1	pin 7	FCF7

Although Fig. 1.6 has been built around the addresses &FCF0 to &FCF7, we could have chosen any other set of eight *contiguous* addresses in Fred's user application band (&FCC0 to &FCFE). For example, suppose for some reason we wished to position the decoder in the eight addresses &FCE0 to &FCE7. The third hex digit would now be E (binary 1110) instead of F (binary 1111). The only change, therefore, would be a logic 0 on address line A4 instead of a logic 1. Thus the circuit remains the same except for one extra inverter in between A4 and the NAND gate.

Note from Fig. 1.6 that the data bus is *not involved*. Switching on the selected advice is simply a case of mentioning the address in a machine code instruction; any data transfers by READ or WRITE action are incidental to device action. We could say that the device is 'address' rather than 'data' driven.

Sending parallel data externally

Some devices only require a single logic line to activate them (simple lamp or electric motor). Others, may require a number of data lines as, for example, an 8-bit digital to analogue converter. Driving such devices would involve the data bus as well as the address bus. As far as address

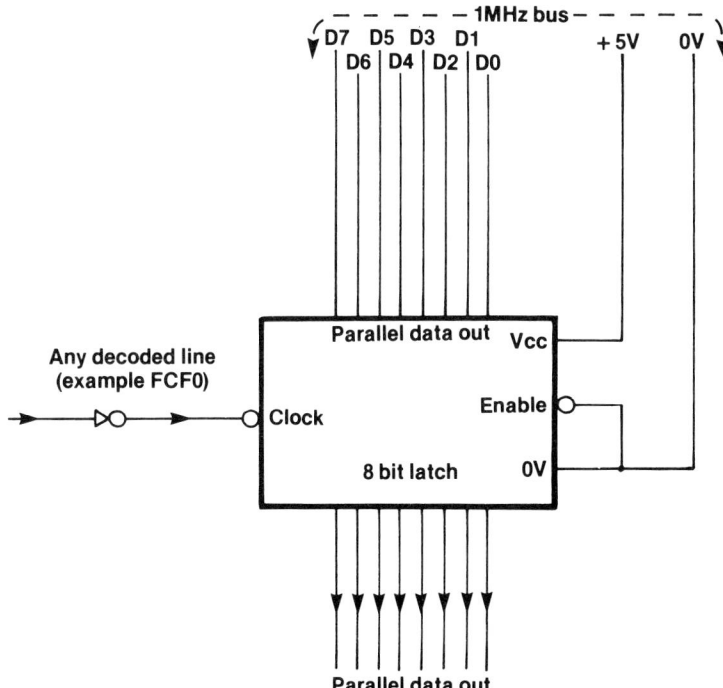

Fig. 1.7. An 8-bit latch as an example of a device.

decoding is concerned, we could enable the device from any one of the outputs in Fig. 1.6 or, in fact, up to eight separate ones if the necessity arises. Figure 1.7 shows how the device-select action is combined with the data bus.

An 8-bit latch is a kind of *buffer* between the data source (in this case the data bus) and the device which requires it. The device only accepts the data when a terminal called the clock changes state. Because the clock input in Fig. 1.7 has a bubble, clocking the data takes place when the change is from logic 1 to logic 0. In the quiescent state (device not yet selected) the parallel data out is that which remained from the last time the latch was clocked: it is 'historic' data. However, whenever &FCF0 is addressed (goes from logic 0 to logic 1), the inverter in the line causes the clock to go from logic 1 to logic 0. The information on the data bus then passes through to the parallel output lines. To summarise: when &FCF0 is addressed, the device immediately receives new information from the data bus, *overwriting the previous information*. As a matter of interest, the machine code line to place the contents of the accumulator into the output lines is:

STA &FCF0

The system recognises the instruction is to act on the 1 MHz bus devices because the first two hex digits of the address is the Fred page.

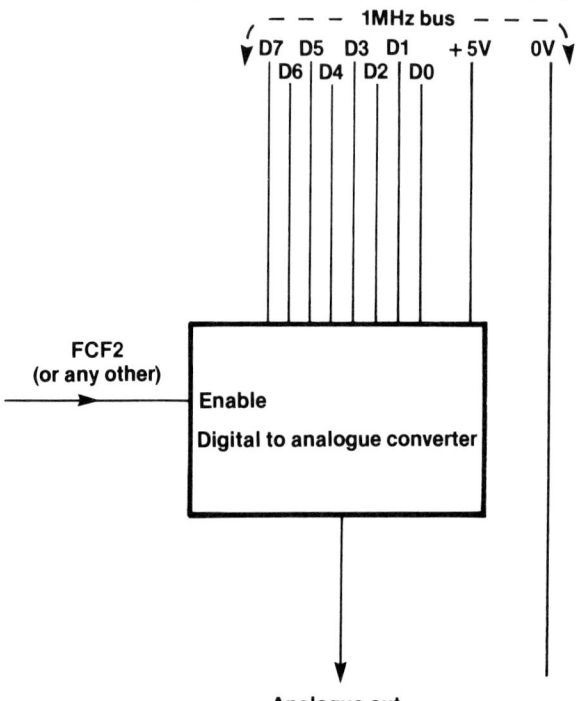

Fig. 1.8. Converting digital information to analogue output.

Figure 1.8 is another example of a device requiring the data bus, which is needed, of course, for receiving the digital data.

Although the BBC machine is not equipped with a digital to analogue converter, it is easy to hook one on the 1 MHz bus. There are several types available so the diagram contains only sufficient detail for the understanding of the system. The diagram shows the data bus directly connected to the D/A converter and enabled by one of the decoded addresses. This, of course, could be one of the lines from a 74LS138 (as shown earlier in Fig. 1.6). An instruction to produce analogue output could be:

STA &FCF2

This will cause the output voltage to assume a value *proportional* to the digital number in the accumulator.

Using the R/NW line

Up to this point, the devices described have all delivered outputs, from the computer to the outside world. However, many systems may include one or more input devices passing data from the outside world to the computer. One obvious example is an analogue to digital converter. There are two dangers inherent in the design of input devices. The first is obvious: make sure that the voltages coming from the outside world are *within the allowed maximum* (usually within the range 0 V to 5 V). The second danger is more obscure. If an input device is enabled, it normally places data on the address bus. Thus the instruction should READ from the data bus (an LDA for example). But if, by mistake, we WRITE (an STA, for example) there is a conflict of loyalties on the data bus because two independent sets of data are trying to gain control. This could damage some of the circuits. The remedy is either to become an infallible programmer (we have never yet met one) or incorporate something on the lines shown in Fig. 1.9.

In Fig. 1.9, a NAND gate is fed by the R/NW line and the decoded device address. The output from the gate is logic 0 only if both inputs are logic 1. Therefore, even if the device address is correct (FCF4 in the example) the R/NW line must be logic 1 which is present only if the instruction is to READ. If, in error, the programmer causes a WRITE action, the R/NW line is turned to logic 0 and the NAND output rises to logic 1. Because the device in Fig. 1.9 has a bubble at the enable input, the input device is not enabled. Thus, it is now impossible to jam the data bus by trying to *write to an input device*. If the device had no enable bubble (and some of them haven't), it would be necessary to include an inverter in the NAND output line. This latter point illustrates how easy it is to be 'one inversion out' when designing logic systems. You can never be just a little bit out (as in analogue design). It is either dead right or dead wrong!

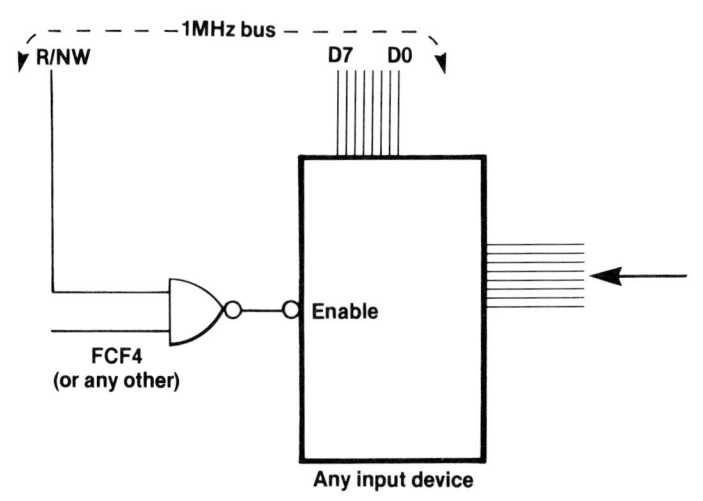

28 Advanced Machine Code Techniques for The BBC Micro

Fig. 1.9. Gating the READ/WRITE line to input devices.

Using Jim to access auxiliary memory

Fred is used for attaching a variety of extra gadgets to the 1 MHz bus. Jim is virtually dedicated to the sole purpose of adding on auxiliary blocks of memory. Up to the full 64K of RAM, ROM or mixtures of RAM and ROM can be page accessed. For full details, it is advisable to obtain the Acorn leaflet on the 1 MHz bus but, in the meantime, Fig. 1.10 shows the general idea.

As mentioned previously, a sixteen-wire bus is required to cover a 64K memory system. Only eight-address wires, A0 to A7, are provided on the 1 MHz bus so it is not surprising that the solution to such a problem involves some strange goings-on. Examining Fig. 1.10 reveals that the *lower order* addresses are supplied by the legitimate address bus. The higher order address, A8 to A15 is obtained by 'borrowing' the data bus. How can the data bus (which is required to pass data to an address) simultaneously supply part of the address as well? The simple answer is that it can't. The secret lies in the 8-bit latch. The programmer *first* supplies the higher order address (the page). This is then automatically clocked into the latch, supplying A8 to A15 in the ROM/RAM. The figure shows that latch clocking is achieved by the special decoded line FCFF. It also shows that the entire ROM/RAM memory structure is only enabled by using the Jim address band, detected by the NPGFD line on the 1 MHz bus. Although the enabling pin is marked 'valid memory address' (instead of 'enable'), the effect is identical.

There is naturally a small penalty to pay for all this jiggery pokery. It takes a little longer to read or write to a location in the extended memory, particularly if the desired address is *outside the current page* (outside the

Architecture of the BBC Machine   29

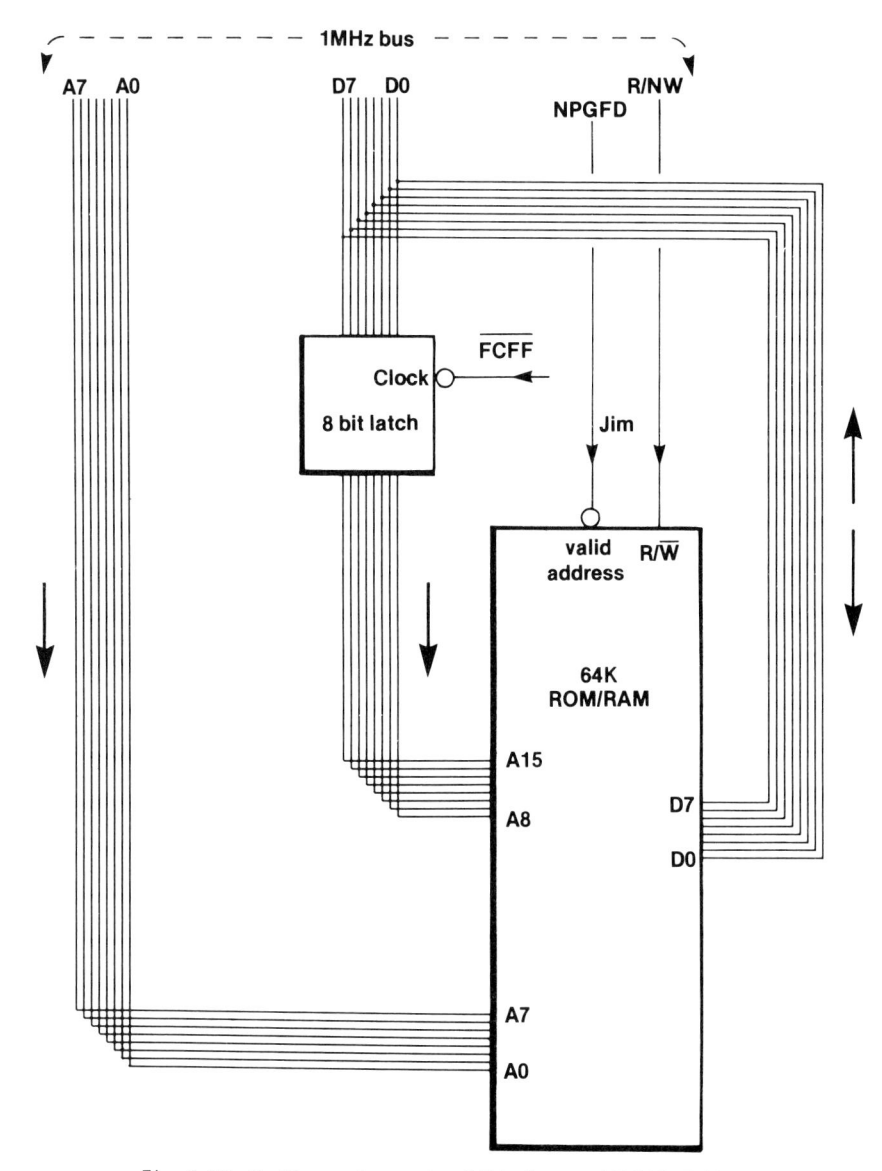

Fig. 1.10. Outline scheme for 64K of paged ROM/RAM.

'page boundary'). Some provisional details of the coding are now given in the hope of clarifying some of these points:

Programming procedure:

• First store the page part of the address in the reserved location &FCFF (called the paging register).

• Then perform the desired data transfer to any position on that page by reading or writing into the address band &FD00 to &FDFF.

30 Advanced Machine Code Techniques for The BBC Micro

Example: to store the number 13 hex in address &3567 of the extended memory.

```
LDA  #&13     \load A with &13
LDX  #&35
STX  &FCFF    \store page address in paging register
STA  &FD67    \store A in address &67 of page &35
```

The *paging register* location, &FCFF is the odd man out in the Fred band because it is used for Jim.

It is unnecessary to keep loading the paging register each time, providing the addresses lie on the same page. If the next address lies on a different page, then the paging register must be reloaded.

Summary

1. Machine code programming can be tackled with more confidence if backed by some knowledge of hardware.
2. If your machine still has the old 0.1 series ROM, get it changed to the 1.2 or any of the 1.X series as soon as possible.
3. The priority on power-up is vested in the ROM occupying the rightmost of the five sockets.
4. The designer's advice is to access the peripheral interfaces by resident subroutines, OSBYTE, OSWORD, etc. This is good advice but need not be taken too seriously during the learning stage of machine code programming.
5. The operating system handles standard peripherals by a process of orderly interrupts.
6. An interrupt request (IRQ) is granted only if the mask bit (in the microprocessor) has not been set to '1'. A non-maskable interrupt, or NMI ignores the mask bit.
7. Parallel interfaces transmit or receive a complete byte at a time, requiring 8 wires to carry the information. Serial interfaces pass only single bits, one after the other, on a single line.
8. The RS423 (an improved version of the older RS232) is a serial interface which can handle certain printers, telephone signals via a modem or act as a data link between other computers.
9. A 6850 chip handles serial and a 6522 chip handles parallel interfacing.
10. The A/D conversion chip, a D7002, allows any one of four varying (analogue) input voltages to be represented as a digital number.
11. The heart of the floppy disk interface is the 8271 controller chip.
12. Memory maps divide the 64K total into 64 pages. A machine address is a four-hex-digit number. The left-hand pair is the page and the right-hand pair the address on the page.

13. One page of memory contains 256 addressable locations (this is exactly 100 in hex notation).
14. Sheila is page FE, occupying the address band &FE00 to &FEFF. It is reserved for accessing all interfaces built into the machine.
15. Fred is page FC, occupying the address range &FC00 to &FCFF. It is reserved for any specialised hardware fed from the 1 MHz bus, such as dealer's test equipment, Teletext, Prestel, etc.
16. A small area of the Fred page is reserved for the user's special applications, &FCC0 to &FCFE.
17. The 1 MHz bus (see Fig. 1.4) provides eight address lines, A0 to A7 and eight data wires via a two-way buffer (IC72). A 5 volt power supply and special lines are also provided.
18. The special lines on the 1 MHz bus include:

    NNMI and NIRQ provide interrupt inputs to the microprocessor. They are activated by logic 0.
    NRST delivers logic 1 during a READ instruction and logic 0 during a WRITE.
    NRST delivers a logic 0 when reset is activated.
    NPGFC delivers a logic 0 whenever page FC (Fred) is addressed.
    NPGFD delivers logic 0 whenever page FD (Jim) is addressed. (The data buffer is only enabled if either Jim or Fred pages are addressed. The 1 MHz clock is an oscillator, sychronised to the 2 MHz microprocessor clock but running at half the frequency.
    Analogue-in is connected to the sound channels. Any signal supplied is *added* to any other programmed sound. It is not a separate channel.

20. Detailed information on the 1 MHz bus can be obtained from Acorn computers.
19. Jim is the FD page, occupying the address range &FD00 to &FDFF. It caters for a 64K memory expansion.
20. Some devices require only a simple ON/OFF drive obtained by a simple decoder from the address bus. The data bus is not required.
21. A 74LS138 is a useful decoding chip, capable of activating any one of eight devices. The address for each device is determined by the '1's and '0's applied to the select and enabling inputs.
22. Devices which deliver data from the outside world (input devices) should be gated with the read/write line (R/NW) in case a WRITE instruction is given in error (see Fig. 1.9).

Self test

1.1 If a ROM or EPROM is 'empty', what hex number appears when you read any location?

32 *Advanced Machine Code Techniques for The BBC Micro*

1.2 You might expect a parallel printer interface to be eight times quicker than a serial. Why is there virtually no difference?

1.3 State an advantage of the RS423 serial interface over the earlier RS232.

1.4 Name a device which could convert, say, atmospheric pressure readings to a proportional voltage.

1.5 What approximate voltage gives full-scale reading at the analogue/digital input.

1.6 What is the highest hex page number?

1.7 What specialised names are given to pages FC,FD and FE.

1.8 The user port and the Centronics printer interface are fed by a 6522 VIA. On which side of the VIA is the user port?

1.9 How would you find out which version of ROM operating system is installed?

1.10 Which instruction in the 6502 will prevent IRQ being granted?

1.11 Passing an ASCII character via the RS423 interface requires ten bits Why?

1.12 What is the approximate voltage across a silicon diode when in forward conduction?

1.13 With reference to Fig. 1.6, what address would activate pin 12 if the inverter to pin 6 was omitted in error?

1.14 With reference to Fig. 1.8, if the maximum output is 2.55 volts, what output voltage is obtained when the digital data is 3F hex?

1.15 With reference to Fig. 1.7, assume the data bus is 4F hex and the latch output is also 4F. Supposing the data bus now changes to 5F, what is the output from the latch prior to the arrival of the clock pulse?

1.16 With reference to Fig. 1.4 some pins on the 6502 have a bar across the label. What is the significance?

1.17 Some logic chips have a pin labelled CE. What does this mean?

1.18 The address band within Fred allotted to User Applications is &FCC0 to &FCFE. How many different addresses are within this band?

1.19 The last address in the Fred band is &FCFF. What is significant about this special address?

1.20 Sheila addresses are reserved for ...?

1.21 Jim addresses are reserved for ...?

1.22 Fred addresses are reserved for ...?

Chapter Two
The 6502 Microprocessor

Useful abbreviations and conventions

lsb = least significant bit.　　msb = most significant bit.
Bit positions within a byte are numbered 7 6 5 4 3 2 1 0.
Bit 0 is the lsb.　　Bit 7 is the msb.
A = the accumulator.　　X = register X.　　Y = register Y.
P = process status register.　　PC = program counter.　　PCL = low byte of PC.
PCH = high byte of PC.　　SP = stack pointer.　　ALU = arithmetic and logic unit.
AR = address register.　　ARL = low byte AR.　　ARH = high byte of AR.

Process status flags:
N = negative (bit 7).　　V = overflow (bit 6).　　B = break (bit 4).
D = BCD (bit 3).　　I = interrupt (bit 2).
Z = zero (bit 1).　　C = carry (bit 0).

The 6502 versus the Z80

The 6502 and the Z80 8-bit microprocessors have retained their popularity with personal computer manufacturers for many years. Their popularity is likely to remain until the approaching 16-bit revolution is established. Both the 6502 and the Z80 have good and bad features which are fairly equally distributed. The Z80 has sometimes been praised as the more powerful of the two but, in the absence of a satisfactory definition of 'power' this praise has little substance. If by 'power' we mean execution speed then neither type is superior. Some types of program can execute faster on the Z80; others execute faster on the 6502. Because of this it is not wise to pay too much attention to 'benchmark' tests. Comparison tests for computers have about the same reliability index as intelligence tests for humans: they tend to test the tester more than the testee. The Z80 has a powerful marketing advantage because of its downward compatibility with the Intel 8080. The widely used disk operating system CP/M, for which an enormous amount of commercial software has been written, is based on the 8080 instruction set, so any microcomputer which runs on the 6502 could be said to be disadvantaged in this respect. The justification for discussing the Z80 at all in this book (which is supposed oriented towards the 6502) is because one of the Second Processor options runs on the Z80. There will be a choice of another 6502, a Z80 or the new 16-bit 16032. Because of this, it is considered reasonable to include occasional references to all three microprocessors. The Motorola 6800 was the ancestor of the 6502. Apart from the indirect addressing modes which are unique to the 6502, they are, in many respects, similar.

6502 architecture

It is possible to delve straight into machine code programming without troubling very much about the technical details of the 6502. Indeed, the introductory book *Discovering BBC Micro Machine Code* plunged straight into a program on page 8. This book is the sequel, intended to fill up some of the gaps left in both the software and hardware treatment. It pays dividends in the long run if the internal behaviour of a microprocessor is understood. It can also be interesting for its own sake.

It is better to begin by reviewing the microprocessor in relation to other main components of the system, as shown in Fig. 2.1. The operating system and BASIC language ROMs each have a capacity of 16K bytes (type number 13128). They are connected across the address and data buses. Note that the address bus is shown split down the middle because it is important always to bear in mind that a 4-hex digit address code is handled by the microprocessor in two halves, the lines A0 to A7 (low-byte) and lines A8 to A15 (high-byte).

The RAM complement is not so straightforward because of the reduced *packing density* within the chip. Each RAM chip in the BBC machine, (type number 4816) stores only 16K bits (not bytes) so it is necessary to use sixteen of these chips to form a storage system of 32K bytes. (The Electron uses four of the new 64K bit RAMs to produce the total 32K bytes.) Another factor contributing to complexity is the 'dynamic' nature of the memory. The correct title for this class of read/write memory is DRAM, the 'D' prefix standing for dynamic. Due to the need for reducing current consumption and maximising packing density, each bit is stored within the inter-electrode capacity of MOS transistors (see Appendix A). The stored information, however, is a transient affair, leaking away in a few milliseconds. Consequently, each stored bit must be periodically *recharged* in order to compensate for the leakage. This process, called 'refreshing' is inherent in the hardware design and is not the responsibility of the programmer. However, the refresh-cycle takes up extra time. DRAMs are

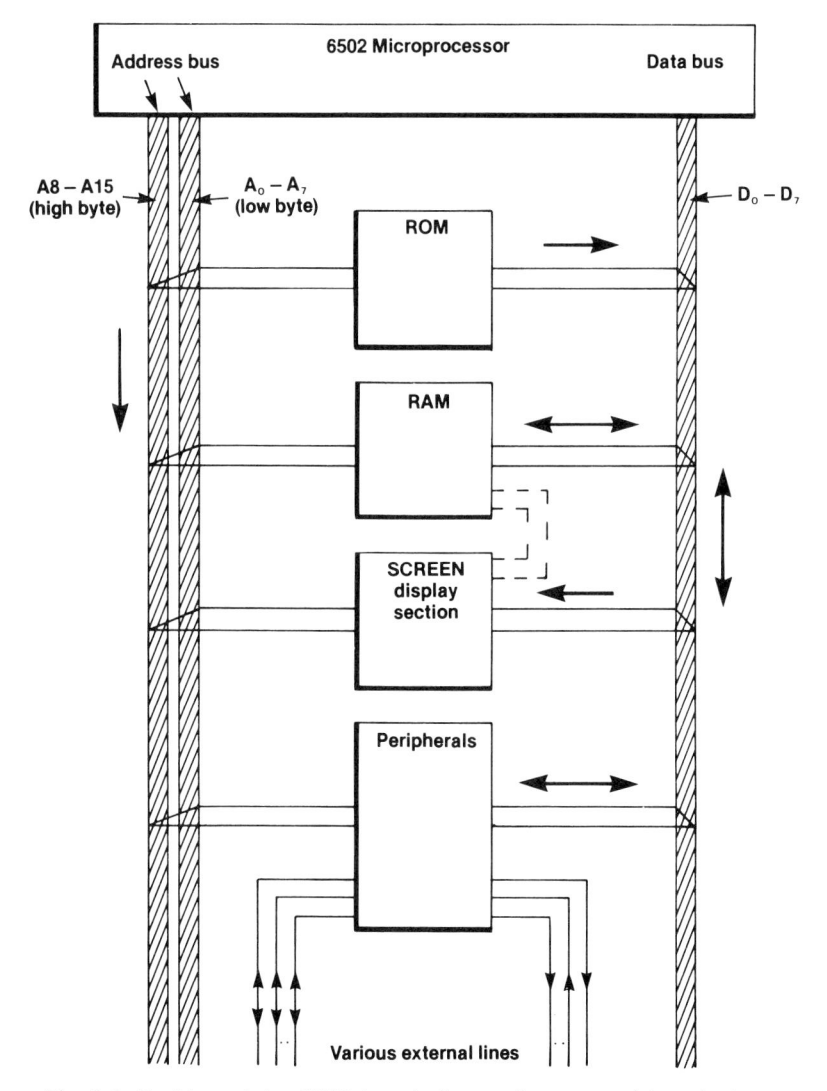

Fig. 2.1. Position of the 6502 in relation to the external bus devices.

therefore a compromise in which access time is sacrificed in order to increase packing density and reduce cost. It is worth mentioning that the BBC and Electron systems are not alone in employing DRAMs. Nearly all microcomputers have, and still do, use them. The alternative would be to use static RAMs but the cost would be prohibitive and they would occupy a greater space on circuit boards. Having noted this, DRAMs will still be referred to as RAMs: distinction is academic. Note that, unlike the ROM chips, the feed to the data bus is *bidirectional*.

36 Advanced Machine Code Techniques for The BBC Micro

6502 systems are memory-mapped so it is not surprising that keyboard, screen display and the input/output interfaces are strung across the address and data buses as if they were memory chips. In the case of the screen display, the dotted line on the figure indicates the additional data path between the area of RAM dedicated to the screen display circuits. To avoid cluttering the diagram, the various signal lines forming the 'control bus' are not shown.

Inside the 6502

Figure 2.2 shows reasonable, but by no means complete, details of the paths between the various registers. Such paths within the microprocessor are often called *highways* because they ramify over the chip area to provide a kind of long distance communication.

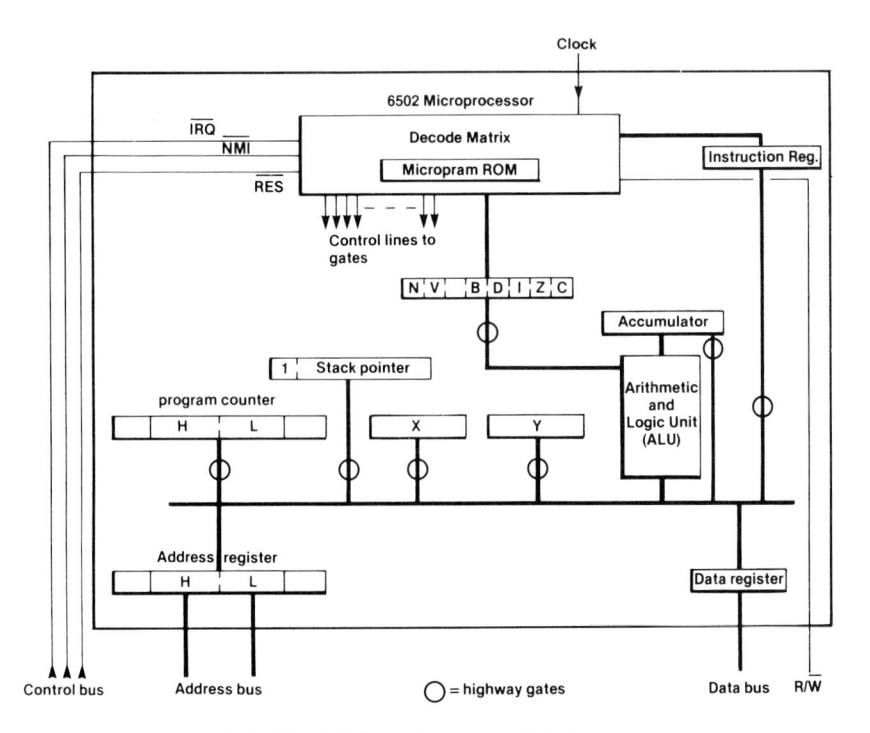

Fig. 2.2. 6502 registers and highways.

The chaos is only apparent. Control lines (not shown) operate the input and output gates of each separate register, ensuring that only one pair is allowed access to the highway at any one time. For example, during the machine code instruction TAX, only register A output gate and register X input gate are open to the data highway, allowing the contents of A to be transferred to X.

The majority of instructions we give to microprocessors are *data transfers*, either between internal registers or between registers and the external RAM, ROM or peripherals. Some instructions, such as ADC (add with carry) perform arithmetical operations on the data but the data still has to be fetched from somewhere else. Even a simple instruction like INX (increment contents of X) involves a transfer because the X register is not equipped for altering itself. Instead, the contents of X must be transferred along the highway to the arithmetic section and subsequently returned.

Directly programmable internal registers

It is assumed that many readers will already be aware of the various registers and their functions but, for the sake of continuity a brief description follows together with the standard abbreviations subsequently used in all references. A distinction is made between *directly programmable* and the other registers which, although playing a vital role, remain in the background, unseen by the programmer.

Accumulator (A)
This register has a supreme role. It is the only one capable of performing arithmetic processing. This is evident from Fig. 2.2 which shows that, in addition to the usual connection to the highway, there is a direct and *exclusive* link to the Arithmetic and Logic Unit (ALU). It is involved in transfers to and from memory and acts as interim data storage during arithmetic and logic operations. For example, during a simple addition of two numbers (ADC), the first number must pass to the accumulator and is then 'entered' to a holding register within the ALU. The second number then enters A, the addition is carried out and the result sent back to A. Those used to scientific calculators in the Hewlett-Packard range will recognise the inherent Reverse Polish (RP) action.

It is worth digressing a little to explain RP. A Polish mathematician proposed a new method of expressing arithmetic, the essence of which was placing the operator (+, −, × etc.) after, instead of in between, variables. For example, instead of writing A+B to indicate addition, he proposed that it should be written AB+. Because his name was quite unpronounceable (and almost unspellable in English) his system has become known simply as Reverse Polish Notation (RPN or simply RP). The influence of von Neumann on the evolution of the computer was mentioned in Chapter 1. He suggested that the arithmetic system of digital computers would operate most efficiently if based on RPN. Thus the ALU of the BBC machine, in common with nearly all other computers, requires the two variables first; the add operator is then activated and the result passed to A, replacing the previous contents.

The dominance of the accumulator over other registers is evident from the instruction set of the 6502. However, the fact that only *one accumulator* is present gives ammunition for the protagonists of the rival Z80 which boasts eight accumulator-type registers. A single accumulator does tend to be restrictive in organising efficient machine code.

The X and Y registers
Like the accumulator, the X register and the Y register (subsequently referred to as X and Y) are both 8 bits wide. They have three primary uses in programming.

(1) They make up for the inconvenience of the solitary accumulator. Important data residing in A can be transferred temporarily by the use of TAX or TAY and later, when A is free, transferred back using TXA or TYA.

(2) They can act as up-counters or down-counters for setting up machine code loops. This is due to the ease with which they can be incremented or decremented by the instructions INX, DEX, INY or DEY. It is curious that the designers failed to provide an equivalent instruction for incrementing or decrementing A. The only way is by the relatively inefficient method of adding or subtracting 1, using ADC or SBC.

(3) They are fundamental to the technique known as *address modification* by indexing. When using an indexed addressing mode (denoted in assembly form by a comma followed by X or Y), the data in the X or Y register is automatically *added* to the data in the operand.

The resultant is interpreted as the address of the required data. This idea was pioneered by a team at Manchester University and, at the time, represented a huge step forward in computer science. They called the index register the 'B box', presumably to differentiate it from the accumulator A. Previous to this, altering the operand address in loops was cumbersome. It involved loading the operand from inside the program, incrementing it and then storing it back in the original position. In other words, it was necessary to alter the program in order to modify an address. Indexed addressing is so much cleaner to work with and certainly less error-prone. Most of the indexable instructions in the 6502 allow a choice of using either X or Y for indexing. Although indexed addressing is later dealt with in detail, there is no harm in a little anticipation for the benefit of those who are new to the idea. So, consider an example in which register X contains 30, and we write LDA 100,X.

The simple instruction LDA 130, however, would have the equivalent effect. They would both load the contents of address 130 into A. The advantage of the indexed over the simpler form will be apparent when organising loops involving action on consecutive addresses.

This discussion should help to explain why the address bus, as well as the data bus, has access to the ALU. This should be understandable now it is recognised that the index register contents have to be added to the operand. After all, address modification by indexing produces a computed address and only the ALU can truly compute.

The process status register (P)

If we define a register as an internal memory location for holding or processing data, then the process status register (P) is not a register at all. It is, in fact, a collection of isolated *flip-flops* (see Appendix A), each capable of storing one bit. Each bit is called a 'flag' because it conveys certain information in yes/no form either for the benefit of the machine or the programmer. After most instructions, the relevant flags are updated, depending on the result. There is no connection, either in the hardware or software aspects, between different flags. In spite of this, it is convenient and conventional to refer to it as a register. It is important to the programmer to understand the exact significance of each flag, under what conditions they are set or reset, which are under the control of the microprocessor and which are directly programmable.

The N bit: If this is 1, the last result contained a 1 in bit 7 position. The N bit is often misleadingly called the 'sign bit' because two's complement arithmetic recognises bit 7 as the sign rather than magnitude. If the number is unsigned binary, the N flag merely indicates the state of bit 7. It is automatically set or reset and is not directly programmable. BMI (branch if minus) and BPL (branch if plus) are the relevant branch instructions conditional on the state of the N bit. Most instructions leave the N bit updated as part of the execution routine The notable exceptions being STA, STX, STY, TXA, and all branch and jump instructions (see Appendix C for complete coverage). LSR is unique in that the N bit is always reset to 0, irrespective of the result.

The V bit: If this bit is 1, it indicates that the last arithmetic instruction caused *two's complement overflow* due to the result being outside the capacity of a single byte. It can be tested by the conditional branch instructions, BVS or BVC. It is of no significance to the programmer when using unsigned binary because bit 7 of the result represents magnitude rather than sign. In this case, it can be ignored. However, the V bit also plays a major role in the BIT test instruction, assuming the same state as bit 6 of the data being tested.

It is possible to directly clear the V bit to 0 by the instruction CLV although there is no corresponding instruction to directly set it to 1. Only the instructions ADC, SBC, BIT, PLP, RTI and CLV affect the V bit.

The B bit: This is set to 1 when a BRK instruction is encountered. Its significance is limited almost entirely to *interrupt* sequences. It cannot be directly programmed.

The D bit: The 6502 can perform arithmetic on straightforward binary numbers or on BCD (Binary Coded Decimal) numbers. The programmer decides this by the use of either SED (set decimal) which makes D = 1 or CLD (clear decimal) which makes D = 0. The arithmetic mode currently in use *remains* until the D bit is altered. The default mode is D = 0. The instructions which affect the D bit are CLD, SED, PLP, and RTI.

The I bit: This is called the interrupt *mask* bit or the interrupt *inhibit*. It is inspected by the microprocessor when an interrupt request is received from a peripheral source. If it is 1, the request is not granted. It can be directly set to 1 by SEI (set interrupt) or cleared to 0 by CLI (clear interrupt). These instructions are vital when designing the software for peripheral interfaces, most of which will be interrupt-driven. The instructions which affect the I bit are BRK, CLI, SEI, PLP and RTI.

The Z bit: This is the zero bit, and is set to 1 when a result is 0. This is worth emphasising strongly because it is often interpreted back to front. If a result is non-zero, the Z bit goes to 0. It can be tested by the branch instructions, BEQ (branch if equal to zero) or BNE (branch if not equal to zero). There are no instructions which can directly effect it. Most instructions affect the Z bit. The exceptions include TXS, STA, STX, STY and the branch and jump instructions.

The C bit: This is the *carry* bit, and is set to 1 when a carry out from the msb is detected. Instead of the bit 'dropping on to the floor' it is popped into the C bit. It can also be thought of as the *ninth bit*, particularly in shift and rotate instructions. It can be tested by the branch instructions BCS (branch if carry set) or BCC (branch if carry clear). It can also be directly programmed by SEC which sets C to 1 or CLC which clears C to 0. Instructions which affect the C bit are ADC, SBC, ASL, LSR, ROL, ROR, SEC, CLC, PLP, RTI, CMP, CPX and CPY.

It is clear from the above that the process status register flags have a profound effect on program behaviour. The majority of errors encountered, particularly when setting the terminating conditions for loop exit, are due to misinterpreting the behaviour of the flag bits. Unless you are already confident in this area you would do well to reread the above treatment several times.

The stack pointer (SP)
This is an 8-bit register, dedicated to the automatic control of a special area in *page one in RAM* memory designated the 'stack'. Its function is as an address generator. It is impossible to describe the stack pointer fully without describing the stack itself. Because the stack is so important in its own right, discussion of its anatomy will be postponed. It is sufficient at this point to grasp the following essentials:

(1) The contents of SP are interpreted by the microprocessor as the address of the currently vacant location in the stack.

(2) To ensure the address is always on page 1, rather than page 0, a permanent 1 is hardwired at the msb end of SP acting as a ninth bit. Thus, if SP itself contains 0000 0011 (0003 hex), the address is interpreted as if it were 1 0000 0011 (0103 hex). That is to say, address 3 on page 1 rather than address 3 on page 0.

(3) SP can be loaded initially to any address on page 1 but the method is a little cumbersome. There is no actual instruction to load SP directly. It is necessary first to load X and then transfer it to SP by the instruction TXS. This may seem a chore but in practice it may only have to be done once, during the initialisation phase of a complete machine code program. In fact, it would be generally unwise to tamper with SP at all when using the assembler because it will have been initialised by the ROM operating system. However, if you are brave enough to attempt circumvention, SP is normally initialised to FF hex in order to utilise the entire stack area.

(4) Once initialised, the use of the stack is simplicity itself. If you want temporarily to save the contents of the accumulator, without having to specify a storage address, just push it on to the stack with PHA (Push A). To retrieve it again, pull it back with PLA (Pull A). It is not possible to push X or Y directly but it can be done piecemeal by first using TXA or TYA.

(5) The stack is a LIFO, meaning Last In First Out, memory so you must pull data back with this in mind. After every push, SP decrements by 1 in order for the next push to operate on a new vacant location. When data is to be pulled back, SP first increments by 1 (in order to point to the last stored item) before the pull operates. The stack pointer automatically 'rises' with each push and 'falls' with each pull so there is no need to bother with SP (see Fig. 2.3). You can forget the existence of the stack pointer providing you remember that the *last item pushed* onto the stack from A will always be the *first item pulled* back into A.

(6) The stack can only hold one page – 256 bytes, that is. If you overflow the stack, there is no friendly warning as in BASIC. All that happens is a 'wrap around' effect. For example, if SP is initially set to FF hex and data keeps piling on the stack, SP eventually reduces to 00. The next decrement wraps around to FF again causing weird and unexpected results. However, a 256 byte stack is normally more than ample for most programs and overflow conditions should be rare.

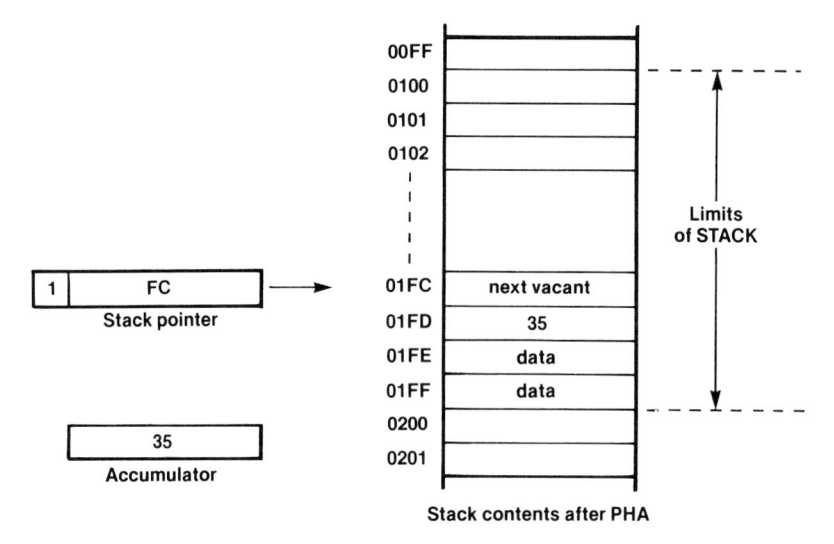

42 *Advanced Machine Code Techniques for The BBC Micro*

Fig. 2.3. The stack and stack pointer.

(7) In addition to its use as a temporary dumping ground for general work, the stack plays a vital role in both *subroutines* and *interrupts*. When a subroutine is called by means of JSR, the two bytes forming the return address (which will be in the program counter) are pushed onto the stack — high byte first, low byte second. When the subroutine ends (with RTS), the return address is pulled back from the stack (low byte first, high byte second) and passed to the program counter, allowing the body of the program to resume again.

Registers which are not directly programmable

In any microprocessor, some of the most important registers remain transparent (or at least translucent) to the programmer. That is to say, instructions are not provided which make direct reference to them. In fact, the more important a register, the less likely is the programmer allowed direct access. In the 6502, the unseen registers (refer back to Fig. 2.2) are the Program Counter (PC), the two address registers ADL, ADH and the Instruction Register (IR).

The Program Counter (PC)
This enjoys the honour of being the only 16-bit register in the 6502. If there is an established register hierarchy, then PC is the undisputed candidate so its function deserves strong emphasis:

> The contents of the Program Counter is always the address of the next instruction byte to be executed.

The 16-bit length allows reference to any address in the entire 64K range.

Once a stored program is commanded to 'start execution', the following automatic sequence begins:

(1) The contents of PC is transferred to the address bus and the first instruction byte at that address is loaded into the computer and 'processed'.
(2) The PC then increments by 1.
(3) The PC is again transferred to the address bus and the next instruction byte is loaded and 'processed'.

The sequence continues indefinitely, sweeping through the program bytes like a scythe until halted legitimately or an illegal code is reached. The sequence makes no distinction whatsoever between program and data. It is up to the programmer to arrange the instruction bytes in consecutive address order and organise either a break (BRK) or an orderly return to the operating system loop. If the PC is allowed to reach data bytes it will interpret these as instructions which the 6502 will either attempt to execute or crash in despair.

It is all very well describing the sequence but how does PC know where the program starts? When entering a program under the direction of the assembler, there is no problem. It is simply a case of knowing the starting address of a program and assigning this to the *reserved variable* P%. In other words, P% appears to the user of the assembler as PC. But this convenience is by courtesy of the software built into the operating system ROM. As a matter of fact, the actual mechanism of loading the PC gives rise to a disturbing question which strikes at the root of stored program sequence control. This is the question: How is it possible to load PC with the starting address of the program unless there is already a program capable of performing the load action?

This is a chicken and egg situation because we can't fall back on the 'operating system'. The operating system is also a program so how was this loaded originally? There have been, and still are, various solutions to the problem although we are only concerned here with the method inherent in the 6502 microprocessor. When the reset line (RES) is momentarily grounded (usually arranged to coincide with the closing of the power-on switch) the following series of events take place:

(1) All peripherals connected to the reset line are initialised to an orderly 'start-up' state. The interrupt mask is set to 1 to prevent the possibility of an interrupt during the start-up sequence.
(2) PC is loaded with the data which happens to be resident in the special addresses &FFFC (low byte) and &FFFD (high byte). These are called the start-up vectors.
(3) PC commences program execution because it now contains the *starting address* of the program.

From the above, it is evident that the writers of the operating system must ensure that the correct starting address is in &FFFC and &FFFD. It is equally evident that they must be in ROM (RAM can only be loaded with data by a program which already exists). Note that the concept of a vectored address allows the system programmer complete freedom to position the program anywhere. It would have been easier, of course, for microprocessor designers to lay down a mandatory starting address, say, 'all programs must start at address &0000'. This would allow PC to be initialised by a simple zero reset. However, the vectored address approach is flexible and we should remember that infinite flexibility has always been the goal of computer scientists. There are three vectored addresses in the 6502 and, for completeness, these are shown in the following table:

6502 vectored addresses	
Vector address	Function
&FFFA and &FFFB	Non-maskable interrupt
&FFFC and &FFFD	Start-up/reset
&FFFE and &FFFF	Interrupt request

Although PC ensures that instructions are normally accessed and executed in consecutive address order, there are times when the sequence must be broken. When a jump or conditional branch instruction is encountered, the current contents of PC are altered drastically. In the case of an absolute jump, the entire contents of PC are replaced by the instruction operand. Branch instructions, however, use relative addressing rather than absolute. The operand is in the nature of an offset which is added to, rather than replacing, the existing contents of PC. Since the offset is in two's complement binary (allowing positive or negative numbers) it is still possible to branch forward or backward.

The Instruction Register (IR)

The first byte of all machine code instructions is the operation code (abbreviated to 'op-code'). The code, which is different for every instruction and addressing mode, carries two vital pieces of information:

(1) What kind of operation is required.
(2) How many operand bytes (if any) are still required to complete the instruction.

On receipt of the code from memory (known as the FETCH phase) it is routed via the highways to IR where it is held pending execution. If the decoding reveals that the instruction requires no further operand bytes (such as TXA, TAX etc.), the instruction sequence enters the EXECUTE phase. If, on the other hand, decoding reveals that one or more operand bytes must follow, the sequence remains in the FETCH phase until the complete instruction has been received from memory.

The 6502 Microprocessor 45

The Data Register (DR)
The data bus carries information downwards from the microprocessor when *writing* to memory and upwards to the microprocessor when *reading* from memory. Because of this, DR operates as a *bidirectional* holding register, controlled by the R/W line. You will remember, from earlier discussions, that when R/W is in the high state (logic 1) the DR would be switched to the READ direction, and to the WRITE direction when in the low state (logic 0). The power levels on the raw bus are weak and external buffers may be needed to boost the power. A full 64K of memory with additional peripheral loads could lead to degradation of logic levels (see Appendix A).

Whilst on the subject of the data bus, it is convenient to discuss the effect of data-jamming. It is essential that all memory and peripheral devices connected directly to the data bus are equipped with 'tristate' outputs. That is to say, when the devices are in the disabled state, their connections to the data bus should be electrically impotent. Tristate devices ensure this by effectively open-circuiting the outputs during the disabled state.

The Address Register (ARL and ARH)
A 4-hex digit address describes a 16-bit logic pattern on the address wires A0 to A15. The address information can originate from several possible sources. It could originate from A, the output of the ALU or even the data bus. From whatever source, it will eventually be routed along the highway, ending up in the address register. This register is split into two halves, each contributing a byte to the two-byte address. The lower order byte (A0 to A7) is held in ARL and the high order byte (A8 to A15) in ARH. As discussed earlier, the high byte determines the page address and the low byte the address on the page. The individual lines on the address bus are direct outputs of the registers. They are, of course, always outputs so the R/W control line is not involved. It should also be noted that, unlike the data bus, devices connected to the address bus need not be tristate. This is because the address bus is always an output from the microprocessor intended to feed only the address decode circuits of memory or peripheral devices. Only the address registers can supply the bus so there is no possibility of data jamming by alternative logic voltage sources.

The microprogram

The term 'microprogram' has nothing to do with programs written for a microcomputer. In fact, microprograms are those which are buried inside the silicon of the microprocessor chip itself! It may surprise some readers that every instruction in the repertoire (about 200 in the 6502) requires its own special microprogram. A simple machine code instruction like LDA &72 is simple only from the viewpoint of the human intellect. In contrast,

46 *Advanced Machine Code Techniques for The BBC Micro*

logic circuits (which are baffled if required to answer any question with other than yes or no) require considerable assistance in dealing with LDA &72. They need micro-instructions, fed one at a time in order to open and close the appropriate register gates and activate the control lines. These micro-instructions must be given in the correct sequential order for every individual instruction. Since a sequential set of instructions is, by definition, a program, then it becomes evident that the earlier statement is justified: *Every instruction needs its own microprogram.*

We do not propose to examine in detail each of these microprograms. This would take more space than this book allows. However, it is interesting to examine a possible microprogram for the simple instruction mentioned previously: LDA &72 will LoaD A with the data stored at address &72 on page 0 hex. This instruction consists of two bytes, which we will assume are residing at addresses &2E34, &2E35. The microprogram will first have to fetch these two bytes from memory.

The FETCH phase:

PC, having just dealt with the last byte of the preceding instruction, will already have been incremented to &2E34. A typical sequence would be:

(1) The contents of PC pass to ARL and ARH.
(2) The R/W line goes or remains high, causing the op-code (LDA) to be read from memory and passed, via the data bus, to DR.
(3) The contents of DR are then passed to IR and the instruction is decoded. From this decoding, the system now 'knows' there is a single operand byte to follow. PC is incremented to &2E35.
(4) The contents of PC pass to ARL and ARH.
(5) The memory is again read, causing the first operand byte (&72) to enter DR.
(6) PC is again incremented.

The complete instruction is now lodged in the microprocessor registers, ending the FETCH phase. The EXECUTE phase now begins.

The EXECUTE phase:
(7) The operand (&72) in DR is passed, via the highway, to ADL. ADH is cleared to zero (because it is a page 0 address).
(8) The memory is read, and the data at address &72 is passed to DR.
(9) The contents of DR are passed to A.

The instruction has now been executed with the PC left pointing to the address of the first byte of the next instruction.

The instruction chosen in the example was particularly simple and yet the microprogram was quite involved. It is left to the imagination to visualise the microprogram for ADC (&72), X (post-indexed indirect addressing).

Microprogrammers are a specialist breed and usually employed on the design staff of the chip manufacturer. It is fortunate that the brief outline above on microprogramming was included as a topic of interest only. The normal machine code programmer takes each complete instruction for granted and is oblivious to the existence of the internal microprogram steps. If we call machine code a low-level language, then microprogramming is at ground-level!

The decoding matrix

Figure 2.2 shows the decode matrix. Its function is to accept the op-code held in IR, decode it, and finally output a pattern of bits on the various gate and timing controls. This pattern will be different for every step in the microprogram. If this function is analysed carefully, we may come to the conclusion that the decode matrix will behave like a miniature computer with a number of fixed programs inside. We can relate IR to the 'program counter'. The op-code is only the starting address of the relevant microprogram. The 'words' read out from the ROM are the bit patterns supplying the various register gates and controls. These patterns will vary for each step of the microprogram. The gate controls are all hardwired to the various registers. This wiring is omitted from Fig. 2.2 to prevent an already complex diagram from becoming incomprehensible.

Sub-pulses of the clock

It is not always appreciated that the clock pulses, which in the 6502 are running at 2 MHz ($0.5\mu s$ period), are split up within the decode matrix. Several sub-pulses are formed, each sub-pulse initiating each step of the microprograms. Within the matrix, the clock pulses are merely the 'low-frequency' envelope of the sub-pulses.

The Arithmetic and Logic Unit

Addition, subtraction and logical instructions will obviously be the responsibility of the ALU. However, in the interests of versatility, nearly all data is made to pass through the ALU irrespective of the particular instruction. For example, data can pass through the ALU without change by adding zero. This may seem time-wasting but is justifiable from a wider viewpoint of a wider system. For example, address modification by indexing involves adding the contents of X or Y to the operand so the ALU is directly involved.

The 6502 is incapable of multiplication, division or exponential operations. It is not alone in this respect. It is very rare to find 8-bit microprocessors capable of performing any arithmetic instructions other

48 *Advanced Machine Code Techniques for The BBC Micro*

than addition. Even subtraction is achieved by the roundabout way of adding the complement.

Before criticising these limitations, it should be remembered that the microprocessor was designed with the primary objective of controlling electrically operated devices and a primitive instruction repertoire was quite sufficient for the purpose. It was never intended to be the brain of a general purpose computer. However, if a machine can add, it is fairly easy to write subroutines which can multiply, divide and handle exponentials. Users of BASIC, or indeed most other high level languages, are unaware of the primitive capabilities of the microprocessor although they have to pay for it by reduced execution speed. Software solutions are always much slower than hardware implementation.

The new breed of 16-bit microprocessors are virtually second generation products many of which are including instructions which perform direct multiplication and division at an impressive speed.

The design of an ALU is based on a parallel binary adder which can be considered as the prototype. With this as a basic building block, it is a relatively simple exercise in logic to arrange gates for implementing exclusive-or (EOR), logical anding (AND) and the inclusive-or (ORA) functions. Finally, it would only require 'function select' inputs to complete the transformation. Four of these, driven by the output word from the control matrix, could activate any one of 16 functions.

Software Interrupt (BRK)

The details of all machine code instructions are given in the relevant chapter but it is convenient at this stage to introduce the BRK instruction. Interrupts are normally the prerogative of peripheral devices but BRK is software initiated. Superficially, it just stops the computer but a dig beneath the surface reveals some interesting side-effects. The instruction takes 7 clock cycles to complete the following steps:

(1) It sets the B flag in the process status register (P).
(2) Adds 2 to PC.
(3) Sets the I and B bit in P then pushes P on stack.
(4) Loads contents of &FFFE into PCL and FFFF into PCH.

The motive behind this seeming complexity is to aid the writing of software error traps during program development. It is common practice to put BRK at strategic 'bug-hazard' points. This would be useless if the sole function of break was to kill all program flow completely. However, it will be seen from the above that a convenient loop-hole is prepared. Providing a routine is written, with the start address residing in the Break Vector at &FFFE/&FFFF, control is automatically diverted to the routine rather than stopping dead. The routine must establish, by pulling P back from the stack, that the B bit was set as a result of a true BRK rather than a genuine peripheral interrupt.

Summary

1. Both the Electron and the BBC machine use the 6502 and both use the same machine code assembler.
2. The 6502 does not allow disk software written under CP/M. To utilise CP/M, the BBC Second Processor controlled by the Z80 microprocessor is required.
3. The BBC machine uses sixteen type 4816 chips to form 32K of RAM.
4. All internal registers communicate by means of input/output gates at the entrance to the highways. The gate controls ensure that only data from one register output occupies a common highway.
5. Not all registers in the 6502 are directly programmable.
6. The single accumulator (A) is the only register equipped with arithmetic facilities. There are no incrementing or decrementing instructions.
7. X and Y registers are used as transfer registers to and from A, loop counters and indexed addressing modes.
8. Address modification by indexing consists of adding X (or Y) to the operand address.
9. The process status register (P) is a collection of seven independent flag bits, each signalling some important result. Most instructions keep P updated. Conditional branch instructions depend on certain flags.
10. The N flag = 1 if bit 7 is set. The Z bit = 1 on a zero result. Neither are directly programmable.
11. The V bit = 1 on a two's complement overflow result. It can be ignored if the data is unsigned binary. The V bit copies bit 6 during the BIT test. It can be directly programmed by CLV and SEV.
12. The B bit = 1 if an interrupt occurs as a result of BRK.
13. The D bit can only be directly programmed. SED makes D = 1 causing subsequent numerical data to be processed in BCD format. CLD makes D = 0 causing subsequent numerical data to be processed in BCD format.
14. SEI sets the I bit, preventing interrupt when requested by IRQ. It is cleared by CLI.
15. The C bit sets to 1 on detecting a carry-out from the msb. The C bit can act as a ninth data bit.
16. The stack is any dedicated area in page 1 of RAM. PSH pushes A to stack. PLA pulls A back from stack.
17. The address of the next vacant stack address is maintained by SP.
18. SP is automatically incremented after a push and decremented before a pull. This causes the stack to rise and fall.

19. The contents of SP can be initialised or changed only by means of TXS.
20. Access to the stack must obey the rule, last in – first out.
21. The stack is used by subroutines to hold the return address, pending RTS.
22. The program counter (PC) is the only 16-bit register and is not directly programmable. It is in supreme control of the program sequence by always pointing to the next byte in the program.
23. PC is altered directly by JMP. An offset may be added by relative address action during conditional branches.
24. A pulse on the reset line (RST) initialises peripheral devices to zero. PC is then loaded by the contents of the address pointed to by the start-up vector at &FFFC, &FFFD.
25. The instruction register (IR) holds the op-code fetched from memory.
26. The op-code defines the instruction type and carries information on the number of operand bytes to follow.
27. The data register (DR) is a bidirectional buffer between the data bus and the highways.
28. Devices which deliver outputs to the data bus must be tristate.
29. The address register is in two halves, ADL and ADH, holding low and high bytes of address respectively.
30. Each instruction is fetched and executed by an individual microprogram.
31. Microprograms are built into the 6502, and selected by the op-code currently resident in IR.
32. Each step of the microprogram outputs a series of bits on the control lines, opening the appropriate highway gates, R/W lines, etc. in the correct sequence.
33. A microprogram is divided into the FETCH phase which, apart from the number of bytes fetched, will be similar for all instructions. The EXECUTE phase is different for each instruction.
34. The 2 MHz clock pulses are subdivided within the decode matrix to form many sub-pulses. Sub-pulses are used for timing the individual steps of a microprogram.
35. The ALU is built round a parallel binary adder. Subtraction is achieved by adding the two's complement. EOR, ORA and AND operations are incorporated by modified addition.
36. Multiplication, division and exponentiation is not catered for. They are relegated to software solutions.
37. BRK provides software interrupt. It sets the B bit and I bit, pushes the status register to stack and loads the contents of the break-vector locations into PC.

Self test

2.1 What kind of RAMs require refreshing?
2.2 Why are static RAMs unpopular in microcomputers?
2.3 What is meant by 'memory-mapped peripherals'?
2.4 How is incrementation performed in the X and Y registers?
2.5 In what important respect does the accumulator differ from other registers.
2.6 What is the effective address (in hex) if Y contains &04 and the instruction is LDA &2CFF,Y.
2.7 Why is the process status register a non-typical register?
2.8 Which flag bits can be directly programmed?
2.9 There are two flag bits which can only be changed by direct programming. Which are they?
2.10 Which flag bits cannot be directly programmed?
2.11 Under what circumstances can a programmer safely ignore the status of the V bit?
2.12 Apart from detecting overflow, what other significance has the V bit?
2.13 If the Z bit is 0, what can you deduce from this?
2.14 Which flag can be treated as a 'ninth' bit?
2.15 Whereabouts in the system is the stack?
2.16 How can the stack pointer be initially loaded?
2.17 Is the stack pointer automatically incremented before or after PLA?
2.18 If data items A, B and C are pushed onto the stack in that order, which item is pulled back first?
2.19 During a subroutine call by JSR, the two-byte return address is pushed to stack. Which byte is pushed first, high or low byte?
2.20 From which register does the return address (mentioned in 2.19) originate?
2.21 What address is left in the program counter after a byte is fetched?
2.22 Name the control line which defines the direction of the data register?
2.23 How does a microprogram differ from a conventional program?
2.24 In what register is the op-code held during decoding?
2.25 How can a programmer detect whether an interrupt was caused by a peripheral request or by software?
2.26 For which microprocessor instruction set was CP/M written?

Chapter Three
The 6502 Instructions and Addressing Modes

Initial terms and definitions

Some readers will be aware of the following points but repetition is not always valueless. In any case, the terms used to describe aspects of machine code are far from standardised. The previous book, *Discovering BBC Micro Machine Code*, examined each separate instruction in reasonable detail and it would be pointless to go over the same ground here. Instead, the complete instruction set is relegated to Appendix C which should be consulted frequently during reading this and subsequent chapters. When programming in higher level language such as BASIC, an individual order to the computer is called a *statement*. For example, Energy = Mass*C^2 is an example of a statement.

In machine code, orders given to the computer are by means of *instructions*. Instructions are primitive and many are needed to form the familiar high level statements. An instruction will normally consist of an *op-code* to indicate the required action and an *operand* to indicate where the data is to be found. Sometimes, the location of the data will be obvious from the op-code but, in the general case, an operand is required.

There are several ways in which the operand can specify the location of the data. They are known as *addressing modes* and there are thirteen of them in the 6502 although not all of these are available to every instruction. Because one byte is used for the op-code it would be possible to have 256 different ones. However, 90 of the possible combinations are reserved for 'future expansion' (illegal in other words). This leaves 166 valid instructions to choose from. The task of selecting the most suitable op-code is less bewildering than it appears from the figures. There are only 56 *completely different* instructions. It is the available addressing modes for each instruction which multiply the choice.

The op-codes are specified by means of a pair of hex digits. There is a different op-code for every variation of addressing mode. However, the hex coding is really of academic interest because all machine code on the BBC machine will be entered by means of the resident assembler. The details of the assembler will be discussed fully in Chapter 4. The most useful property of an assembler is the facility to enter op-codes in three-letter *mnemonic* form. The desired addressing mode is indicated by the form in which the operand is written. The repertoire of instructions is set out formally in Appendix C. Consequently, the purpose of this chapter will be to explain the symbols, to define the addressing modes and to offer guidelines on the choice of a particular instruction and the most suitable method of addressing.

Factors influencing choice

It is not easy to give a specific answer to the question 'What is the correct instruction to use here?' The choice is very often a compromise between execution speed, memory economy and the demands of structure. Newcomers to machine code may be quite satisfied if their subroutine works at all but it soon becomes apparent that there are good and not so good variants. It is popularly supposed that a program written in machine code will always be much faster and take less memory than the BASIC version. This is a reasonable generalisation but not a universal truth. A poorly written machine code program could be slower than the BASIC equivalent. Even if it is faster, it is well to remember that a speed advantage, to have any real meaning, must be assessed on human, rather than machine, time scales. If a BASIC version runs in one second and the machine code version runs in a millisecond, the advantage is academic rather than visible. The items of information needed to assess the merits of each instruction are as follows:

(1) What does it do? This information is conveyed by a three-letter mnemonic such as LDA or ADC. Although the mnemonic itself conveys a reasonable idea of what the instruction does, it is primarily intended as an aid to the interpretation of a listing. It cannot cover all the subtleties. It is necessary to augment the mnemonic by either a verbal definition or by a loosely standardised format known as *operational symbols* (discussed later).

(2) What addressing modes are available?

(3) What flags in the process status register are altered (updated)? Ignorance or confusion in this area is the cause of many an intractable bug.

(4) How many clock cycles does it consume? The BBC machine runs at 2 MHz so each clock cycle is half a microsecond. The number of clock cycles is influenced more by the addressing mode than the actual instruction. Clock cycle time is particularly critical if the instruction is within a loop which revolves many times. Outside a loop, it is seldom important enough to influence choice.

(5) How many bytes are in the instruction? All instructions take at least one byte because they all have an op-code. The operand, however, can be absent altogether, one byte long, or two bytes long. Knowledge of the

number of bytes required can be helpful. For example, it can be a matter of doubt in certain circumstances whether to write &004B or &4B in the operand. They are mathematically the same but an incorrect choice can cause havoc to the program.

(6) What is the hex op-code? Programming will always be performed with the aid of the assembler which uses mnemonic op-codes. However, it is still necessary at times to be aware of the hex coding for every instruction because the assembled machine code program will include it. It is easy to use an incorrect address mode by mistake when writing the operand but the hex code, which is specific for the addressing mode, might highlight the error during debugging. It is interesting, but not particularly rewarding, to write out the hex code in binary. It gives an insight into the mind of the microprocessor designer because some intriguing patterns emerge which can give a clue to the microprogram within the chip.

(7) What is the correct syntax for the operand? This depends on the addressing mode and the rules are rigid, more so than in BASIC. The assembler does its best but it would be foolish to add user-friendliness to its list of virtues. Make a mistake and you are on your own!

Operational symbols

Universities have traditionally considered computing and data processing subjects to be the prerogative of the mathematics department. The computer is useful as a tool in mathematics so it was considered only natural that computing should be taught by mathematicians. Whether this has helped or hindered progress may be arguable. There is no denying that a mathematical brain was behind the establishment of operational symbols.

How do we describe exactly what an instruction will do, bearing in mind that there must be one, and only one, interpretation? Normal language is one way; perhaps the obvious way. But, to a mathematician, normal language lacks precision and is difficult to formulate concisely without using a lot of ifs and buts. Operational symbols are concise and unequivocal. They explain what the instruction does but make no attempt to explain the meaning of the operand. This is understandable because the meaning of an operand depends only on the addressing mode chosen. For example, the instruction LDA will have the same operation symbols whether it is using immediate, zero-page, absolute, indexed or indirect addressing. The general pattern of operational symbols is of the form:

Action → Result

The arrow denotes the direction of data transfer and is preferable to the = sign sometimes used. The abbreviations used for the registers are those already used but M is used to represent the data specified by the operand.

As a simple example, the instruction STA could be described as follows:

A → M

This means 'Store a copy of the contents of the accumulator in the address specified by the operand'. Note that the arrow *points from the source to the destination* and only the destination contents are over-written by the new data; the source data is preserved.

To take a little more complex example, the instruction ADC could be described concisely as follows:

A+M+C → A

This means 'Add together the present contents of the accumulator, the data specified by the operand, and the carry bit, then place the result in the accumulator'.

The shift and rotate instructions are fearsome looking. For example, the instruction ASL (which is Arithmetic Shift Left) has the operational symbolism:

C ← (7...0) ← 0

The bracketed expression indicates the bits within a byte numbered 0 to 7. The action shows that a zero enters from the right and overspill from bit 7 goes into the carry.

Classification of instructions

There are many ways of classifying instructions. Appendix C simply lists them in alphabetical order by mnemonic group. This is useful as a quick reference but is by no means a scientific classification. Appendix C2 classifies them according to the flags affected in the processor status register and can be quite useful. Appendix C4 is an attempt to classify them according to 'popularity'. It is undeniable that some instructions out of the 56 are used a lot, some are used at times and a few are used spasmodically. Unfortunately, the choice of instructions to perform a given task is very much an individual affair. Some programmers have a particular liking for a certain subset. Indeed, it is often possible to recognise a friend's handiwork from the listing which can be almost a fingerprint. Because of the individual character, Appendix C4 can be no more than the author's personal choice although it might help those who are initially bewildered.

In this chapter, the instructions will be introduced (rather than classified), according to need. No account will yet be taken of the various addressing modes under each mnemonic.

56 *Advanced Machine Code Techniques for The BBC Micro*

Finding temporary homes for data

Due to the single accumulator in the 6502, it is often necessary to find a temporary home for existing data. There are several choices:

(1) Transfer A to another register by the use of TAX or TAY and later restore by TXA or TYA. This is the simple and speedy solution because they are both single-byte instructions, taking only two clock cycles. The trouble is that existing data in the X and Y registers may also be valuable and must not be overwritten. X and Y are often totally committed for indexing or loop counting.

(2) Push A to stack by using PHA and retrieve later by PLA. These are single-byte instructions but they take three clock cycles. It is important to bear in mind the LIFO (last in first out) nature of the stack. Mistakes in the order of retrieval could result in false data entering A. Another danger, of course, is stack overflow although this should be a comparatively rare event.

(3) Store A in a memory location by use of STA and retrieve it with LDA. This will take three clock cycles if the location is on page zero and four on any other page (indexing and indirect addressing can take five or six cycles).

Performing arithmetic

There are only two direct arithmetical instructions, ADC and SBC for addition and subtraction respectively. The carry is always involved and, to avoid introducing garbage carries left over from a previous operation, it is important to be aware of the following rules:

(1) Before using ADC, the carry should normally be *cleared* with CLC.
(2) Before using SBC, the carry should normally be *set* with SEC.

Although in some circumstances the carry can be treated as the 'ninth bit', it should be borne in mind that this is purely a way of looking at it. Obviously, this ninth bit is not transferred by STA, TAX or TAY.

Addition and subtraction of single byte numbers are, of course, severely limited in the range of the result (255 in unsigned binary and +127 and −128 in two's complement binary). Fortunately, the carry bit allows double or multiple byte numbers to be added or subtracted because it can act as the continuity element between the msb of one byte and the lsb of the next. Thus, the carry is only cleared before the two lower order bytes are added. The higher order byte additions will include the carry over (if any) from any previous process so it would be fatal to clear the carry first.

It is important not to forget that there are two arithmetic modes depending on the D flag being set or cleared. The default condition is D = 0, which is the normal two's complement binary arithmetic mode. It is wise, though, to ensure the default condition by initialising with CLD at the head of a program. On the rare occasions when decimal (BCD) mode is required then the initialisation begins with SED, but remember this mode *continues until cancelled again*.

Multiplication and division is possible by a tongue-in-the-cheek method using ASL and LSR respectively. The operations are limited to integral powers of two. Watch must be kept on overspill from the msb in multiplication and the lsb in division.

Subject to overspill into the carry, shifting left by ASL will multiply by two each time so four consecutive ASL operations will multiply the existing data by 16. Division by two is achieved by LSR although we must remember that the overspill from the right (from the lsb) goes into the carry. As a matter of interest, the reason why LSR is named Logical Shift Right is due to this very reason. It is arithmetically absurd for carry status to be in the lsb position, hence it is deemed to be 'logical' shift. This is in contrast to ASL (Arithmetic Shift Left) where the carry action is at the msb end. Unless the programmer is sure, from previous knowledge of the data, multiplication and division by these instructions must check for the presence of a carry after each use. There will be exceptions, of course, such as when multiple-byte precision is used. In these circumstances, the carry will be providing continuity between the component bytes when used in conjunction with ROL or ROR.

Clearing memory and registers

There are no instructions in the 6502 which can clear any of the registers or memory locations to zero. The usual way to clear registers is to store zero in them. To clear memory locations, a previously zeroed register can be stored in them. Those who are fascinated by novelty may be attracted by the following little snippet:

> Exclusive-oring data with itself always results in all zeros.

For example, if A contains &9D and we write EOR #&9D, the accumulator result is &00. (To confirm, write out the example in binary form.)

Up-counting and down-counting

Counting is essentially an adding-by-one operation and implies 'up-counting'. It is also called *incrementing*. Down-counting is subtracting by one. It is also called *decrementing*. The X and Y registers can be counted up or down by the single byte instructions INX, INY, DEX and DEY, each taking only two clock cycles. Data in memory can be incremented or decremented by means of INC or DEC but not economically. They each take five to seven cycles depending on the addressing mode in use.

The accumulator is left out in the cold, lacking an increment or decrement instruction. It can, of course, be done by adding or subtracting 1 which, like DEX or INX only takes two clock cycles, but it requires two bytes even for the immediate addressing mode. There is also the possibility that the carry might have to be cleared first which, if forgotten, could lead to a mystery bug. An alternative is some roundabout method such as TAX then INX then TXA, providing of course, that X (or Y) is free.

Counting is an essential part of loop control. The number of loop revs can be achieved either by starting with N and *counting down to zero* or starting with 1 and *counting up to N*. The advantage of the count down method is that testing for loop exit can be achieved with BNE or BPL. Unfortunately, it is very easy to be 'one out' in the count down. If we count up to N, an extra comparison instruction such as CPX, CPY or CMP is required to check the exit condition but the method may have the advantage of seeming more 'natural' and errors by one are less likely.

Processing particular bits

There will be times when it will be required to operate on one or more particular bits within a byte, rather than on the entire byte. We may wish to ensure, say, that bit 3 is set to 1 without altering the remaining bits. The possible operations fall into three main groups, *clearing* bits to zero, *setting* bits to 1 and finally, *changing* bits. This is achieved by using one of the three 'logical' instructions AND, ORA and EOR in conjunction with the appropriate mask word in the operand. The action is always on the accumulator.

To clear selected bits:
Use AND with an operand mask as follows: '1's in the mask will leave corresponding bits unchanged. '0's in the mask will ensure that corresponding bits are 0.

To set selected bits:
Use ORA with an operand mask as follows: '0's in the mask will leave corresponding bits unchanged. '1's in the mask will ensure that corresponding bits are 1.

To change selected bits:
Use EOR with operand mask as follows: '0's in the mask will leave corresponding bits unchanged. '1's in the mask will ensure that corresponding bits are changed.

The explanation for the above behaviour can be found in Appendix A

The 6502 Instructions and Addressing Modes 59

under the heading Logic Gates. However, the following examples may help in understanding how to work out the correct mask:

(a) To ensure that bit 5 in the accumulator is a 0, use AND #&DF (the mask in binary is 1101 1111).
(b) To ensure that bits 2 and 6 in the accumulator are '1's, use ORA #&44 (the mask in binary is 0100 0100).
(c) To ensure that bit 3 in the accumulator is changed, use EOR #&08 (the mask in binary is 0000 1000).

One's complement of accumulator

It is sometimes necessary to *flip* all the bits in a byte (i.e. produce the one's complement). Assuming the data is already in the accumulator, this can be done by exclusive-oring as follows:

    EOR #&FF or EOR &255

Two's complement of accumulator

The two's complement is obtained by adding 1 to the above. Unfortunately, we can't add the 1 by incrementing because the result is in the accumulator. The only way is to follow with ADC #1, making sure to clear the carry first. The coding is as follows:

    EOR #&FF
    CLC
    ADC #1

Since the two's complement of X is 0−X, an alternative method is simply to subtract the number from zero. This is, by definition, the two's complement but would entail storing the data first before loading the accumulator with 0.

Finding the state of a particular bit

It is sometimes important, particularly in peripheral control, to find out the state of one particular bit within a byte. This can be done by loading the byte into the accumulator, erasing all bits except the one of interest, then testing for zero. If the result is non-zero, the bit must have been a 1. For example, suppose we are interested in bit 3, the coding could be:

    LDA data
    AND #08 (0000 1000)
    BNE etc.

An alternative method, which only works if bit 6 or bit 7 is involved, is the BIT test. For example, we can start by writing:

    BIT data   ('data' is an arbitrary address)

This copies bit 6 and bit 7 of the data into the V and N bits respectively. This can be followed by BVS or BMI as required. The BIT instruction takes 3 clock cycles if data is on page zero but otherwise 4 cycles. As a bonus, the bit test also logically ANDs the data into the accumulator. If this is a nuisance rather than a bonus, the accumulator should be stored first. Because of this, use of the BIT test is not a commonly used instruction.

Besides the three logical instructions AND, ORA and EOR, the shift and rotate instructions LSR, ASL, ROR and ROL are also used to play around with bits. LSR and ASL should be thought of as 'open-loop' operations because bits are lost if the carry is already full. In contrast, ROR and ROL are 'closed-loop' because the bit pattern circulates. They can all play an important role in peripheral work and some off-beat requirements. The shift and rotate instructions are unique in having 'accumulator' addressing. Thus, they can act on the accumulator or a memory location. If the action is required on the accumulator, the mnemonic must be followed by A. For example, to shift the accumulator right, we must write LSR A. When using accumulator addressing, no operand is necessary (the 'A' is not a true operand and does not consume a byte). Because of this, it should be noted (because it is a common mistake) that the shift and rotate instructions must either have an operand or an 'A'. For example, a naked LSR is illegal.

Double-byte multiplication

This provides a useful exercise in shift and rotate operations. Although ASL and ROL both multiply by two, the carry can be a problem if they are not chosen wisely. No carry must be allowed to enter the lower order byte from the right so ASL is appropriate. On the other hand, the higher order byte must take into consideration the carry from the right so ROL must be used. Assuming the data is in two bytes of memory, the coding would be:

    ASL low-byte
    ROL high-byte

Double-byte division

The opposite is required here. Thus, the higher order byte must be attacked first and a carry must not be allowed to enter from the left. This suggests LSR as the first step. The lower order byte must receive a carry (if any) from the left so the correct instruction here is ROR. Assuming that the data is in two bytes of memory, the coding is therefore:

    LSR high-byte
    ROR low-byte

Branching techniques

The equivalent of the dreaded GOTO in BASIC is JMP. The jump to a new part of the program is unconditional and, because JMP has a two-byte operand, can reach any part of the 64K memory map. Appendix C lists seven conditional branch instructions. A common cause of a programming bug is an incorrectly used branch test allowing an unexpected loophole. The following points are worth emphasising:

(1) Branch instructions themselves have *no effect* on the processor status register. Thus, two different branch instructions can follow one another so the original data can be tested for two conditions.
(2) BMI or BPL should only be used if data is represented in two's complement binary. They are meaningless in unsigned binary because there is no differentiation into positive or negative sets.
(3) Before using a branch, make certain that the *last operation* actually updates the bits you are testing. In other words, check up on Appendix C2 which includes a classification of all instructions according to their effect on the processor flag bits. For example, it may be pointless to use BCC after DEX because only the N and Z flag bits are updated.

The limits of +127 byte forward or −128 bytes backwards have been covered elsewhere. If the branch is beyond range (which should not be often) the customary solution is to combine the branch with a JMP. For example, suppose the branch is to be BNE LOOP and the label 'LOOP' is out of range. The conventional way out is as follows:

```
    BEQ SKIP
    JMP LOOP
.SKIP
```

Note that the opposite test (BEQ) is used instead of BNE so the jump is leap-frogged to the label SKIP.

Comparisons

It is often required to compare two numbers in order to set the status flags without altering the contents of the register. There are three instructions which perform this task, all of which set the N, Z and C flags:

CMP, which compares memory with the contents of the accumulator.
CPX, which compares memory with the contents of the X register.
CPY, which compares memory with the contents of the Y register.

The comparisons are done by subtracting the memory data from a copy of the register in question. The operational symbolism is therefore A−M, X−M or Y−M respectively. It is easy to get mixed up with the direction of the subtraction, so note carefully that the subtraction is from the register. A suitable branch instruction must follow a comparison (otherwise there would be no point in asking for the comparison). It is possible to get in

62 *Advanced Machine Code Techniques for The BBC Micro*

some funny mix-ups. The following examples may help in choosing the correct branch:

(1) To check if the register is *less* than memory, follow with BCC.
(2) To check if the register is *equal* to memory, follow with BEQ.
(3) To check if the register is *greater* than memory, follow with BEQ first then BCS.
(4) To check if the register is *greater than or equal to* memory, follow with BCS.

Addressing modes

Commencing with a definition, an addressing mode is the significance to be attached to the operand part of the instruction. Addressing modes available on the 6502 can be conveniently divided into three groups: non-indexed, simple indexed, and indirect indexed. Most of these modes may already be familiar to most readers, especially those who have read *Discovering BBC Micro Machine Code*. However, some revision or restatements are advisable, if only to maintain continuity during the lead-up to the rather nasty (nasty to grasp, that is) indirect addressing modes. Appendix C3 classifies instructions according to the addressing modes available.

Implied addressing
This is the simplest addressing mode in the repertoire because memory is not involved, neither is an operand required. They are all single byte instructions, conveying full information by the op-code alone. They all refer to internal operations on the 6502 registers. Because most of them only take two clock cycles, they are, or should be, the popular choice wherever possible.

Instructions which allow implied addressing and consume only two clock cycles are: CLC, CLD, CLI, CLV, DEX, DEY, INX, INY, NOP, SEC, SED, SEI, TAX, TAY, TSX, TXA and TXS.

The following take more than two clock cycles: BRK, PHA, PHP, PLA, PLP, RTI, and RTS.

Immediate addressing
Memory is not involved because the operand is the data. All instructions using immediate addressing consume two bytes: one for the op-code and one for the operand. The standard assembler prefix to denote this mode is the symbol (#). For example:

LDA #32 or LDA #&20

Both are using immediate addressing. The first example is loading the decimal number 32 into the accumulator while the second example loads hex 20. Whether to use hex or decimal is optional but the guiding rule is to choose the more natural form for the purpose in use. For normal numerical work, decimal would be the preferred notation but for AND, EOR or ORA masks, hexadecimal has more meaning. Although it may seem to be stating the obvious, the largest numerical operand is 255 or &FF because immediate addressing only allows a single byte operand. Risking another obvious statement, the assembler would be very unhappy if we tried to load negative numbers in the form LDA #–32.

Immediate addressing is used for constants, particularly in conjunction with comparison instructions at the end of a loop as, for example, CMP #20. The constant must, of course, be known to the programmer at the time of writing. In BASIC, we are usually extolled to avoid constants within the body of the program, the advice being to assign them to a variable at the head of the program. Such advice is not necessarily sound when applied to machine code because this would mean a trip to memory to obtain the data. The power of immediate addressing lies in the fact that memory is not involved: the data is *immediately* available in the instruction, providing, as said before, the programmer knows it at the time of writing.

There are eleven instructions which allow immediate addressing: ADC, AND, CMP, CPX, CPY, EOR, LDA, LDX, LDY, ORA and SBC.

Absolute addressing

We should begin by sorting out some of the confusing terms used by different authorities. The term 'direct' addressing is often used loosely when the operand refers to the *address* of data, rather than the data itself. Thus, the instruction LDA &0034 is an example of 'direct' addressing (note there is no '#' prefix).The instruction causes the contents of address &0034 to be placed in the accumulator. However, bearing in mind that 6502 has a 64K memory map, it will be evident that addresses between &0000 and &00FF would result in an inefficient use of memory space if the full four-hex digit address were mandatory. Since the data bus is only eight bits wide, the microprocessor would need to make two trips down the address and up the data bus to collect the full operand. The first two leading zeros are useless passengers.

To improve the efficiency, the address space is broken down into two domains. As mentioned in an earlier chapter, addresses within the range &0000 to &00FF are designated the page zero domain, to distinguish them from all other addresses &0100 to &FFFF. With regard to the terms used, the Motorola 6800 (the ancestor of the 6502) used the term 'direct' addressing instead of zero-page addressing and 'extended' addressing to cover the rest. Many machine code programmers, brought up on the 6800, had to readjust to the change in terminology. Returning to the 6502, the term 'absolute' addressing is applied to addresses anywhere in the 64K memory map. In other words, absolute addressing requires four hex digits, while zero-page addressing only requires two. Instructions using absolute addressing require three bytes, one for the op-code and two for the operand.

There are 21 instructions which allow absolute addressing. These are: ADC, AND, ASL, BIT, CMP, CPX, CPY, DEC, EOR, INC, JMP, JSR, LDA, LDX, LDY, LSR, ORA, ROL, STA, STX and STY.

Zero-page addressing

The concept of zero-page (sometimes called page-zero) is so important that it justifies emphasising the boundaries once again.

> Zero-page is the address range &00 to &FF or 0 to 255

There are reasons why this page deserves special treatment. There are obvious speed advantages, due to the single byte operand. This also leads to a saving in program memory space. Another reason is that the more complex addressing modes (to be dealt with later) require address pointers which must be in zero-page. Perhaps the most disappointing aspect is the scarcity of available space. The operating system, not surprisingly, occupies the vast majority of zero-page. In fact there are only *thirty-two* locations guaranteed free under all circumstances in the BBC machine:

> Free space in zero-page is between &70 and &8F inclusive

Because of the restricted space, it is essential, before planning any ambitious machine code systems, to choose zero-page locations with care. The apparent speed advantage is not, in itself, sufficient to justify squandering locations. In fact, it is sound philosophy to treat zero-page locations in the same light as registers – as valuable and scarce commodities. A good rule is to use zero-page for the most frequently used variable data. Sometimes, it may be wise to use zero-page for data within a loop, even if it means temporarily transferring it from an absolute address and then back again. The advantage of this approach may be appreciated more readily if we examine a few figures. Suppose a variable data item, located in an absolute address, is in the middle of a long loop which revolves 10000 times. Suppose we then transfer it temporarily to zero-page before entering the loop by using:

    LDA &xxxx   (absolute, 4 clock cycles)
    STA &xx   (zero-page, 3 clock cycles)

After the loop ends, the status quo can be regained with:

    LDA &xx   (zero-page, 3 clock cycles)
    STA &xxxx   (absolute, 4 clock cycles)

The four extra instructions for the complete transfer have taken a total of

The 6502 Instructions and Addressing Modes **65**

14 clock cycles and consumed an extra 10 bytes of programming space. The saving within the loop, however, would be 1 cycle per rev, leading to a total saving of 10000−14 = 9986 clock cycles. We shall see later that indirect address pointers in zero-page will take two bytes each and many of these may be required in a program of even moderate complexity.

Relative addressing

The intimate details of relative addressing are only of vital importance if the only method of entry is via a machine code monitor. Since the BBC machine has the advantage of assembler input, it is not necessary to spend quite so much time on the subject. It would not be wise, however, to skip the subject altogether. If we did, the hex columns of the assembler output could often look mysterious.

Relative addressing is only used with *branch* instructions. In fact, forgetting the assembler for a moment, relative addressing is the only method possible in branch instructions. Using hex machine code as an example,

    BEQ &04

The literal meaning is 'If equal to zero, branch 4 bytes forward'. The term 'relative' refers to the program counter. If the branch conditions are satisfied, the program counter (which always contains the address of the next program byte) has 04 added to it. This causes the next byte executed to be 04 bytes ahead, relative to the previous position. In other words, the operand indicates the number of bytes to be skipped. To branch backward, the two's complement is required (see Appendix A) so, to branch 04 bytes back, the instruction would be BEQ &FC. Clearly, the calculation of the correct operand is an error-prone exercise. The assembler takes all the drudgery out of relative addressing by allowing the operand to be a label instead of a relative address. We can use,

    BEQ Loop

This works, subject to the proviso that the line, to which we wish to branch, is prefixed with the 'Loop' label (naturally, the choice of label is arbitrary). The assembler is hiding from us the fact that relative addressing is being used. Instead, it appears as a simple 'branch to label' operation which is far less error-prone than grappling with relative addressing.

As for the timings of relative addressing, these will depend on whether or not the branch is taken. If taken, a branch takes 3 clock cycles or, if across a page boundary, 4 clock cycles. If it is not taken, the branch takes 2 clock cycles.

The extra cycle when a page boundary is crossed is due to the alteration to the *high*- as well as low-byte of the addresses. If speed is very critical, a programmer should watch the hexadecimal assembly listing closely to see if a page boundary is crossed. For example, suppose the program counter was showing &05FC prior to a branch. If the relative branch is &04 ahead, the new program counter reading would be &0600, therefore there has been a boundary crossing between page 5 to page 6 which consumes an extra clock cycle. If such a branch was in the middle of a loop which revolves N times, it would be sensible to manipulate the coding, or alternatively relocate, so that the branch range was limited to the same page, and saving N clock cycles. It is surprising how attention to such small details can result in a material gain in execution speed. Although terribly wasteful in terms of memory, it is better to cut loops out altogether and resort to straight-in-line coding if speed is absolutely vital. In most cases, this will be little more than an idealistic solution.

Indexed addressing

Although briefly discussed elsewhere, the concept of indexed addressing deserves detailed treatment. As far as the BBC assembler is concerned, the indexing mode is denoted by a *comma* following the operand, followed in turn by X or Y. For example:

LDA &2356,X or LDA &75,Y

Both are examples of indexed addressing but the first is using an absolute address and the second is using a zero-page address. The contents of the X (or Y) register is automatically added to the operand address before the instruction operates on the resultant address. It is well to recap on the terms used in indexed addressing:

(a) The base address is the address as stated in the operand.
(b) The relative address is the contents of index register (X or Y).
(c) The absolute address is the sum of the base and relative addresses.

As an example, assume that X contains 3 and that the instruction LDA &34,X is written. The *base* address is 34, the *relative* address is 3 and the *absolute* address is 34+3=37. Alternatively, the term 'effective' is often used in place of 'absolute'.

Two forms of indexed addressing are recognised:

(1) *Absolute indexed*, when the operand is any address in the 64K memory map. The instructions allowing X as the index register are ADC, AND, ASL, CMP, DEC, EOR, INC, LDA, LDY, LSR, ORA, ROL, SBC, and STA. The Y index register can be used in ADC, AND, CMP, EOR, LDA, LDX, ORA, SBC and STA.

(2) *Zero-page indexed*, when the operand is on page-zero. The instructions which allow X as the index register are ADC, AND, ASL, CMP, DEC, EOR, INC, LDA, LDY, LSR, ORA, ROL, SBC, STA and STY. There are only two instructions which allow the Y register for indexing. They are LDX and STX.

A mysterious bug can occur when using zero-page indexed addressing if the contents of X plus the operand address come to more than 255 or &FF. Clearly the single byte operand cannot hold numbers of this value so a wrap-around takes place. For example, if the instruction is LDA &FE and X contains 2, the arithmetical sum would be &100. The wrap-around action, however, will mean that the first hex digit is dropped and the absolute address will be &00 instead of &100.

Indexing allows any item in a block of data to be addressed by suitable adjustment of the index register. The operand of an indexed instruction (the base address) can be the address of the first item in the block or the last, depending on convenience or the programmer's whim. For example, if the base address is to be the start of the block, the index register can be incremented (by INX) within the loop until the last item is reached. On the other hand, it may be more convenient to choose the end of the data as the base address, in which case the index register is decremented (by DEX) until the first item is reached. Decrementation of the index register towards zero is generally recognised to be the more efficient method because the end-of-loop test can be carried out by a simple branch, such as BNE. The incrementation method demands a comparison (CPX or CPY) before the branch test. However, program legibility is sometimes more important than speed. There is a natural inclination to count up towards a finite limit rather than to count down towards zero and there is less chance of being 1 out in the count.

Besides accessing a data block sequentially, indexing is useful for *look-up tables*. For example, imagine a table of sines (or other mathematical functions) between, say, 0 and 89 degrees to be stored in a data block and the base address is where sin(zero) is located. The table can be accessed by

    LDA base, X

If the required angle is in X, the sine of the angle will be in the accumulator. The limitation of 8 bits for each sine will only give an accuracy to about two decimal places unless multi-byte working is used. Also, the programmer must take account of the decimal point when interpreting the result. Obviously, it would be absurd to use this method in place of the resident BASIC trig functions unless high speed access is vital.

Indexing is really address modification made easy. Besides being interesting, it is worth examining an alternative method (which was, historically, used before index registers were thought of) involving direct modification of the operand. This consists of loading the operand of an instruction into the accumulator (or other register), changing its value and then returning it to the previous location. To see how this works, consider the following line:

    STA blogs

The operand has an arbitrary symbolic address. If this were in a loop and we wished to store the next item in blogs+1 without using indexing, it could be achieved as follows:

```
.Modify STA blogs
        INC Modify+1
```

Note that the original line has now been given an arbitrary label 'Modify' which is where the op-code STA is stored, so blogs must be located in the next address, modify+1. The next line increments the contents of blogs+1 so we have achieved 'address modification' by a roundabout method. If the change is to be more than just a simple increment – say, adding 7 – the coding could be as follows:

```
.Modify STA   blogs
        LDA   Modify+1
        ADC   #7
        STA   Modify+1
```

Such direct alteration of an operand by the program itself is sometimes useful, but it is not a practice to be recommended. Listings of machine code are never easy to follow and these sorts of tricks can only add to the general confusion. It is worth emphasising that the primary function of an index register lies in the ability to alter the *effect* of an operand and without *altering the operand* itself. One disadvantage of the 6502, which soon becomes evident in the early stages of programming, is the limit of 8 bits. This, of course, restricts the range of addresses which can be scanned by indexing even when absolute indexing is used.

Indirect addressing

Mastering any subject consists of systematically overcoming the various intellectual hurdles which appear during a course of study. Student drop-outs may occur when a hurdle is reached which is just too high. In machine code programming, there are many hurdles to overcome but the one which is responsible for the greatest student drop-out ratio is the concept of *indirect addressing*. Indexing is relatively easy to grasp once the advantages of address modification are realised but the following definition may help in understanding why difficulties arise in indirect addressing.

> An indirect address is the address of an address.

In assembly language, indirect addressing is indicated by enclosing the operand in parentheses as follows:

    LDA (operand)

Note that although the operand is indeed an address, it is where the computer must go to find the address of the data. We shall continue for the moment to use LDA in examples, but it should be mentioned that simple indirect addressing as described above is only available with one instruction, JMP. Providing this is borne in mind, there is no harm in continuing with LDA in the initial stages. Consider the instruction:

LDA (&70)

Because of the parentheses, &70 is an indirect address, referring the computer to go to a *double-byte* address &70 (low-byte) and &71 (high-byte). This double-byte address is known as the *address pointer* because it 'points' to where the required data is located. Continuing with the examples, suppose that address &70 contains &35 and address &71 contains &0D. Returning now to the original instruction, LDA (&70), it should now be apparent that the contents of address &0D35 will be loaded into the accumulator. We will further assume that &0D35 contains &56

Let us recap, using this example to illustrate the terms once more:

The instruction was LDA (&70).
The indirect address is &70.
The address pointer is &0D35.
The data pointed to and finally loaded into the accumulator is &56.

Figure 3.1 may help in the understanding of the above example.

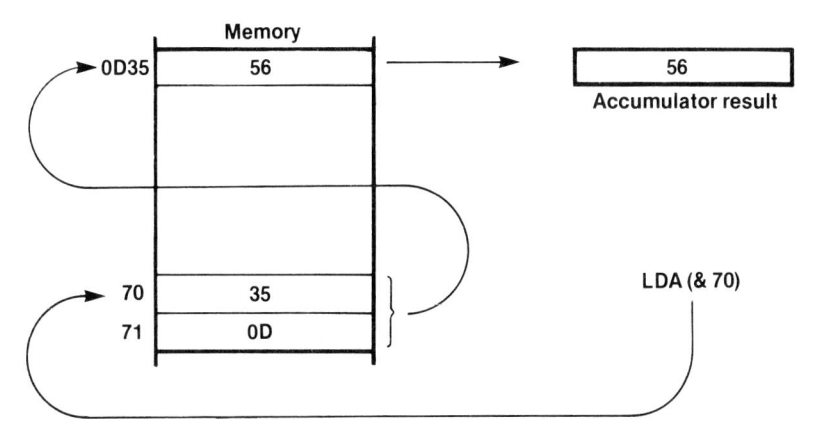

Fig. 3.1. Data flow in indirect addressing.

When first introduced to the idea of indirect addressing, it is difficult to grasp the use of it. It appears to be a complicated and tortuous path to follow, merely to place data in the accumulator. For instance, it is understandable, and pertinent, to ask why the line in the above example couldn't have been written in the simpler absolute addressing form:

LDA &0D35

After all, it may be argued, both forms would have identical effects. They would both load the same item of data into the accumulator, but the second form would not be wasting a valuable location (&70) in zero-page and would certainly be quicker to execute. The answer to this lies in the ability of indirect addressing to alter the effect of an operand without altering the operand itself. You will remember that this quality was the fundamental justification for the use of indexed addressing. If the address pointer is changed in any instruction using indirect addressing, the effect of the instruction acts on a different location. This has far-reaching advantages, particularly when writing general purpose machine code subroutines. Clearly, when writing a subroutine intended to act on a block of data, it would be restrictive to force the writer of the program using the subroutine to always place the data in a fixed memory block. However, with indirect addressing, all that is necessary is for the main program to know where the address pointer is (&70 and &71 in our previous example) and load it with the starting address of the data block. This flexibility means that the writer of the machine code subroutine need have no knowledge of the whereabouts of the eventual data block.

Before proceeding further, it should be remembered that the descriptions so far have been simplified by assuming that a 6502 has the instruction LDA (operand). Apart from the single instruction, JMP, simple indirect addressing is not supported. Instead, we have the added benefit (and unfortunately, the added complication) of indirect addressing combined with indexing. In fact, there are two forms to choose from, called 'indirect indexed' and 'indexed indirect'.

Indirect indexed addressing

This is the form most often required. Only the Y index register is allowed in this mode. The assembler form is:

   LDA (operand), Y

The operand is single byte and therefore can only refer to a zero-page address.

The only difference between this mode and simple indirect addressing is the addition of the Y register contents to the address pointer. That is to say, the operand still defines where a double-byte pointer is located but the pointer is modified by the *addition of the Y register contents*. As an example, assume that the following line is written:

   LDA (&70), Y

Also assume that the contents of address &70 contains &35, address &71 contains &0D and the Y register contains &02. The effective address pointer will be &0D35 + &02 = &0D37. The effect of the instruction is therefore to load the contents of address &0D37 into the accumulator. The example figures can be used to define a few more terms connected with indirect indexing:

The instruction was LDA (&70), Y.
The base address pointer was &0D35.
The relative offset in Y was &02.
The effective address pointer was &0D37.

Figure 3.2 illustrates the example.

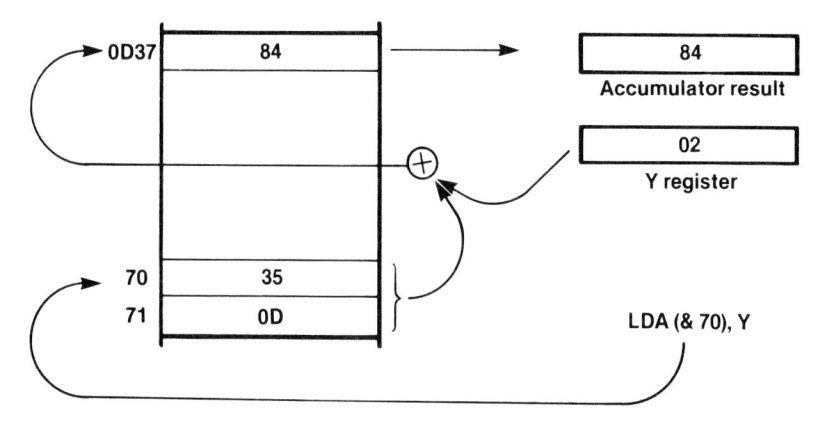

Fig. 3.2. Data flow in indirect indexed addressing.

Indirect indexed addressing allows the effect of the operand to be altered in either of two ways, by changing the base address pointer, by altering the contents of the Y register or both. The index register should be looked upon as an optional extra because there is no need to use it actively. For example, if Y is reset to &00, the instruction,

LDA (&70), Y

has the same effect as the simple (but fictitious) indirect addressing example given earlier:

LDA (&70)

However, an obvious use of indirect indexing lies in *sequencing through a block of data items* by incrementing or decrementing the Y register. It is helpful to distinguish simple indexed loops from indirect indexed loops by considering under what circumstances they would be used:

(a) Use simple indexing if the base address is known and constant.
(b) Use indirect indexing if the base address is not known at the time of writing or is liable to require changing.

One advantage of indirect addressing not yet mentioned is the ability to reach any part of the 64K memory map by use of a *single-byte* operand. This is because the address pointer in zero-page is double-byte (16 bits).

The following example is outline coding to perform a process on a block of memory with just sufficient detail to illustrate indirect indexed addressing. Assume that the address of the first data item has been prior assigned to the address pointer in &70 (low-byte) and &71 (high-byte) and the length of the block minus 1 is 20.

```
        LDY #20
.data   LDA (&70),Y
        .
        .
        process
        .
        .
        DEY
        BPL data
        .
        rest of program
```

The example should require little explanation, except perhaps to note that the indexing proceeds downwards towards zero, so the processing begins with the last data item and finishes with the first. As mentioned earlier, a downwards scan enables the end of the loop to be tested without the use of a CPY.

Some variations in the jargon exist. The alternative name for indirect indexed (and in some ways more informative) is 'post-indexed' indirect addressing because the indexing is done after the indirect address has been found. Also, address pointers are sometimes called *address vectors*.

Indirect indexed addressing is available with ADC, AND, CMP, EOR, LDA, ORA, SBC, and STA. They all take 5 clock cycles except STA which takes 6. If a page boundary is crossed, they take an extra clock cycle.

Indexed indirect addressing

This mode doesn't enjoy quite the same measure of popularity as indirect indexed. The assembler form is:

   LDA (operand, X)

Note carefully the position of the parentheses, that X is inside instead of outside and only X is allowed for indexing. As before, the operand must be single-byte so can only refer to a zero-page address.

X is shown within parentheses to emphasise the manner in which indexing is carried out. The behaviour of indexed indirect addressing is as follows:

> The address of the pointer in indexed indirect addressing is the sum of the operand and the contents of X.

This definition may explain why an alternative name of this mode is 'pre-indexed' indirect addressing. To aid understanding, first study the following numerical example:

The 6502 Instructions and Addressing Modes 73

LDA (&70,X)

In the first instance, assume that X is zero. The pointer is then the double byte address which happens to be in &70 (low-byte) and &71 (high-byte). However, if we assume that X contains &02, the address pointer is located at the double-byte address &72 and &73. Proceeding with this example, suppose that &72 contains &35 and &73 contains &0D, the instruction would load the accumulator with the contents of address &0D35. The example is illustrated in Fig. 3.3.

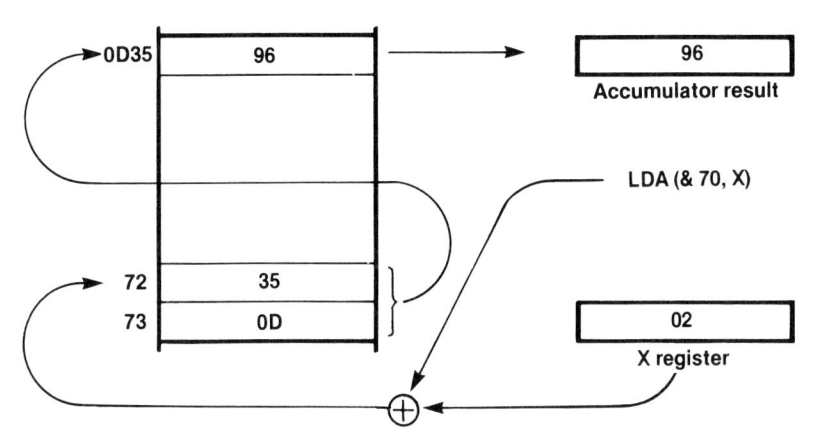

Fig. 3.3. Data flow in indexed indirect addressing.

Until familiarity is gained, it is easy to get mixed up with the two indirect modes because of the relatively superficial differences in the assembler form. In order to emphasise the difference in form and effect, it is worth viewing the two side by side:

Indirect indexed (post-indexed indirect) addressing keeps the pointer at a constant location but uses Y indexing to modify the pointer value.

Indexed indirect (pre-indexed indirect) addressing uses X indexing to modify the operand, and hence, the location of the address pointer.

As hinted earlier, indexed indirect addressing is not a commonly used mode. One area in which it is valuable is in handling peripheral interrupts. The course of a program can often depend on the particular peripheral which has requested interrupt. For example, the data sent to a printer will originate from a different area than the data sent to a digital-to-analogue converter. Assuming there are two peripherals on line, then we can arrange to have two separate address pointers to service them, located in zero-page. Suppose these double-byte addresses occupy the four locations &72, &73

and &74, &75 and consider the following line:

  STA (&70,X)

The value placed in X must be that which modifies the operand to locate the desired address pointer. Care should be taken when calculating the value of X. The indirect address pointer is a two-byte address, so X must be changed by two at a time, otherwise the instruction above will define the high-byte instead of the low-byte. For example, if X is initially zero, the address pointer selected is located at &72, &73. If X is incremented only once, there is a foul-up because the address pointer is taken to be &73, &74 which is the high-byte of the first pointer and the low-byte of the second.

Apart from handling peripherals, indexed indirect addressing can be used to simulate the CASE statement found in some of the structured languages or the ON GOTO in BASIC. Control can be switched to separate machine code processes, each switched by a unique address pointer. The value in X determines which process is activated.

Indexed indirect addressing is available with ADC, AND, CMP, EOR, LDA, ORA, SBC and STA.

Summary

1. A machine code instruction always has an op-code but not all have operands.
2. The op-code defines the required action; the operand indicates where data is to be found.
3. Addressing modes are various ways in which operands express location of data.
4. The computer recognises only binary op-codes expressed as two hex digits but the resident assembler allows three-letter mnemonic groups.
5. The precise effect of an instruction is more concise if written in operational symbolism rather than words.
6. During transfers, source data remains intact but old data at the destination is overwritten.
7. In normal use, the carry is cleared before adding but set before subtracting.
8. In double or multiple byte arithmetic, clear carry only before adding the lowest order bytes and set carry only before subtracting the lowest order bytes.
9. Memory or registers are cleared by a load zero. There are no CLR instructions.
10. There are no instructions to increment or decrement A.
11. Use AND to clear, ORA to set and EOR to change selected bits within a byte.
12. To flip over all bits, exclusive-or with &FF.

The 6502 Instructions and Addressing Modes

13. To produce two's complement, flip first and then add 1.
14. To find the state of a single bit, mask out uninteresting bits using AND and test for zero.
15. The BIT test copies bit 6 and 7 of the data into V and N bits respectively and ANDs the data into A.
16. LSR has the carry bit at the lsb end; ASR has the carry bit at the msb end.
17. Only shift and rotate instructions have accumulator-addressing.
18. In double-byte multiplication, use ASL for low-order and ROL for high-order byte.
19. In double-byte division, use LSR first for the high-order then ROR for the low-order byte.
20. The current state of the process status register determines whether or not a branch takes place.
21. Branch instructions themselves do not affect the process status register.
22. BMI and BPL are only useful if two's complement binary is used.
23. If the branch is out of range, combine with JMP.
24. In comparisons (CMP, CPX or CPY), the data is subtracted from the register in order to set flags but the original contents are restored.
25. To check if the register is less, use BCC; to check if equal use BEQ; to check if greater, use BEQ first then BCS.
26. Implied addressing has no operand.
27. Immediate addressing is when the operand, which must be single byte, is the data.
28. Absolute addressing is when the operand, which must be double-byte, is the address of the data.
29. Zero-page addressing is when the operand, which must be single byte, is the page-zero address of the data.
30. There are only 32 addresses guaranteed left free by the operating system, &70 to &8F inclusive.
31. Relative addressing, used only with branch instructions, is when the operand signifies how many bytes away is the next instruction.
32. Two's complement arithmetic is used to cover forward and backward branches. With the assembler, branch-to-label is possible.
33. Absolute indexed addressing is when the operand (which must be double byte) plus the index register, is the address of the data.
34. Zero-page indexed addressing is when the operand (which must be single byte) plus the index register, is the address of the data.
35. In an indexed instruction, the operand defines the base address, the index register the relative address. The sum of the two is the absolute or 'effective' address.
36. The operand in simple indirect addressing is the address of the lower order byte of a two-byte address pointer. Only JMP offers this mode.
37. JMP excepted, address pointers can only reside in zero-page (page-zero).

76 *Advanced Machine Code Techniques for The BBC Micro*

38. Indirectly indexed addressing modifies the address pointer by the addition of Y. The assembler operand format is (operand), Y.
39. Indexed indirect addressing modifies the address of the address pointer by the addition of the X register. The operand assembler format is (operand,X).
40. Address pointers are also called vectors.

Self test

3.1 Using three lines, multiply data in the accumulator by 3.
3.2 Write the instruction to clear bit 5 in the accumulator.
3.3 Write the instruction to change bits 3 and 6 in the accumulator.
3.4 Write the instruction to set bit 2 in the accumulator.
3.5 If the accumulator initially contains 17, what will it contain (in hex) after EOR #&FF?
3.6 What is wrong with LDA #&23DF?
3.7 Which 6502 register is involved in relative addressing?
3.8 In the BBC machine, where are the 32 free locations in page-zero (answer in decimal address range)?
3.9 If the effective address in the instruction EOR &73,X is &84, what is the relative address in hex?
3.10 Name the one instruction in the 6502 which offers non-indexed indirect addressing.
3.11 Which index register is allowed in indexed indirect addressing?
3.12 What addressing mode is being used in STA (&75),Y?
3.13 In the instruction ADC (&73),Y where is the high-byte of the address pointer located if Y contains 6?
3.14 In the instruction ADC (&73,X) where is the low-byte of the address pointer located if X contains 6?
3.15 What is an alternative name for indexed indirect addressing?

Chapter Four
Handling the Resident Assembler

The assembler format

An *assembler* is essentially a piece of software which aids the writing of machine code. Most personal computers offer only the crudest facilities for using machine code. Some only have a 'machine code monitor'. Others are even less equipped and the only way to enter a machine code program is by means of a boring and error-prone series of POKEs. It is not surprising that few owners of such machines develop a strong attraction for machine code. Of course, assemblers for most popular microcomputers are available on tape or disk but it is a sad fact of life that external software which has to be loaded, particularly from tape, is often too much trouble. Initially, it may be used with enthusiasm but the inevitable 'tape-inertia' syndrome eventually relegates the tape to its coffin.

Assemblers vary in sophistication and the facilities offered for debugging. It is unusual for a personal computer to be equipped with a *resident* assembler. No doubt manufacture's of machines for this market have previously assumed that few buyers, other than the completely dedicated, would be interested in any programming language other than BASIC. Acorn, conscious that interest in machine code would grow, included a resident assembler in the Atom, a practice which they have continued in the BBC machine.

The assembler used is unique because it is 'wedged' inside the BASIC chip. The position of the assembler inside the language system ensures easy transition between BASIC and machine coding. Machine code splices within a BASIC program are recognised by the *large square brackets*[and]. (These appear on the screen as left- and right-pointing arrows in Mode 7 on the BBC machine.) Although the assembler lacks many of the refinements found in traditional mainframe-oriented software, it is perfectly adequate and quite easy to use. In fact, some features of its design could be considered superior to classical assemblers. Although many readers will already be familiar with the facilities offered, it is necessary, for the sake of continuity, to devote a little space to the following overview.

78 *Advanced Machine Code Techniques for The BBC Micro*

Mnemonic op-codes

Bearing in mind the function of an assembler defined at the beginning of this chapter, the foremost requirement of any assembler is the substitution of *meaningful* letter groups for the instruction op-codes. Thus, to transfer X to A, the hex machine code is &8A (see Appendix C1). The assembler allows us to write TXA instead. All mnemonic op-codes are three-letter groups.

Numerical operands

Numerical values in operands are assumed to be decimal. If the number is to be interpreted as hex, they must be prefixed with the & character.

Operand variables

The most remarkable and useful property of the assembler is the lattitude allowed with variables. The following deserves emphasis:

> Any legitimate BASIC variable or expression can be used in the operand.

Examples:
```
100 LDA LOCK
110 LDA LOCK+1
120 LDA #ASC("Y")
130 LDA #BASE DIV 256
140 LDA #BASE MOD 256
150 LDA #SQR(4)
```

These are all expressions which the assembler will accept although the following common sense provisos apply:

(1) The operand expression must be capable of intelligent decoding. That is to say, the resultant must be an address or data acceptable as an *operand*.
(2) Registers (A, in the above examples) can only hold *one* byte so it will be up to the programmer to ensure that the data, represented by the variables, is within this limit.
(3) It is essential that the variables be *pre-defined* in the BASIC program area. For example, we cannot write A=30 inside an area enclosed by the square brackets [.....].
(4) Although BASIC expressions can be used, BASIC commands are most definitely illegal. The assembler would ruthlessly reject lines like PRINT A or DEF PROCsort. BASIC commands or statements must be confined to the BASIC area.

BASIC variables and expressions can also be used in jump operands such as:

```
JMP START+7
```

Handling the Resident Assembler

This will cause a jump to the address found by adding 7 to the contents of the variable START.

Branch labels

The previous chapter, dealing with branch instructions and relative addressing, stressed the difficulties associated with counting the number of bytes forward or backwards to reach the desired branch destination. The assembler, to a large extent, offers relief by allowing the use of *labels*. Thus the assembler disguises the inherent relative addressing and substitutes a straightforward 'branch to label'. For example, we can write:

```
BNE Sort
```

Here 'Sort' is the branch operand, referring to a label appearing somewhere in the program.

The label is recognised as such by the assembler because it must *begin* with a full-stop as shown in the following example:

```
CLC
.BACK LDA Number1
ADC Number2
BEQ Finish
ROR A
BNE BACK
.Finish RTS
```

The coding obviously has no practical value so it would be pointless to key in. Note the full-stop before the two labels and note also that there must be no full-stop when the label is an operand directive. The layout is valid but considerable latitude is allowed. For example, it could be re-written as follows:

```
CLC
.BACK
LDA Number1
ADC Number2
BEQ Finish
ROR A
BNE BACK
.Finish RTS
```

Notice that the label can stand alone or be on the same line as the instruction, providing there is at least one space separation. The label, although existing within the assembled coding, can also be considered to be a normal BASIC variable. It is, after all, an address and therefore a simple numeric. We could, for instance, discover this address (when out of the assembler and back in BASIC) by writing PRINT BACK or PRINT Finish. A problem arises, which we shall deal with later, when assembling coding in which branches are made to forward positions.

Remarks

Remarks, which programmers feel are necessary to explain coding, must be distinguished by either the semicolon or the back slash (\). For example:

LDA (pointer,Y) \Indirect loading

We shall use the back slash because it seems a more meaingful symbol and also because the semicolon is strongly associated with the PRINT statement in BASIC. Remember that the back slash in the BBC machine Mode 7 appears on the screen as a funny '½' character.

Multi-statements

As in BASIC, more than one assembly instruction can be placed on one line by using the full colon as a separator. For example:

**[
CLC:ADC Number:ADC #4:RTS
]**

It must be appreciated that the square brackets, which enclose assembly coding, have the status of an instruction, even though they are categorised as 'pseudo instructions'.

Writing many statements per line is popular in BASIC because programs appear shorter in length and less bytes are squandered in storing line numbers. In assembly code, although the length of the program still appears less, there is no real saving because the action of assembly produces the same final object program. Another disadvantage of multi-statements per line is the decrease in readability. A program written in assembly code is not exactly an easy thing to decipher (even for the writer!) and cramming a lot on one line increases the confusion, besides leaving less room for remarks.

Storing assembly code

When writing a BASIC program, we have no worries about where it will be stored in memory. It is left entirely to the operating system, which stores it in accordance with built-in rules. However, when a piece of assembly code is written, the assembler has no such built-in authority. It is up to the programmer to provide guidance on the desired starting location of the program in memory. Naturally, the guidance given must steer clear of the RAM space already earmarked by the operating system. There are several reasonably free areas in the BBC machine, besides space made artificially by shifting the BASIC text and variable areas around. Before discussing the details of free spaces, it is important to stress the vital importance of one of the special resident integer variables P%. As readers are already aware, the

Handling the Resident Assembler 81

complete set of these twenty-seven special variables are labelled @%,A% ... Z%. They all occupy fixed locations and can be picked up at any time by the operating system or assembler. Returning to P%,

> The contents of P% are taken as the address of the next item of machine code.

Thus, to locate a program anywhere in memory, it is simply a case of loading the starting address of the first byte into P%. After each byte is stored, P% is automatically incremented by one in readiness for the next byte. In fact, it is convenient to relate P% to the microprocessor program counter.

The setting of P% must be carried out in the BASIC part of the composite program. For example:

```
10 P%=&0D00
20 [
30     \
40     \
50     \Assembly coding
60     \
70     \
80 ]
90 REM rest of BASIC
```

This would store the first byte of assembly code (wedged between BASIC) in the hex address 0D00. It is possible to use variable names when loading P% so we could have written the top bit of the previous example as:

```
10 START%=&0D00
20 100 P%=START%
```

Instead of committing P% to a fixed machine address, it is possible to delegate some of the responsibility to the operating system. Page 237 of the BBC User Guide tells us that the Dimension statement can be twisted a little in order to accommodate byte arrays. For example:

```
DIM START% 99
P%=START%
```

This will reserve 100 bytes for assembly code, the first byte located in START% (START% is, of course an arbitrary name). It is important to recognise the unusual character of the DIM statement in line 100. There are indeed two variations from the normal BASIC statement for dimensioning arrays. The first point to notice is the absence of the brackets around the 99 although the space before 99 is mandatory. The second point, less vital but still useful to know, is that START% should not be thought of as the 'name of the array'. It is merely the labelled address of where the first byte is stored. The storage area, like the normal DIM statement, is 'dynamic'. That is to say, it moves up or down depending on the number of lines in the BASIC area. However, the actual machine address of the first byte in the example above can always be ascertained by a command, such as PRINT START%. The snag in using the DIM statement is the fact that you have to make an intelligent guess as to the number of bytes in your coding. The best way is to make a preliminary estimate and then add, say, twenty more for luck because it doesn't matter if you over-estimate. However, if you are a stickler for having things dead right, it is easy to count the bytes after the final debugging and alter the DIM number accordingly.

Other ways of finding space for assembly code are by the use of the *pseudo variables* TOP and PAGE. Space (for example 256 bytes) can be found below the BASIC program by using PAGE in the following manner:

```
100 PAGE=PAGE+256
110 P%=PAGE-256
```

The first line pushes PAGE upwards, and therefore the start of the BASIC program. This will reserve 256 bytes for the assembly coding which, as line 110 suggests, starts at the old PAGE position. If we wish to reserve some of the assembly area for, say, 20 data bytes, line 110 can be written as:

```
110 P%=PAGE-236
```

This leaves 20 bytes for data, the first item being in PAGE and the last in PAGE+19. The assembly program will follow, beginning at PAGE +20.

If we use LOMEM, the program and/or data can be positioned between TOP (the top of the BASIC program) and LOMEM (where BASIC stores its variables). (See the memory map on page 501 of the BBC User Guide.) For example:

```
100 LOMEM=LOMEM+256
110 P%=TOP
```

This will reserve 256 bytes for assembly coding, the first byte being in TOP. The User Guide warns us not to attempt to alter LOMEM in the middle of a program or the interpreter will lose track of the variables.

Fixed locations which are potentially free
There is nothing wrong with storing assembly programs and data 'dynamically' as described above. However, storing in a fixed location has, at least, a psychological advantage. You always know exactly where the program is stored and this can be comforting. The trouble with fixed storage in the BBC Micro is its scarcity.

The BBC machine has plenty of fixed free space providing that some of

Handling the Resident Assembler

the normal and expansion facilities are sacrificed. For example, page &0D is perfectly safe and is actually described in the User Guide as space for 'user-supplied resident routines'. Unfortunately, this is subject to the proviso that no disk interface is used. It is also possible to use page &C0 if we are prepared to sacrifice user-defined character definitions. Page &B0 is yet another page available but this time we will lose the facility of programming those delightful red function keys. Use of any of these pages will therefore depend on individual needs, but it is useful to know that three contiguous pages are potentially free, representing a total memory range &0B00 to &0DFF. This is a hefty 768 bytes which, in machine code terms, is capable of supporting a complex program.

However, for those with disk or other expansion options it is advisable to steer clear of fixed locations altogether. It is safer to use the DIM statement. Any subsequent programs given which use fixed locations (to simplify explanations) can always be modified to DIM methods.

Operating the assembler code

To execute a BASIC program, we use the keyword RUN. To execute a machine code program we use the keyword CALL. Both RUN and CALL are BASIC keywords, a fact which serves to emphasise the close relationship between the assembler and the BASIC interpreter. The simple word CALL is very powerful because it combines the role of parameter-passing with machine code execution. Before delving into great detail, it is useful to study the following sequence of events starting with the source code and ending with the final execution:

1. *A source code listing*

```
10 P%=&0D01
20 [
30 LDA #99
40 STA &0DFF
50 ]
60 PRINT:PRINT"The contents of &0DFF
is ";?&0DFF
```

Line 10 positions the code in page &0D, a quite arbitrary decision. Lines 30 and 40 are the assembly code which loads the accumulator with decimal 99 then stores it in &0DFF. Line 60 is BASIC and prints out the contents of this address, using the byte indirection operator.

2. *Running the program*

When we type RUN, the result is:

84 *Advanced Machine Code Techniques for The BBC Micro*

```
0D00
0D00  A9 63      LDA #99
0D02  8D FF 0D   STA &0DFF
```

The contents of address &0DFF is 13.

This is the work of the assembler and indeed is called an *assembly listing*. It has produced the correct machine code from our mnemonic source code. The first column is the hex address of the *first byte* on *that line*. The second column is the hex machine code consisting of the op-code, followed by the operand. Notice that the two-byte operand is low-byte, high-byte form and appears back to front. The third column is our original source code.

Note carefully that we have RUN but the machine code doesn't appear to have worked because the printout is 13 instead of the expected 99. This is because the machine code has only been assembled – that is to say, it has only been converted from our source code to a pure machine code form. But we have not yet told the code to be executed! Thus, the 'answer' we got of 13 was merely garbage that happened to be in &0DFF. If you try it, you will have a different garbage number (unless the law of averages break down). So, we need another step.

3. *Executing the machine code with CALL*

   CALL &0D01

Nothing visible happens but the machine code has been executed. To prove it, RUN the program again. This will produce exactly the same results as the previous RUN but with one important difference. The BASIC line at the bottom will now read:

   The contents of address &0D01 is 99

The steps shown above have deliberately been separated in order to emphasise the difference between the assembly and the call processes. In practice, the CALL would normally be included under a line number in the program rather than activated by a separate command. For example, the listing above could be written:

```
10 P%=&0D01
20 [
30 LDA #99
40 STA &0DFF
45 RTS
50 ]
55 CALL &0D01
60 PRINT:PRINT"The contents of &0DFF
   is ";?&0DFF
70 END
```

Apart from the extra CALL line, notice that RTS has been squeezed in. This should be considered the normal way to terminate machine code routines in order to ensure smooth control *back to BASIC* after the code has been executed. Without RTS, an error message from the assembler might (probably will) appear. Now when we type RUN, the program will automatically assemble the code, line 55 will execute it and RTS returns control back to BASIC at line 60.

Controlling the assembler output
The *pseudo operation* OPT controls the activities of the assembler. It is fully described in the User Guide but is repeated (with less detail) here.

The format is OPT pass, where pass is a variable which can be 0, 1, 2 or 3.

If pass=0, the assembly listing is suppressed and no errors are reported.
If pass=1, only assembly errors are suppressed.
If pass=2, only assembly listing is suppressed.
If pass=3, nothing is suppressed

It is important to remember that OPT is not a BASIC keyword, consequently it is only legal within the square bracket area. If OPT is not used, it defaults to OPT 3. Since the previous examples have not used OPT, the assembly listing appeared and assembly errors might also have appeared. It is often inconvenient and purposeless to display these except during the development and debugging stage.

The forward branch problem and 2-pass assembly
If a branch instruction directs control backwards to a labelled line, the assembler can cope immediately because it has picked up the address of the label on the way. However, if the branch directs to a forward address, the assembler is confused. To see why, imagine what happens in the following piece of code:

```
110  BNE exit
120     :
130     :
140  .exit
```

The main job of the assembler is to change mnemonic op-codes and operands into equivalent hex numbers and addresses. So what happens when it reaches line 110? It can easily look up its conversion table to find the hex code for BNE (it is D0). But it can't determine the hex address of the operand because it hasn't yet reached line 140. Its intelligence is just not equal to the situation, so it gives up.

The BBC assembler is not peculiar in this respect. It is a common problem in all but the most sophisticated versions. The standard way out is

86 *Advanced Machine Code Techniques for The BBC Micro*

to give the assembler two goes at it, a trick known as two-pass assembly. The first pass collects all the labels and addresses and the second pass uses them to produce the final assembly.

It would be boring and error-prone if the operator always had to assemble programs twice. Fortunately, the FOR/NEXT loop in BASIC can be left to do the donkey-work. The following piece of code includes a simple forward branch and illustrates the two-pass assembly technique:

```
100 FOR pass=0 TO 3 STEP 3
110 P%=&0D00
120 [
130 OPT pass
140 LDA #3
150 CMP #3
160 BEQ Finish
170 NOP
180 .Finish RTS
190 ]
200 NEXT pass
210 CALL &0D00
220 END
```

The code itself is purposeless and barely worth explaining. It is easy to see that the forward branch, (the object of the example), will always take place. Line 170 could have been any useless instruction so NOP is exceptionally well-qualified. Note the following points:

(1) The FOR loop ensures that OPT 0 applies during the first pass. We don't want a listing and we certainly don't want the inevitable error 'unknown label' to appear.

2. During the second pass, OPT 3 applies so the assembly listing appears and any errors (there shouldn't be any now) are reported.

3. The assigning of P% is *inside* the FOR loop. This ensures that the second pass starts again on the same piece of code. If P% was assigned before the FOR statement, the second pass would try and assemble code following on from the first pass with unpleasant results.

(4) The NEXT statement which closes the FOR loop must be *outside* the square brackets.

(5) If assembly code is intermixed with BASIC lines, it is necessary to include an appropriate OPT *each time*, otherwise it would default to OPT 3.

Using variable names

The facility to predefine memory locations with BASIC variables and use them in assembly code should be exploited to the full. Any dodge which makes assembly code look less formidable is worthwhile, even if it does squander a few BASIC lines. For example:

Number 1=&70
Number 2=&71

Having defined these locations, the variable names can be used in assembly operands, rather than absolute hex addresses. The following example, which adds two numbers (limited to single byte), illustrates some of the interchanges possible between BASIC and assembler:

```
 10 DIM START% 40
 20 CLS
 30 INPUT"Enter first number "Number1
 40 INPUT"Enter second number "Number2
 50 Result=&70
 60 P%=START%
 70 [
 80 CLC
 90 LDA #Number1
100 ADC #Number2
110 STA Result
120 RTS
130 ]
140 CALL START%
150 PRINT ?Result
```

Just for a change, the program is stored by courtesy of DIM, instead of using fixed free space. It is easy to get mixed up with the address of data and the data itself. For example, it may not be obvious why lines 90 and 100 must have the hash mark denoting immediate addressing. Note also that line 150 prints the contents of 'Result'. If 'Result' was printed, it would be an address rather than data in that address.

Macros

A *macro* is short for macro-instruction, a facility offered in some assemblers, whereby a block of instructions performing some task can be defined by name, and later treated as if it were a single instruction. Superficially, this description resembles an ordinary subroutine so it is important to compare them with a view to spotting the differences.

A subroutine is written once, stored in some fixed location and called up by a special jump (JSR). A macro, on the other hand, is assembled in machine code *each time* it is used in the body of the program. For example, suppose the following is a macro in a fictitious (and using an equally fictitious format) machine:

88 *Advanced Machine Code Techniques for The BBC Micro*

```
Macro TDX.
DEX
DEX
DEX
End Macro
```

The macro is first defined and given some arbitrary name (TDX in example). The macro is then written (three consecutive decrements in the example). The macro is then terminated. From now on, anytime we use TDX, the assembler will include the three instructions in the coding. Note that there is no 'jump' action. The macro is inserted in line every time. Because there is no time wasted in calling and returning from a subroutine, a macro has a higher execution speed.

```
>LIST
   10 REM Procedures used as macros
   20 DIM START% 40
   30 P%=START%
   40 [:LDA #1:]
   50 PROCshiftleft3
   60 [:STA &70:]
   70 PROCshiftleft3
   80 [:STA &71
   90 RTS
  100 ]
  110 CALL START%
  120 PRINT?&70
  130 PRINT?&71
  140 END
  150 DEF PROCshiftleft3
  160 [:ASL A:ASL A:ASL A:]
  170 ENDPROC

>RUN
19EF
19EF A9 01     LDA #1
19F1
19F1 0A        ASL A
19F2 0A        ASL A
19F3 0A        ASL A
19F4
19F4 85 70     STA &70
19F6
19F6 0A        ASL A
19F7 0A        ASL A
19F8 0A        ASL A
19F9
19F9 85 71     STA &71
19FB 60        RTS
           8
          64
```

Program 4.1. Procedures used as macros.

Handling the Resident Assembler

Now for the crunch. There is no macro facility in the BBC machine, at least not directly. However, it is possible to wangle it by exploiting BBC BASIC's most powerful asset, the *Procedure*. Instead of naming a macro, we name a procedure. Defining the macro is replaced by DEF PROCname. Naturally, we must define the procedure in BASIC and use it in BASIC, but the assembler is undaunted providing the square brackets are used correctly.

To illustrate, Program 4.1 loads the accumulator with 1 and then uses a simple 'macro' to produce three shift lefts on the accumulator. The macro is used twice, so the accumulator is shifted 6 times. After RUN, the assembly listing appears. You will notice that the three ASL instructions are indeed assembled in-line each time the 'macro' is used. This example should emphasise the difference between macros and subroutines. We have stated that a macro is faster and yet, from the assembly listing it is not too obvious why. Actually, the time it takes actually to assemble macros may indeed be longer than assembling the equivalent subroutine. Once assembled (which only has to be done once) however, the execution is faster with macros because no time is wasted in jumping and returning (JSR takes 6 clock cycles and so does RTS). Against this, however, it should be realised that macros use up memory for the assembly code *each time* they are called.

The main hazard, when using procedures to simulate macros, is failing to observe the rules of the square brackets when dodging in and out of BASIC. The brackets can be round the wrong way or in the wrong places. Program 4.1 above uses a standardised format with the brackets enclosing the procedure call and on the same line.

As with normal procedure calls and definitions, it is possible to pass formal parameters into the assembly enclosure. For example, we can define a procedure as follows:

```
500 DEF PROCsubtract(number1,number2)
510 [
520 SEC
530 LDA number1
540 SBC number2
550 ]
560 ENDPROC
```

Once such a procedure is defined, it can be used to subtract, say, contents of Tax from Gross by using:

PROCsubtract (Gross, Tax)

Naturally, such a simple procedure can only handle a single byte subtraction but this is irrelevant – it is the principle that matters.

Conditional assembly
This technique, like macros, is commonplace in professional mainframe assemblers. It simply means that certain changes can be made in assembly code without having to reassemble each time. Again like macros, it is not

directly available on the BBC machine but can be simulated by a mixture of BASIC and machine code. As a simple example, it may be that during program development we would like to try the effect of X=4 or X=40 in the same program. A simple IF/THEN/ELSE spliced in the right place would do the job nicely:

IF Speed=slow THEN [: LDX #4:]ELSE[: LDX #40:]

Passing parameters via registers

There are various ways of passing parameters from the main program (which could be BASIC) to a machine code subroutine. The simplest, but not always the most advisable, is via registers. The three most important resident subroutines, OSRDCH, OSWRCH and OSBYTE (discussed in a later chapter) all use registers for parameter passing. OSRDCH and OSWRCH use the accumulator; OSBYTE uses the accumulator and the X and Y index registers.

Apart from the enforced use in resident subroutines, registers are not the ideal medium for passing parameters. The 6502 is not generous as far as they will already be holding variable data – although, of course, the stack can be used as a temporary store while the registers are being used. Fortunately, alternatives are available in the shape of the USR and CALL statements.

Passing parameters with CALL

The CALL statement is far more powerful than has been indicated earlier in the chapter. For example, we can use:

CALL NAME, G%, A$, Blogs

This shows that, in addition to actually calling (executing) machine code, it is possible to pass a variety of mixed parameters (integer variables, string variables and floating point variables and even single byte numbers) to the assembly code. Essential information on the parameters is passed to a special memory block located in the BBC machine at &0600 onwards. This block contains the following information:

&0600	number of parameters passed in CALL statement
&0601	low byte address of first parameter
&0602	high byte address of first parameter
&0603	code for parameter type
&0604	low byte address of second parameter
&0605	high byte address of second parameter
&0606	code for parameter type

Handling the Resident Assembler 91

&0607	low byte address of third parameter
&0608	high byte address of third parameter
&0609	code for parameter type

This sequence is repeated for any further parameters.
The parameter code which has been referred to above is as follows:

    0   8-bit byte (example ?Z)
    4   32-bit integer variable (example Volts%)
    5   5 byte floating-point number (example Blogs)
    81   string variable (example Name$)
    80   string at a defined address (example $Name)

The reference above to simple variables, also applies to array variables: For example, A%(3), C(3) or B$(5).

The parameter block format always begins with the number of variables attached to the CALL. Thereafter, three bytes of information are given for each variable. If, for example, there are five variables in all, there will be 1+(3×5)=16 bytes of information, starting at &0600 and ending at &060F. It is worth stressing that the information given is not the data itself but the address to which the data has been transferred. These addresses are not constant and only the operating system will be aware of them. When such a situation arises (in which only addresses are given) the data can be easily obtained by the use of indirect addressing. All that needs to be done is to treat the address information as pointers which can be passed to page-zero for use by indirect address action. It is possible to avoid indirect addressing to obtain this data by a series of LDAs and STAs but it is messy and inefficient.

It is easy to be confused by all this so it is essential to attack the subject in gentle steps. We begin by writing a few lines of code just to test that the CALL statement is indeed operating as described above. This code is shown in Program 4.2.

To keep the first example simple, only one parameter is passed in line 20. It is spread out in hex in order to appreciate the result more readily. Since we are demonstrating CALL, there must be some bit of machine code to call, so to maintain simplicity it is sufficient to use a NOP (we are not, at this stage, interested in the particular code). Line 90 is in BASIC and calls up the code, passing G% to the system. Lines 110 to 130 print out (in hex) the contents of the parameter block. On first running the program, it stops at line 140 and displays the assembly code and the contents of the parameter block which have the following significance:

    1   number of parameters passed (just G%)
    1C   low-byte address of where the first byte of G% is stored
    4   high-byte address
    4   parameter code (4=four-byte integer)

92 *Advanced Machine Code Techniques for The BBC Micro*

```
>LIST
   10 REM Passing variables via CALL
   20 G%=&01234567
   30 P%=&0D00
   40 START=P%
   50 [
   60 NOP
   70 RTS
   80 ]
   90 CALL START,G%
  100 PRINT
  110 FOR Block=&0600 TO &0603
  120 PRINT~?Block
  130 NEXT
  140 END
  150 Pointer=&041C
  160 FOR Data=Pointer TO Pointer+3
  170 PRINT ~Data,~?Data
  180 NEXT

>RUN
0D00
0D00 EA         NOP
0D01 60         RTS

            1
           1C
            4
            4
>GOTO150
          41C         67
          41D         45
          41E         23
          41F          1
```

Program 4.2. Passing variables via the CALL statement.

Thus, we are now in the position of knowing that our data has been stored in address &041C. You may see from this why it was necessary to stop the program at line 140. The preliminary RUN gave us the address information. A GOTO 150 then executes the bottom program which displays the contents of the four addresses &041C to &041F. The original G% has therefore been successfully recovered although in the conventional reverse order (low-byte first). It would have been possible to use the indirection operator (!) instead of the FOR/NEXT loops but the display would have packed horizontally instead of being in more readable, vertical separation steps.

The next program (Program 4.3) goes a step further by showing indirect address pointers picking up parameter data from the call statement. The

Handling the Resident Assembler 93

```
>LIST
   10   REM Passing variables via CALL (2
)
   20   POINTER=&70
   30   RESULT=&80
   40   START=&0C00
   50   P%=START
   60   [
   70   LDA &0601 \Store LB/HB
   80   STA POINTER    \Address of volts
   90   LDA &0602      \in zero page
  100   STA POINTER+1
  110   LDA #0
  120   LDA (POINTER),Y \indirect address
  130   STA RESULT
  140   RTS
  150   ]
  160   INPUT"ENTER INTEGER "Volts%
  170   CALL START,Volts%
  180   PRINT"THE INTEGER PASSED WAS "?RE
SULT
```

Program 4.3. Passing variables and use of indirect address pointers.

idea is to pass the address given in the parameter block at &0600, 0601 to the page zero addresses &70, &71 where they will act as the address pointer. The program is best understood by starting at the three lines of BASIC at the bottom (160 to 180 inclusive). The objective, again deliberately kept simple, is to input an integer variable (Volts%), pass it through the CALL procedure and print it out again, merely to prove the points described above. At the top of the program three preliminary assignments are made but you should particularly note line 20. It is a convention that the label, assigned to the lowest byte, is used to refer to the whole number, irrespective of the number of bytes. Lines 70 to 100 transfer the address information (where Volts% is stored) into the two zero-page addresses. Notice the economy of using POINTER and POINTER+1 for the low- and high-byte respectively. This is why only the low-byte pointer was assigned in line 20. This little dodge is useful and will appear frequently in subsequent examples.

Line 120 is the most important of all because it illustrates the beauty of indirect addressing. Index register Y is first cleared because it has no meaning in this context. All we want is simple indirect addressing without indexing. Although indirect indexed addressing is used, we could have substituted indexed indirect addressing – providing that the X register, instead of the Y register, was cleared initially.

Proceeding another step further, Program 4.4 adds two single-byte numbers, both of them passed via the CALL statement. BASIC is used to input the two numbers into A% and B% and then passed to the system by means of CALL ADD, A%, B%. Since there are two variables, we reserve space for the address pointers in page-zero. The two assignments

```
>LIST
   10 REM 8-bit integer addition
   20 MODE 4
   30 FIRST=&70:SECOND=&72
   40 RESULT=&80
   50 ADD=&0C00
   60 FOR PASS=0 TO 3 STEP 3
   70 P%=ADD
   80 [OPT PASS
   90 LDA &0601
  100 STA FIRST
  110 LDA &0602
  120 STA FIRST+1
  130 LDA &0604
  140 STA SECOND
  150 LDA &0605
  160 STA SECOND+1
  170 LDY #0
  180 CLC
  190 LDA (FIRST),Y \Add pos integers
  200 ADC (SECOND),Y \indirect address
  210 STA RESULT,Y  \Indexed address
  220 RTS:]
  230 NEXT
  240 PRINT
  250 PRINT"Addition of two unsigned int
egers ":PRINT
  260 INPUT"First unsigned integer ",A%
  270 INPUT"Second unsigned integer ",B%
  280 CALL ADD,A%,B%
  290 PRINT"Addition= ";?RESULT
```

Program 4.4. Single-byte addition.

for this (appropriately labelled 'FIRST' and 'SECOND') are made in line 30. Space is also reserved for RESULT in line 40. Lines 90 to 120 transfer the address information of A% in &0601, &0602 to &70 and &71. Lines 130 to 160 perform a similar task for B%. After clearing Y and the carry bit, lines 190 to 210 perform the addition, again using indirect addressing.

Although unnecessary (there are no forward branches in the assembly code), the two pass assembly process has been included for the first time. It is a good habit to cultivate, even when unnecessary, in order to maintain consistency in program layout.

Passing variables by means of USR

Although CALL is ideal for passing parameters to the assembler, it lacks the facility for directly returning parameters back from the assembler. The USR function is sometimes a more convenient, although less versatile,

Handling the Resident Assembler 95

option. The general format of the USR function is as follows:

Result=USR (calling address)
Examples: D%=USR (START), Blogs= USR(&0D00)

Unlike CALL, the parameters to be passed must first be assigned to the four resident integer variables. A%,X%,Y% and C%. When USR is used, the information in these variables is transferred to the microprocessor registers of the same name with C% going into the Carry flag. The transfer is subject to the following provisos:

(1) Only the low order bytes of A%,X% and Y% can be passed to A,X and Y registers.
(2) Only the least significant bit of C% can be passed to the C flag in the processor status register.

```
>LIST
   10 REM 8bit INTEGER ADDITION
   20 REM DEMONSTRATING USR
   30 MODE4
   40 STORE=&70
   50 ADD=&0C00
   60 FOR PASS=0 TO 3 STEP 3
   70 P%=ADD
   80 [OPT PASS
   90 STX STORE      \STORE X REG
  100 LDX #0         \SET HIGH BYTE TO 0
  110 CLC
  120 ADC STORE
  130 BCC FINISH     \INCREMENT RESULT
  140 INX            \HIGH BYTE IF CARRY
  150 .FINISH        \IS SET
  160 RTS:]
  170 NEXT PASS
  180 PRINT
  190 PRINT"ADDITION OF TWO UNSIGNED 8bi
t INTEGERS"
  200 PRINT
  210 INPUT"FIRST UNSIGNED 8bit INTEGER
",A%
  220 INPUT"SECOND UNSIGNED 8bit INTEGER
",X%
  230 RESULT=USR(&0C00)
  240 RESULT=RESULT AND &0000FFFF
  250 REM MASK OUT UNWANTED BITS
  260 PRINT"ADDITION= ";RESULT
```

Program 4.5. 8-bit integer addition called by USR.

After exit from the assembly code, a four-byte integer is returned to the result-variable *supplied by the user.* This integer is the composite contents of the four registers P, Y, X, A in that order. For example, suppose we used:

    Blogs=USR (START)

Suppose also that the assembly code, on exit, left the registers with the following contents:

    A=&FC, X=&67, Y=&FF and P (the process status register)=&03

On exit, the variable Blogs would contain &03FF67FC which, you will do well to note, is in the reverse order. The fact that the contents of the P register form the most significant byte of the result is, in some respects, unfortunate. This register is normally dedicated to flag bits and some degree of fiddling is necessary if it is ever called upon (indirectly) to contribute meaningful numerical information to the result-parameter.

Program 4.5 illustrates the use of USR by adding two single-byte numbers in A% and X% respectively. The two numbers entered from the keyboard are placed in A% and X% by the BASIC lines 210, 220 before calling the code with USR. When two single-byte numbers are added, the result may spill over to two bytes but never more. Therefore the two higher order bytes of the four-byte result are so much garbage. Line 240 erases these bytes by use of the AND mask. There were no difficulties with the P register because it held one of the garbage bytes. However, many programs would require data contribution from P. There are only two instructions, PHP and PLP, which have direct action on the total contents of P. These can only push and pull to and from the stack. If we assume that the data to be placed in P initially rests in A, the following two lines of code illustrate a simple way out:

```
PHA    \Push A to stack
PLP    \pull A to P
```

Although the method looks simple, there is a hidden danger. It can turn out to be a hazardous business to interfere with the processor status, particularly if the program allows interrupts. The original status, however, is restored by an RTS but care may be needed to preserve P before using the above.

USR or CALL?

The respective merits of USR and CALL can be summarised as follows:

CALL:
(a) CALL can pass any number of parameters, limited only by the available space from &0600 onwards.
(b) The parameters are not restricted to integers. They can be any of the data forms, including string array variables.

(c) The magnitude of the variables passed is not restricted to single bytes.
(d) There is no provision in the CALL format for directly passing a result parameter (if there is one) back to the calling program. It must be arranged within the coding.

USR:
(a) Only three single-byte integers and one isolated bit can be passed as parameters to the subroutine.
(b) A four-byte result can be directly returned.

Indirection operators

The indirection operators form a grey area between high level language and machine code. They are similar to PEEK and POKE operations in traditional BASIC but are more versatile. However, this versatility is obtained at the expense of user-friendliness. The symbolism and format used can feel awkward for users hooked on BASIC. As far as machine code is concerned, the indirection operators are a boon because of the ease with which byte data can be pushed around memory. The definitions and format are well described in the user guides so only a brief outline (for the sake of continuity) is justified.

There are three operators and all may be taken to mean 'the contents of ...'. For example, ?&0D00, means 'the contents of address &0D00'. A 'word' is taken to mean four bytes at consecutive addresses.

Byte indirection (?)
Word indirection (!)
String indirection ($)

All three operators must be placed before the address to which they refer. Some examples follow:

Byte indirection
(a) ?&X=&23 (b) ?&0D00=5 (c) ?current=&456 (d) ?208=46 (e) PRINT ?X (f) PRINT ~&0C00
Note in (c) above that only the lower order byte (56) is assigned to 'current'; the 4 is dropped because there is no room for it in a single byte.

Word indirection
One example is sufficient:
!&0D00=&23456789
89 goes into &0D00, 67 into &0D01, 45 in &0D02 and 23 in &0D03.

String indirection
$&0D00="ABC" is an example worth examining in detail. The ASCII code for A (65) will be poked into &0D00, ASCII for B (66) in &0D01 and

ASCII for C in &0D02. Note that the dollar sign comes first to distinguish it from a normal string variable.

Saving and loading machine code

If the machine code is written within a BASIC program enclosed in the usual square brackets, it can be saved or loaded in the normal way (SAVE"name" or LOAD"name"). However, once the machine code has been assembled (and you know the address of the first byte), it can be saved and loaded separately from the BASIC parts. The formats are as follows:

To save machine code:
*SAVE"name" start-address end-address+1 (addresses will be assumed hex). For example, if a machine code subroutine called "sort" is located between &0D00 and &0D20 inclusive, it can be saved by:

   *SAVE"sort" 0D00 0D21

There is an alternative format:

   *SAVE"sort" starting-address number-of-bytes

The above example would then read:

   *SAVE"sort" 0D00 +21

To load machine code:
The format is:

   *LOAD"name"

The code will be loaded into the same address band as when saved. An alternative format is:

   *LOAD"name" first-address

This is used (rarely) if, for some reason, it is required to load the code into a hex address, different to that used when the code was saved.

To run machine code:
The majority of machine code is likely to be called from within an outline BASIC program. If, however, the code is self-supporting it can be run by using:

   *RUN "name"

Summary
   1. Assembly code within BASIC must be enclosed within [ ].
   2. Hex op-codes are replaced by three-letter mnemonic groups.

Handling the Resident Assembler **99**

3. All numerics are assumed decimal unless preceded by &.
4. Operands can be absolute numeric or any legitimate BASIC variable expression but not BASIC commands.
5. Registers can only hold one byte so any excess high order operand digits are dropped.
6. BASIC variables cannot be assigned within assembly code.
7. Conditional branch destination can be to a symbolic label.
8. A branch destination label must be preceded by the full-stop. There must be no full-stop when the label is in the operand position.
9. Each statement on the same line must have the full colon as a delimiter.
10. P% is special. The contents will be the address of the first byte of the assembly code.
11. Assembly code can be located by either absolute addressing, by modified DIM statement, below BASIC by using PAGE or between the end of BASIC program and the start of the 'variable space' by use of LOMEM.
12. The BASIC keyword RUN assembles any machine code present but only CALL can execute it.
13. CALL can be a statement within BASIC or a separate command.
14. OPT is a pseudo operation (not a BASIC keyword) so is valid only within the square brackets.
15. OPT defaults to OPT 3 which instructs the assembler to produce a listing and to report any errors.
16. A fully debugged, tested program would normally be run under OPT 0.
17. Assembly code which contains a branch to a forward (higher) address requires two passes through the assembler.
18. A P% assignment must be inside the FOR loop for two-pass assembly.
19. Macros, although not directly available in the assembler, can be implemented by using procedures.
20. The square brackets, denoting assembly code are legal within DEF PROC.
21. Macros, implemented by procedures, require a temporary exit from the assembler.
22. Conditional assembly is not directly available but can be implemented by the IF THEN ELSE structure.
23. Parameters can be passed to assembly subroutines by CALL or USR.
24. In the BBC machine, the address band beginning at &0600 is the parameter-block used by CALL.
25. The parameter-block contains only the address of the parameters not the parameters themselves.
26. The parameter begins with the number of parameters. Three items for each parameter then follow.
27. The first and second items give the low- and high-byte address and the third gives the parameter type.

28. The parameter type code is 0 for single byte, 4 for four-byte integer, 5 for five-byte floating point variable.
29. The parameter type code 80 is for defined address strings and 81 is for normal string variables.
30. Because the CALL parameter block contains only addresses of data, the data is easily recovered by using indirect addressing.
31. Before using indirect addressing, Y (or X) are usually zeroed and parameter addresses transferred to page zero.
32. Parameters passed by USR are by A%, X%, Y% into the same named 6502 registers. The lsb of C% is passed to the carry bit in P (process status register).
33. The result of USR action (if any) is passed to any designated integer variable.
34. The USR result is the combined contents of P, Y, X and A as they were on exit from the subroutine.
35. The most significant byte of the USR result is that contributed by P.
36. Indirection operators ?, !, $ before a variable refer to single-byte, four-byte and string respectively.
37. The presence of * before SAVE or LOAD indicates that the actions refer to assembly code programs.
38. Provision exists within *LOAD for loading assembly programs into a different address block from that used when *SAVE was used.
39. When using *SAVE, either the last address+1 of the block is stated or the number of bytes.

Self Test

4.1 What is the error in the following segment of code?

LDA Number:. Label CLC:ADC #&20:BNE .Label

4.2 RUN, CALL and OPT. Which of these are pseudo-operations?
4.3 What is the default number in OPT n?
4.4 If the only branch instruction in a code section was BNE &83, would it require two-pass assembly?
4.5 Some code is called with CALL name F%, Blogs. State:

(a) The hex number stored in address &0600.
(b) The contents of address &0603.
(c) The contents of address &0606.

4.6 The result variable, returned by a USR call, was &12345678.

(a) What number was in the X register?
(b) What number was in the process status register?

4.7 Using the word indirection operator, write a BASIC statement which will print out in hex the contents of address 34587.

Chapter Five
Multi-byte Loops

Two-byte operations

Single-byte working is ideal for illustrating the basic principles of the 6502 or, indeed any other 8-bit microprocessor. However, machine code programs of practical value must assume that numbers will greatly exceed the capacity of a single byte. Multi-byte (or multi-precision) working is the software solution. In other words, an 8-bit microprocessor can by using suitable software, simulate a microprocessor of (theoretically) any desirable word length. There are penalties, of course, the most important being increased execution time and extra programming involved in arranging the component bytes. The programs in this chapter are kept simple since they are only intended as guidance on the formation of loops involving rev counts greater than 255.

Incrementing a two-byte number
Incrementing the loop counter (in cases where the number of revs round the loop exceeds 256) poses problems associated with two-byte numbers. The following segment of code is a simple solution:

```
    INC NUMBER
    BNE SKIP
    INC NUMBER+1
.SKIP
```

NUMBER is the low order byte of the loop counter and NUMBER+1 the high order byte. While the count remains less than 255, only the low order byte is incremented because of the branch to SKIP

Decrementing a two-byte number
The following is as economical (in execution time) as any:

```
    SEC
    LDA NUMBER
    SBC #1
    STA NUMBER
    BCS SKIP
    DEC NUMBER+1
.SKIP
```

Note that SBC is used for decrementing the low-order byte instead of DEC. This is because:

(a) DEC will not affect the carry flag.
(b) The Z flag cannot be used because the high-byte is only decremented when the low-byte has passed through zero.

Adding two single-byte numbers

Even when the numbers are individually within the capacity of a single byte, a double-byte result must be allowed for. The following segment allows for this:

```
LDA #0
STA SUM+1
CLC
LDA NUMBER1
ADC NUMBER2
STA SUM
BCC SKIP
INC SUM+1
.SKIP
```

Adding a single-byte number to a double-byte number

The following short program illustrates how a single-byte number can be added to a double-byte number:

```
CLC
LDA NUMBER1
ADC NUMBER2
STA NUMBER1
BCC SKIP
INC NUMBER+1
.SKIP
```

The example programs which follow will pass parameters by means of the CALL statement and, consequently, will take advantage of indirect indexed addressing. It would be possible, and perhaps simpler, to make use of the word-indirection operator. However, the advantages of indirect addressing, the concept of address pointers and the power of the CALL statement justify the extra programming work. This is a useful habit to acquire, since most machine code routines will ultimately be called from BASIC. We shall use the word-indirection operator only in a BASIC print role.

Four-byte operations

Simple four-byte addition

Integer variables in the BBC and Electron occupy four bytes. The flowchart shown in Fig. 5.1 illustrates the addition of two 32-bit integers.

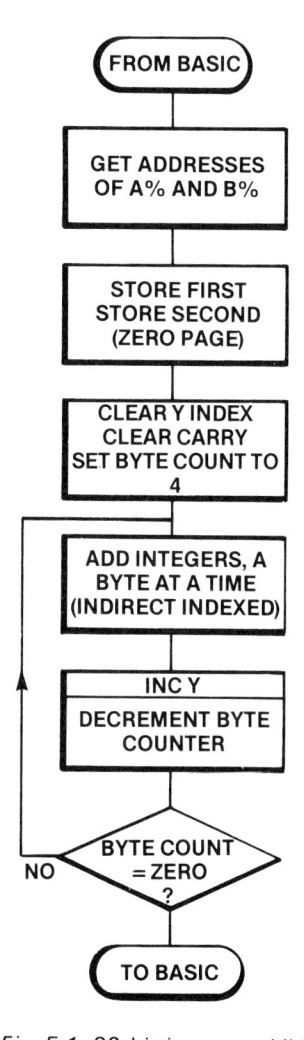

Fig. 5.1. 32-bit integer addition.

The flowchart begins at the point where the two variables to be added (A% and B%) have been received from the CALL statement in BASIC with their addresses passed to the parameter block at &0600. These addresses now become the address pointers 'FIRST' and 'SECOND' which are transferred to zero-page locations.

The four-byte loop is then initialised by:

104 *Advanced Machine Code Techniques for The BBC Micro*

(a) setting the Y index to 0 (ready for the low order byte in each integer),
(b) setting the loop counter (X) to 4,
(c) clearing the carry.

Each time round the loop, the following actions occur:

(a) The corresponding bytes of each integer are added using indirect indexing and taking the carry bit into consideration.
(b) The byte sum is transferred to 'RESULT', this time using indexed addressing.
(c) The Y index is incremented ready for action on the next higher order byte.
(d) The loop counter (X) is decremented.

The loop exits after the most significant byte pair has been added which is

```
>LIST
   10 REM 32bit INTEGER ADDITION
   20 MODE4
   30 FIRST=&70:SECOND=&72
   40 RESULT=&80
   50 ADD=&0C00
   60 FOR PASS=0 TO 2 STEP 2
   70 P%=ADD
   80 [OPT PASS
   90 LDA &0601       \STORE ADDRESSES
  100 STA FIRST       \OF BASIC INTEGERS
  110 LDA &0602       \A% AND B% IN
  120 STA FIRST+1     \ZERO PAGE
  130 LDA &0604
  140 STA SECOND
  150 LDA &0605
  160 STA SECOND+1
  170 LDY #0
  180 LDX #4          \SET BYTE COUNTER
  190 CLC
  200 .ADDLOOP
  210 LDA (FIRST),Y   \ADD INTEGERS
  220 ADC (SECOND),Y  \A BYTE AT A TIME
  230 STA RESULT,Y    \USING INDIRECT
  240 INY             \INDEXED ADDRESSING
  250 DEX             \BRANCH ADDLOOP
  260 BNE ADDLOOP     \IF BYTE CTR=0
  270 RTS:]
  280 NEXT PASS
  290 CLS
  300 INPUT"FIRST INTEGER  ",A%
  310 INPUT"SECOND INTEGER ",B%
  320 CALL ADD,A%,B%
  330 PRINT"ADDITION= ";!&80
```

Program 5.1 32-bit integer addition.

Multi-byte Loops **105**

when the loop count has reached zero. The control then passes back to BASIC.

The complete assembly coding is given in Program 5.1. It can be deduced from line 30 of Program 5.1 that the address pointers FIRST and FIRST+1 occupy &70 and &71. Also SECOND and SECOND+1 address pointers occupy &72 and &73. The RESULT, in &80 and &81 is the data itself, not an address pointer. This is confirmed by line 230 which shows that simple indexed (not indirect) addressing is used for RESULT.

Simple four-byte subtraction

Because of the close similarity with the previous program, a flowchart was not considered necessary, so only the listing is given in Program 5.2.

```
>LIST
   10 REM 32bit INTEGER SUBTRACTION
   20 MODE4
   30 FIRST=&70:SECOND=&72
   40 RESULT=&80
   50 SUBTRACT=&0C00
   60 FOR PASS=0 TO 2 STEP 2
   70 P%=SUBTRACT
   80 [OPT PASS
   90 LDA &0601        \STORE ADDRESSES
  100 STA FIRST        \OF BASIC INTEGERS
  110 LDA &0602        \A% AND B% IN
  120 STA FIRST+1      \ZERO PAGE
  130 LDA &0604
  140 STA SECOND
  150 LDA &0605
  160 STA SECOND+1
  170 LDY #0
  180 LDX #4           \SET BYTE COUNTER
  190 SEC
  200 .ADDLOOP
  210 LDA (FIRST),Y    \SUBTRACT INTEGERS
  220 SBC (SECOND),Y
  230 STA RESULT,Y     \USING INDIRECT
  240 INY              \INDEXED ADDRESSING
  250 DEX              \BRANCH ADDLOOP
  260 BNE ADDLOOP      \IF BYTE CTR<>0
  270 RTS:]
  280 NEXT PASS
  290 CLS
  300 INPUT"FIRST INTEGER  ",A%
  310 INPUT"SECOND INTEGER ",B%
  320 CALL SUBTRACT,A%,B%
  330 PRINT"SUBTRACTION= ";!&80
```

Program 5.2. 32-bit integer subtraction.

Multiple byte loop (up-counting)

It is useful to have a skeleton program for performing a certain process n times where n is not limited to 256. Figure 5.2 shows the outline flowchart,

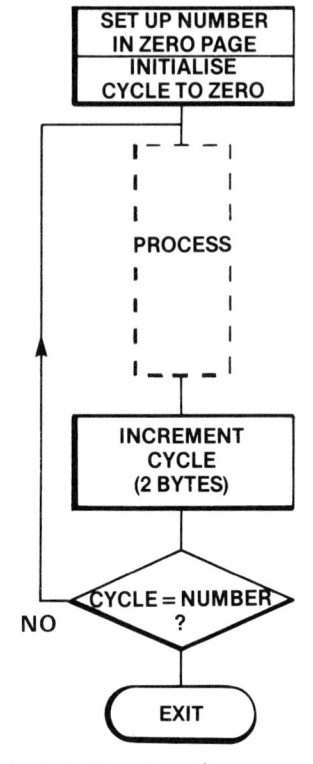

Fig. 5.2. Flowchart for up-count.

with the particular process left undefined. No attempt is made in the flowchart to discriminate between low-byte and high-byte components of CYCLE and NUMBER. To do so would entail extra detail which could weaken, rather than clarify, the impact of the flowchart.

Program 5.3 is an implementation of the flowchart in Fig. 5.2 and will print the letter H on the screen 1024 times.

NUMBER (in Program 5.3) is the number of times the process is to be completed. CYCLE is the current loop count. Line 30 assigns the two bytes of CYCLE to &70 and &71, and NUMBER to &72 and &73. Purely for purposes of illustration, NUMBER has been initialised to a constant value of 1024 by line 40. This is done by setting the low-byte of NUMBER to 0 and the high-byte to 4 (equivalent to 4×256).

The process, used as an example (painting H on the screen), occupies lines 130 and 140 and uses the resident subroutine OSWRCH which is at address &FFEE.

```
>LIST
   10.REM MULTIPLE BYTE LOOP(UPCOUNTING)
   20 MODE4
   30 CYCLE=&70:NUMBER=&72
   40 ?&72=0:?&73=4
   50 START=&0C00
   60 FOR PASS=0 TO 2 STEP 2
   70 P%=START
   80 [OPT PASS
   90 LDA #0         \INITIALISE CYCLE
  100 STA CYCLE      \COUNTER TO ZERO
  110 STA CYCLE+1    \(2 BYTES)
  120 .LOOP
  130 LDA #&48       \PRINT A "H" ON THE
  140 JSR &FFEE      \SCREEN.
  150 INC CYCLE      \INCREMENT THE CYCLE
  160 BNE SKIP       \COUNTER BY 1
  170 INC CYCLE+1    \(2 BYTES)
  180 .SKIP
  190 LDA NUMBER     \COMPARE NUMBER OF
  200 CMP CYCLE      \CYCLES REQD TO CYCLE
  210 BNE LOOP       \COUNTER IF NOT EQUAL
  220 LDA NUMBER+1   \BRANCH TO LOOP
  230 CMP CYCLE+1    \(2 BYTES)
  240 BNE LOOP
  250 RTS:]
  260 NEXT PASS
  270 CALL START
```

Program 5.3. Multiple-byte loop (up-counting).

Multiple-byte loop (down-counting)

Providing the sole criterion is that a process is carried out the requisite number of times, it matters little whether the loop counter starts at zero and increments or starts with a finite number and decrements towards zero. However, as discussed in a previous chapter, the decrement method (down-counting), is both simpler and faster in execution. No comparison instructions appear and therefore there will be no need to assign NUMBER. Program 5.4 is identical in objective to the previous program but uses this down-counting method.

```
>LIST
   10 REM MULTIPLE BYTE LOOP (DOWNCOUNTING)
   20 MODE4
   30 CYCLE=&70
   40 ?&70=0:?&71=4
   50 START=&0C00
   60 FOR PASS=0 TO 2 STEP 2
   70 P%=START
```

Program 5.4. Multiple-byte loop (down-counting).

108 *Advanced Machine Code Techniques for The BBC Micro*

```
 80 [OPT PASS
 90 LDA #&48      \PUT A "H" ON THE
100 JSR &FFEE     \SCREEN
110 SEC
120 LDA CYCLE     \DECREMENT CYCLE
130 SBC #1        \COUNTER BY 1
140 STA CYCLE     \(2 BYTES)
150 BCS SKIP
160 DEC CYCLE+1
170 .SKIP
180 LDA CYCLE
190 BNE START     \COMPARE CYCLE COUNTER
200 LDA CYCLE+1   \TO ZERO, IF NOT EQUAL
210 BNE START     \BRANCH TO START
220 RTS:]
230 NEXT PASS
240 CALL START
```

Program 5.4. contd

It is worth comparing the two programs side by side to dispel lingering doubts as to which is the more elegant.

Adding an array of integers

Program 5.5 adds four-byte integer numbers held in a BASIC array (ARRAY%). For testing purposes only, ARRAY% is filled with random

```
>LIST
 10 REM 32bit INTEGER ARRAY SUMMATION
 20 MODE 4
 30 NUMBER=&70:POINTER=&72
 40 RESULT=&80
 50 SUM=&0C00
 60 FOR PASS=0 TO 2 STEP 2
 70 P%=SUM
 80 [OPT PASS
 90 LDA &0601        \GET NUMBER OF
100 STA RESULT       \INTEGERS IN
110 LDA &0602        \ARRAY
120 STA RESULT+1     \STORE IN NUMBER
130 LDY #0
140 LDA (RESULT),Y
150 STA NUMBER
160 INY
170 LDA (RESULT),Y
180 STA NUMBER+1
190 LDA &0604        \GET START
200 STA POINTER      \ADDRESS OF ARRAY
210 LDA &0605        \STORE IN POINTER
```

Program 5.5. Integer array summation.

Multi-byte Loops 109

```
220 STA POINTER+1
230 LDA #0              \INITIALISE 4
240 STA RESULT          \BYTES FOR RESULT
250 STA RESULT+1        \TO ZERO
260 STA RESULT+2
270 STA RESULT+3
280 .LOOP
290 LDY #0
300 LDX #4              \SET BYTE COUNTER
310 CLC
320 .ADDLOOP            \ADD SUCESSIVE
330 LDA (POINTER),Y     \INTEGERS A BYTE
340 ADC RESULT,Y        \AT A TIME.STORE
350 STA RESULT,Y        \CUMUL'VE RESULT
360 INY
370 DEX                 \DEC BYTE COUNTER
380 BNE ADDLOOP
390 CLC
400 LDA POINTER         \ADD 4 TO POINTER
410 ADC #4
420 STA POINTER
430 BCC SKIP
440 INC POINTER+1
450 .SKIP
460 LDA NUMBER          \DECREMENT
470 SEC                 \NUMBER BY 1
480 SBC #1
490 STA NUMBER
500 BCS SKIP2
510 DEC NUMBER+1
520 .SKIP2
530 LDA NUMBER          \IF NUMBER IS NOT
540 BNE LOOP            \ZERO THEN BRANCH
550 LDA NUMBER+1        \TO LOOP(2 BYTES)
560 BNE LOOP
570 RTS:]
580 NEXT
590 CLS
600 INPUT"HOW MANY RANDOM INTEGERS ",NUMBER%
610 DIM ARRAY%(NUMBER%)
620 FOR N%=1 TO NUMBER%
630 ARRAY%(N%)=RND/100000
640 PRINT ARRAY%(N%)
650 NEXT
660 PRINT:PRINT
670 CALL SUM,NUMBER%,ARRAY%(1)
680 PRINT"SUM= ";!RESULT
690 PRINT:PRINT
700 PRINT"CHECK USING BASIC"
710 PRINT
```

Program 5.5. contd

110 *Advanced Machine Code Techniques for The BBC Micro*

```
720 SUM=0
730 FOR N%=1 TO NUMBER%
740 SUM=SUM+ARRAY%(N%)
750 NEXT
760 PRINT"CHECK= ";SUM
```

>RUN

HOW MANY RANDOM INTEGERS ?5
    681
   20966
   10485
   -2851
   -2610

SUM= 26671

CHECK USING BASIC

CHECK= 26671

Program 5.5. contd

integers of mixed sign, the number of integers being entered by the user. An example computer RUN is shown at the end of the listing. It helps if the flowchart, shown in Fig. 5.3 is studied first.

The program is the first one in this book which illustrates the speed of machine code. When assessing the speed, it should be realised that the filling of the array and the scrolled display of the numbers is carried out in BASIC. The speed referred to applies only to the machine code portion which performs the actual addition. A parallel addition check is carried out in BASIC, primarily for speed comparisons. To compare the machine code speed with the BASIC equivalent, run the program with 4000 integers instead of with 5 as shown in Program 5.5 and note that the machine code sum appears almost instantaneously after the numbers stop scrolling. The BASIC check on the addition takes many seconds. The program should be fairly easy to follow from the comments on the listing. It uses some of the coding blocks previously discussed.

Multi-byte Loops 111

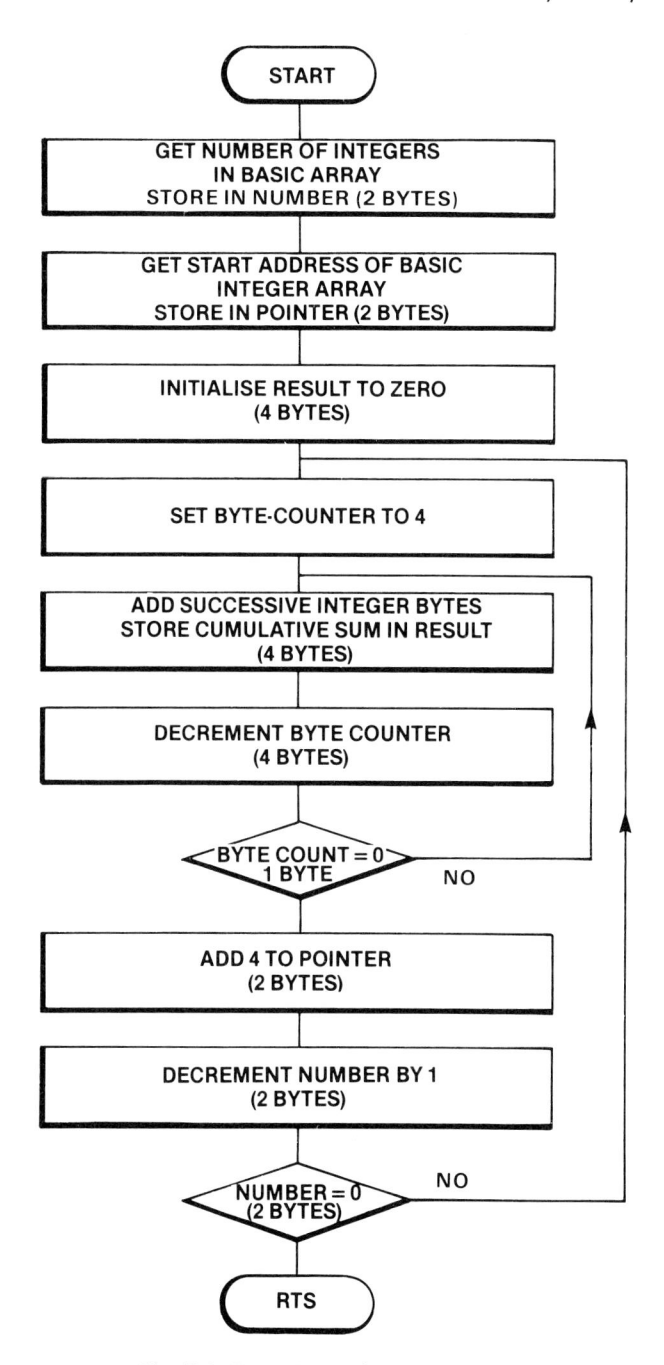

```
                    ┌─────────┐
                    │  START  │
                    └────┬────┘
                         │
         ┌───────────────▼───────────────┐
         │   GET NUMBER OF INTEGERS      │
         │        IN BASIC ARRAY         │
         │    STORE IN NUMBER (2 BYTES)  │
         └───────────────┬───────────────┘
                         │
         ┌───────────────▼───────────────┐
         │  GET START ADDRESS OF BASIC   │
         │         INTEGER ARRAY         │
         │    STORE IN POINTER (2 BYTES) │
         └───────────────┬───────────────┘
                         │
         ┌───────────────▼───────────────┐
         │   INITIALISE RESULT TO ZERO   │
         │           (4 BYTES)           │
         └───────────────┬───────────────┘
                         │
         ┌───────────────▼───────────────┐
         │     SET BYTE-COUNTER TO 4     │◄───┐
         └───────────────┬───────────────┘    │
                         │                    │
         ┌───────────────▼───────────────┐    │
         │  ADD SUCCESSIVE INTEGER BYTES │    │
         │  STORE CUMULATIVE SUM IN RESULT│◄─┐ │
         │           (4 BYTES)           │  │ │
         └───────────────┬───────────────┘  │ │
                         │                  │ │
         ┌───────────────▼───────────────┐  │ │
         │    DECREMENT BYTE COUNTER     │  │ │
         │           (4 BYTES)           │  │ │
         └───────────────┬───────────────┘  │ │
                         │                  │ │
                    ◇────▼────◇             │ │
                  ◇ BYTE COUNT=0 ◇──NO──────┘ │
                  ◇    1 BYTE   ◇             │
                    ◇────┬────◇               │
                         │ YES                │
         ┌───────────────▼───────────────┐    │
         │      ADD 4 TO POINTER         │    │
         │           (2 BYTES)           │    │
         └───────────────┬───────────────┘    │
                         │                    │
         ┌───────────────▼───────────────┐    │
         │     DECREMENT NUMBER BY 1     │    │
         │           (2 BYTES)           │    │
         └───────────────┬───────────────┘    │
                         │                    │
                    ◇────▼────◇               │
                  ◇  NUMBER=0  ◇──NO──────────┘
                  ◇  (2 BYTES) ◇
                    ◇────┬────◇
                         │ YES
                    ┌────▼────┐
                    │   RTS   │
                    └─────────┘
```

Fig. 5.3. Flowchart of Program 5.5.

Summary

1. The 6502, in common with most microprocessors, has a word length of 8-bits, limiting the magnitude of signed integers to +127 and −128 and unsigned integers to 255.
2. The 8-bit word length is merely a hardware limitation, easily overcome by means of software.
3. Separate 8-bit words can be considered 'joined' end to end in order to simulate long word lengths. The simulation is perfect in most respects except execution time.
4. Incrementing a double-byte number proceeds initially with the low-order byte. The high-order byte is incremented only when the count goes over the top from 255 (&FF) to zero (&00).
5. Decrementing a double-byte number is similar but SBC is preferable to DEC because a carry rather than a zero is required for the inner loop test.
6. Most machine code programs are entered from BASIC, so loop parameters can be easily passed by use of CALL.
7. Integer variables in BASIC occupy 4 bytes (32 bits).
8. In signed integer work, the sign bits in the three lower order bytes are ignored. Only the highest order byte carries real sign information.
9. When performing loop counts, it is normally more efficient to count down towards zero rather than up towards a finite number.
10. When estimating the speed of the example programs, remember that the BASIC sections, which call and initialise the machine code, squander most of the execution time.

Self Test

5.1 A two-byte counter is holding 770 decimal. Write the bit pattern in the high-order byte.
5.2 A two-byte counter is holding 1801 decimal. Write the bit pattern in the low-order byte.
5.3 A four-byte counter is holding −1. What hex number is the highest order byte holding?
5.4 Signed integers in the BBC machine occupy four bytes. What is the largest positive number possible (to the nearest million)?
5.5 If two single-byte numbers of opposite sign are added, could the result ever exceed the capacity of a single byte?

Chaper Six
Sort Routines

Apart from personal interest and/or intellectual stimulation, there is little point in adopting a partisan approach to machine code. It is pointless to view BASIC, particularly BBC BASIC, as a language inferior to machine code. The two should complement, rather than rival, each other. Once familiarity and confidence is gained in handling machine code, it will gradually become clear which parts of a BASIC program should be relegated to machine code and which parts can be handled quite adequately in BASIC.

There can be no doubt, however, that one area in data processing which calls out for machine code solutions is sorting data into numerical or alphabetical order. It has been stated that approximately 30% of all commercial computing time is spent on some kind of sorting activity. An ordered system of any kind represents a 'high energy' system. Since the equation for energy in physics is power multiplied by time, we would therefore expect that programs which sort data will make heavy demands on computing time.

The physical power of a given computer is fixed by the hardware, which in turn depends on such things as the clock frequency, word length and the sophistication built into the central processor (in the BBC, the central processor is the 6502). Although in no way meant as criticism, the machine, and indeed most other microcomputers likely to be found in the average home, are slow in terms of 'mips'(million instructions per second). The BBC machine is rated at about 0.5 mips. In contrast, some of the modern mainframe giants have reached a speed approaching 100 mips with a word length of 64 bits and it is confidently expected that this figure will be substantially beaten by the forthcoming breed of fifth generation machines. Returning to present day reality, there is nothing we can do about the limitations imposed by the hardware of our machine. The only method of attack is to use software which takes the fullest advantage of the machine.

This chapter is devoted entirely to the problem of machine code sorting routines. A simple bubble sort, limited to single byte data, was introduced in the previous book, *Discovering BBC Micro Machine Code*. The following programs treat the sorting problem in more detail and will include the sorting of arrays of four-byte BASIC integers, strings, floating point numbers and two- dimensional string arrays. It will also include routines which sort fixed length multi-field records. They are given complete with BASIC parameter passing lines so they can be entered and exhaustively tested. It should be pointed out that the machine code portion of the listings will stand alone as subroutines, providing that:

(a) the correct parameters are passed from any BASIC program;
(b) the code is lodged either in one of the safe areas (not necessarily the areas used in our listings) or dynamically, above or below BASIC, by the use of the DIM statement.

All the programs in this chapter are concerned with sorting data into either numerical or alphabetical order and will be useful in compiling indexes, customer lists, domestic accounts, hobby collections (butterflies, stamps, beetles) etc. They could also be employed as routines within general purpose filing systems to store or retrieve information according to some predetermined order.

Bubble sort of a BASIC integer array

The bubble sort is well-known but often despised because it is slow. It is one of the simplest sort routines to understand and, providing there are not too many elements in the array, can be acceptable if written in machine code. It provides a good starting point for handling multibyte integers.

Because the programs which follow are intended to be used in conjunction with BASIC, via CALL parameters, it is important to understand how the interpreter allocates variable space.

How integer array variables are stored
The four bytes, allocated to each integer array variable, are aranged as follows:

```
sign bit ┐   ←──── increasing memory ────
 (bit 7) ▼
         ┌───────┬───────┬───────┬───────┐
         │ MSB   │       │       │ LSB   │
         │       │       │       │       │
         │  4    │   3   │   2   │   1   │
         └───────┴───────┴───────┴───────┘
```

Sort Routines 115

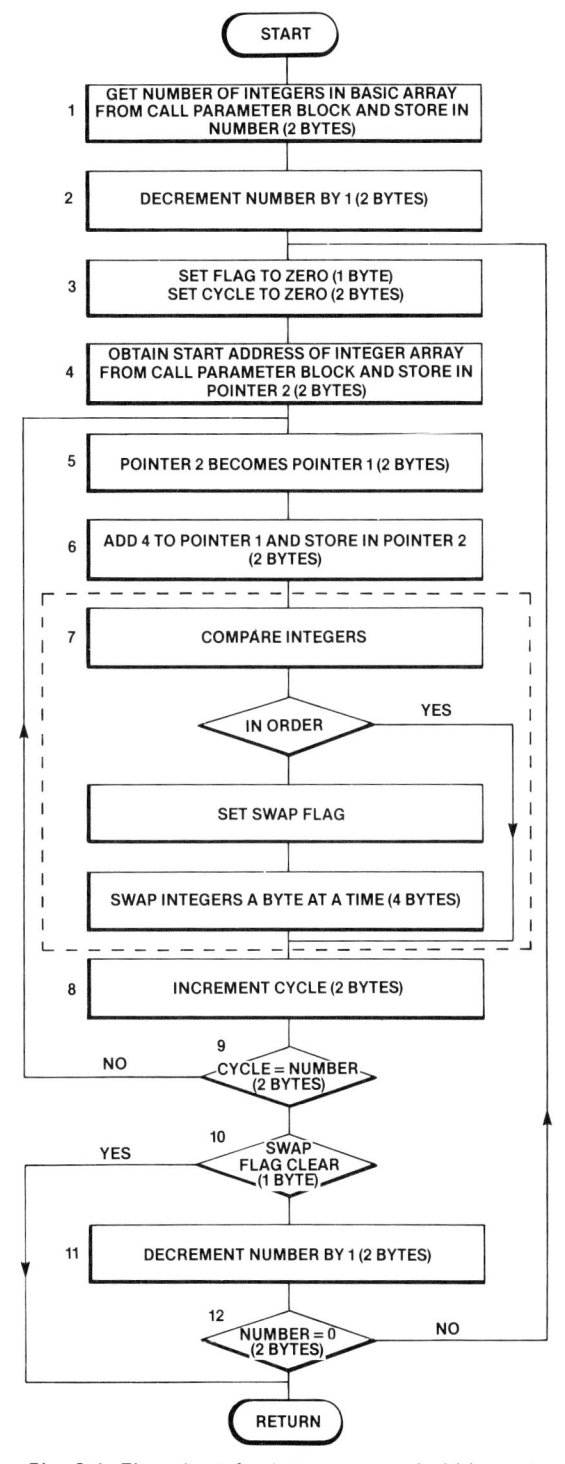

```
                    ┌─────────┐
                    │  START  │
                    └─────────┘
                         │
    ┌────────────────────────────────────────────┐
  1 │ GET NUMBER OF INTEGERS IN BASIC ARRAY      │
    │ FROM CALL PARAMETER BLOCK AND STORE IN     │
    │ NUMBER (2 BYTES)                           │
    └────────────────────────────────────────────┘
                         │
    ┌────────────────────────────────────────────┐
  2 │ DECREMENT NUMBER BY 1 (2 BYTES)            │
    └────────────────────────────────────────────┘
                         │
    ┌────────────────────────────────────────────┐
  3 │ SET FLAG TO ZERO (1 BYTE)                  │
    │ SET CYCLE TO ZERO (2 BYTES)                │
    └────────────────────────────────────────────┘
                         │
    ┌────────────────────────────────────────────┐
  4 │ OBTAIN START ADDRESS OF INTEGER ARRAY      │
    │ FROM CALL PARAMETER BLOCK AND STORE IN     │
    │ POINTER 2 (2 BYTES)                        │
    └────────────────────────────────────────────┘
                         │
    ┌────────────────────────────────────────────┐
  5 │ POINTER 2 BECOMES POINTER 1 (2 BYTES)      │
    └────────────────────────────────────────────┘
                         │
    ┌────────────────────────────────────────────┐
  6 │ ADD 4 TO POINTER 1 AND STORE IN POINTER 2  │
    │ (2 BYTES)                                  │
    └────────────────────────────────────────────┘
                         │
    ┌────────────────────────────────────────────┐
  7 │ COMPARE INTEGERS                           │
    └────────────────────────────────────────────┘
                         │
                    ◇ IN ORDER ◇ ──YES──┐
                         │               │
                   SET SWAP FLAG         │
                         │               │
         SWAP INTEGERS A BYTE AT A TIME (4 BYTES)
                         │               │
    ┌────────────────────────────────────────────┐
  8 │ INCREMENT CYCLE (2 BYTES)                  │
    └────────────────────────────────────────────┘
                         │
              9   ◇ CYCLE = NUMBER ◇ ──NO──┐
                     (2 BYTES)
                         │ YES
             10   ◇ SWAP FLAG CLEAR ◇ ──YES──┐
                     (1 BYTE)
                         │ NO
    ┌────────────────────────────────────────────┐
 11 │ DECREMENT NUMBER BY 1 (2 BYTES)            │
    └────────────────────────────────────────────┘
                         │
             12   ◇ NUMBER = 0 ◇ ──NO──┐
                    (2 BYTES)
                         │ YES
                    ┌─────────┐
                    │ RETURN  │
                    └─────────┘
```

Fig. 6.1. Flowchart for integer array bubble sort.

Each integer of the array is then stored sequentially, so in effect, each element has an address 4 bytes in advance of the previous integer.

The machine code routine is executed from BASIC via the CALL statement:

CALL SORT, NUMBER%, ARRAY% (1)

Of course, the above variable names are arbitrarily chosen but they must be in the above order where:

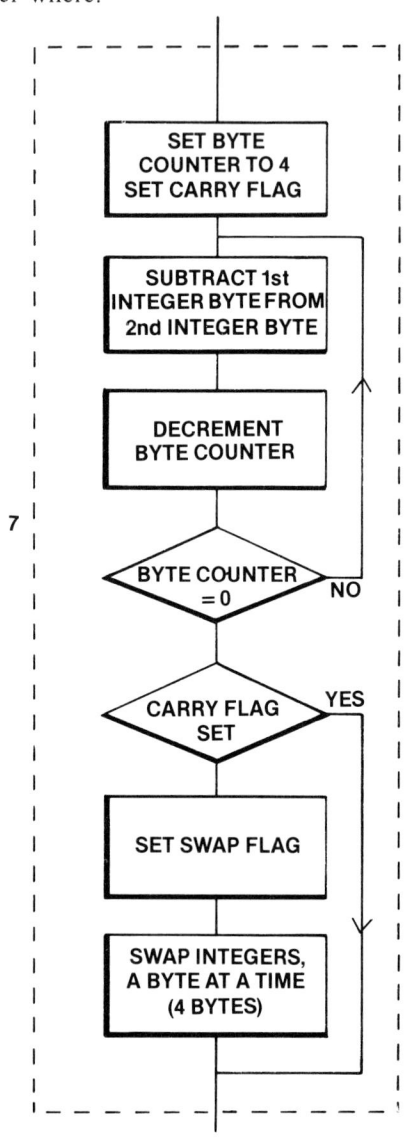

Fig. 6.2. Expansion of block 7 in Fig. 6.1.

Sort Routines 117

SORT=the start address of the routine
NUMBER%=the number of elements in the array
ARRAY% (1) =the first usable element in the array

The zero element is best left vacant for headings, etc.

The flowchart for the routine is given in Fig. 6.1. As can be seen, the algorithm consists basically of an inner control loop and an outer control loop. The pairs of integers are repeatedly incremented, compared (and if necessary swopped) in the inner loop. The largest integer in the list always 'bubbles' through to the last position. It will no longer be necessary to involve this integer again, so the outer loop count may be reduced by one. On the next inner loop series of cycles, the next largest integer 'bubbles' through to the last but one position in the list and so on, until the list is fully sorted. The maximum number of comparisons is approximately equal to half the square of the array size. The execution time can be reduced if the list is not too disordered by the use of a swop flag technique as shown in the flowchart. Note from the flowchart that the blocks have been numbered for reference purposes. Block 7 is shown expanded in Fig. 6.2. The listing corresponding to the flowchart is given in Program 6.1.

```
>LIST
   10 REM BUBBLE SORT OF ARRAY OF
   20 REM 32bit UNSIGNED INTEGERS
   30 NUMBER=&70:CYCLE=&72:POINTER1=&74
   40 POINTER2=&76:FLAG=&78
   50 DIM SORT 500
   60 FOR PASS=0 TO 2 STEP 2
   70 P%=SORT
   80 [OPT PASS          \***************
   90 LDA &0601          \GET NUMBER OF
  100 STA CYCLE          \BASIC INTEGERS
  110 LDA &0602          \IN ARRAY AND
  120 STA CYCLE+1        \STORE IN NUMBER
  130 LDY #1
  140 LDA (CYCLE),Y
  150 STA NUMBER+1
  160 DEY
  170 SEC
  180 LDA (CYCLE),Y      \***************
  190 SBC #1             \DECREMENT
  200 STA NUMBER         \NUMBER
  210 BCS OUTERLOOP
  220 DEC NUMBER+1
  230 .OUTERLOOP         \***************
  240 LDA #0             \INITIALISE
  250 STA FLAG           \SWOP FLAG AND
  260 STA CYCLE          \CYCLE TO ZERO
  270 STA CYCLE+1
  280 LDA &0604          \***************
  290 STA POINTER2       \STORE FIRST INT
```

Program 6.1. Bubble sort of an unsigned 32-bit integer array.

118 Advanced Machine Code Techniques for The BBC Micro

```
300 LDA &0605          \ADDRESS TEMP IN
310 STA POINTER2+1     \POINTER2
320 .INNERLOOP         \***************
330 LDA POINTER2+1     \TRANSFER
340 STA POINTER1+1     \POINTERS
350 LDA POINTER2       \POINTER1 =
360 STA POINTER1       \POINTER2
370 CLC                \***************
380 ADC #4             \ADD 4 TO
390 STA POINTER2       \POINTER 1 AND
400 BCC SKIP           \STORE IN
410 INC POINTER2+1     \POINTER2
420 .SKIP              \***************
430 LDX #4             \SUBTRACT INT'S
440 LDY #0             \A BYTE AT A
450 SEC                \TIME (4 BYTES)
460 .COMPLOOP          \KEEPING TRACK
470 LDA (POINTER2),Y   \OF CARRY FLAG
480 SBC (POINTER1),Y   \AT COMPLETION
490 INY
500 DEX
510 BNE COMPLOOP       \BRANCH NOSWOP
520 BCS NOSWOP         \IF CARRY SET
530 DEY
540 STY FLAG           \SET SWOP FLAG
550 .SWOPLOOP          \***************
560 LDA(POINTER1),Y    \SWOP INTEGERS
570 TAX                \A BYTE AT A
580 LDA(POINTER2),Y    \TIME
590 STA(POINTER1),Y
600 TXA
610 STA(POINTER2),Y
620 DEY
630 BPL SWOPLOOP
640 .NOSWOP
650 INC CYCLE          \***************
660 BNE SKIP2          \INCREMENT
670 INC CYCLE+1        \CYCLE
680 .SKIP2             \***************
690 LDA CYCLE          \COMPARE CYCLE
700 CMP NUMBER         \TO NUMBER. IF
710 BNE INNERLOOP      \<> BRANCH TO
720 LDA CYCLE+1        \INNERLOOP
730 CMP NUMBER+1
740 BNE INNERLOOP
750 LDA FLAG           \IF SW.FLG CLEAR
760 BEQ FLAGCLEAR      \BR. FLAGCLEAR
770 LDA NUMBER         \***************
780 SEC                \DECREMENT
790 SBC #1             \NUMBER
800 STA NUMBER
```

Program 6.1. contd

```
 810 BCS SKIP3
 820 DEC NUMBER+1
 830 .SKIP3              \***************
 840 LDA NUMBER          \COMPARE NUMBER
 850 BNE OUTERLOOP       \TO ZERO
 860 LDA NUMBER+1        \BRANCH IF <> TO
 870 BNE OUTERLOOP       \OUTERLOOP
 880 .FLAGCLEAR
 890 RTS:]
 900 NEXT PASS
 910
 920 REM BASIC IS FOR TESTING ONLY
 930 MODE4
 940 CLS
 950 INPUT"NUMBER OF INTEGERS ",NUMBER%
 960 PRINT
 970 DIM ARRAY%(NUMBER%)
 980 FOR N%=1 TO NUMBER%
 990 ARRAY%(N%)=RND(10000)
1000 PRINT ARRAY%(N%)
1010 NEXT
1020 PRINT
1030 PRINT "SORTING"
1040 PRINT
1050 START%=TIME
1060 CALL SORT,NUMBER%,ARRAY%(1)
1070 time%=TIME-START%
1080 FOR N%=1 TO NUMBER%
1090 PRINT ARRAY%(N%)
1100 NEXT
1110 PRINT
1120 PRINT"SORTING TIME= ";time%/100;"
SECONDS"
```

Program 6.1. contd

Although the listing is supplied with outline remarks, here is a more detailed breakdown:

Lines 30–40 set up the zero-page labelled locations referred to in assembly code.

Lines 90-220 obtain the address of the BASIC variable NUMBER% from the CALL parameter block and temporarily store it in CYCLE. Using indirect indexed addressing, the data is picked up, decremented by 1 and stored in NUMBER and NUMBER+1 (low-byte and high-byte respectively). Note, that zero-page locations must be used for indirect indexed addressing.

Lines 240-270 initialise the swop FLAG and CYCLE counter to zero.

Lines 280–310 store the address of the first integer in the array temporarily in POINTER2. This is picked up from the CALL parameter block.

Lines 320-360 copy POINTER2 contents into POINTER1.

Lines 370-410 add 4 to POINTER1 and store the result in POINTER2. The reason why 4 is added is so that POINTER2 is the address of the next integer in the array: that is to say, 4 bytes onwards.

Line 430 initialises the byte counter to 4. The X register is used for this (see below).

Lines 450-520 subtract the integers with carry, a byte at a time, keeping the result of the fourth bytes in the accumulator. Notice that the X register and DEX is used for byte counting. This is because a CPY instruction would corrupt the carry flag during the subtraction processes. If the carry flag is set at the end of the subtraction, no swop is required. This method only works for unsigned integers.

Line 530 sets the byte counter for the swop process. DEY is used to set this to 3 since the current value of Y is 4.

Line 540 stores the Y register contents as a swop flag in FLAG (any non-zero quantity would do here).

Lines 560 to 630 swop the integers, a byte at a time, starting with the high-byte. Notice that the X register is used as a temporary storage location as this is the most economical in execution time since TAX uses only two machine cycles, whereas the alternatives PHA or STA require 3 cycles.

Lines 650-680 increment the CYCLE counter by 1. The coding given is an economical way to do this in terms of execution time.

Lines 690-740 compare the low-byte of CYCLE and NUMBER. If the result is non-zero, a branch is made to the label INNERLOOP. If the result is zero, the program 'falls through' to compare the high-byte in the same manner.

Lines 750-760 check if the swop FLAG is clear. If so, a branch to FLAGCLEAR is made.

Lines 770-820 decrement NUMBER by 1 (2 bytes, of course).

Lines 840 to 870 check if NUMBER has reached zero, first checking the low-byte with branching to OUTERLOOP if not true, otherwise 'falling through' to compare the high-byte.

Lines 920-1120 are pure BASIC just for test and familiarisation purposes. They first print out a random integer array, call the machine code routine and then print out the sorted result together with the time taken. See Table 6.1 at the end of this chapter for a compendium of timing data.

Bubble sort of a BASIC string array

This routine is capable of sorting a BASIC string array, where the string elements can vary in length up to the legal maximum of 255.

How string arrays are stored

When a string array is set up by the interpreter, four bytes are used in a similar manner to integers. These bytes, are not the strings themselves but

Sort Routines 121

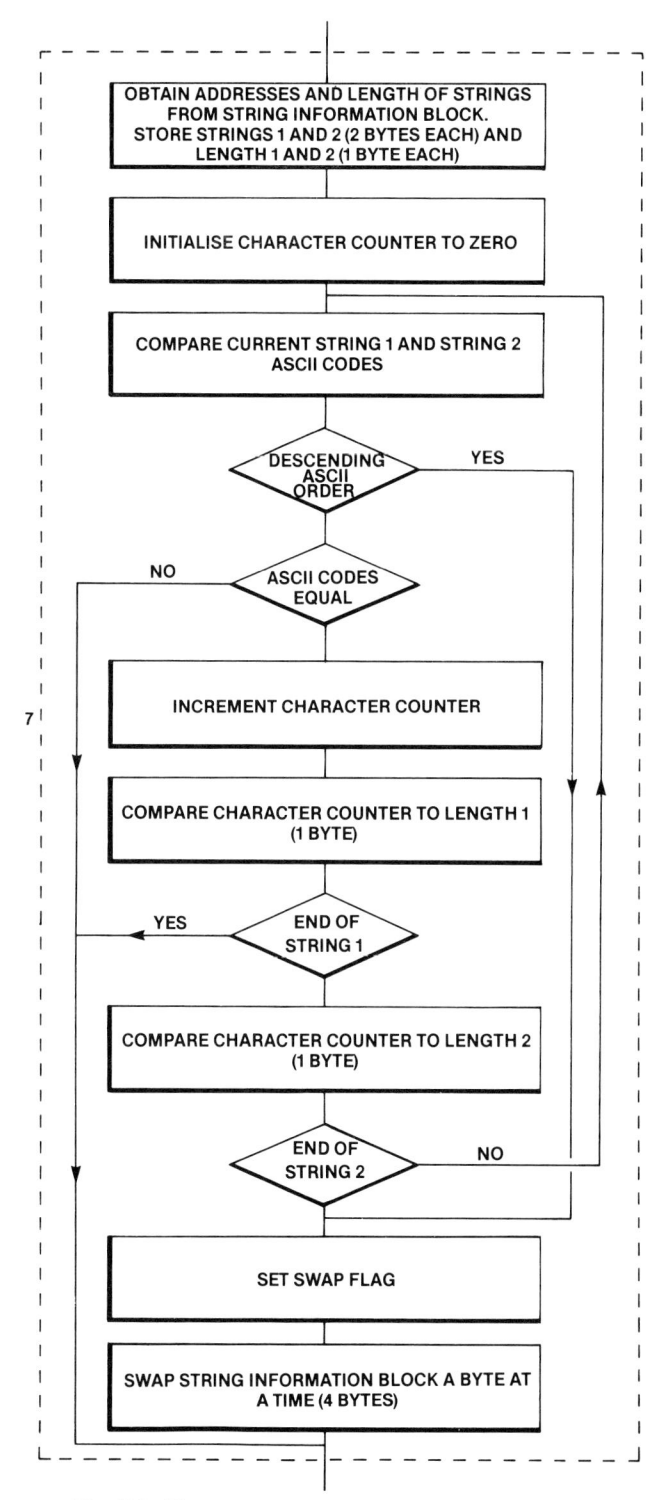

```
┌─────────────────────────────────┐
│ OBTAIN ADDRESSES AND LENGTH OF STRINGS │
│ FROM STRING INFORMATION BLOCK.         │
│ STORE STRINGS 1 AND 2 (2 BYTES EACH) AND│
│ LENGTH 1 AND 2 (1 BYTE EACH)           │
└─────────────────────────────────┘
                │
                ▼
┌─────────────────────────────────┐
│ INITIALISE CHARACTER COUNTER TO ZERO │
└─────────────────────────────────┘
                │
                ▼
┌─────────────────────────────────┐
│ COMPARE CURRENT STRING 1 AND STRING 2 │
│            ASCII CODES                │
└─────────────────────────────────┘
                │
                ▼
        ╱ DESCENDING ╲     YES
       ⟨    ASCII     ⟩─────────►
        ╲   ORDER    ╱
                │ NO
                ▼
  NO    ╱ ASCII CODES ╲
◄───────⟨    EQUAL    ⟩
        ╲             ╱
                │
                ▼
┌─────────────────────────────────┐
│   INCREMENT CHARACTER COUNTER   │
└─────────────────────────────────┘
                │
                ▼
┌─────────────────────────────────┐
│ COMPARE CHARACTER COUNTER TO LENGTH 1 │
│              (1 BYTE)                 │
└─────────────────────────────────┘
                │
                ▼
   YES  ╱  END OF  ╲
◄───────⟨ STRING 1 ⟩
        ╲         ╱
                │
                ▼
┌─────────────────────────────────┐
│ COMPARE CHARACTER COUNTER TO LENGTH 2 │
│              (1 BYTE)                 │
└─────────────────────────────────┘
                │
                ▼
        ╱  END OF  ╲   NO
       ⟨ STRING 2  ⟩─────────►
        ╲          ╱
                │
                ▼
┌─────────────────────────────────┐
│         SET SWAP FLAG           │
└─────────────────────────────────┘
                │
                ▼
┌─────────────────────────────────┐
│ SWAP STRING INFORMATION BLOCK A BYTE AT │
│          A TIME (4 BYTES)               │
└─────────────────────────────────┘
```

Fig. 6.3. Block 7 expansion for string array sort.

length details and the address of where the string is actually stored. These four bytes are referred to as a String Information Block, the details of which follow:

←———— increasing memory ————→

4	3	2	1
string length	maximum length	high-byte	low-byte
		Start address	

The actual string, consisting of the ASCII codes in sequential memory locations, is stored from the starting address given in bytes 1 and 2 above. A string array is formed by a series of such string information blocks, stored sequentially in memory. Therefore, if we want to swop strings (such as during a string sort) it is necessary only to swop the string information blocks since these tell the system where the strings are stored. This makes programs involving machine code sorting much easier to program since most of the work has already been done by the interpreter. Byte 3 of the String Information Block gives the maximum number of characters allowed before discarding original reserved space. This data is rarely used in practice, except in 'housekeeping' or garbage disposal programs and consequently is of no present interest to us. Byte 4 of the String Information Block gives the actual length of the string in bytes (characters).

The CALL parameter block is first set up in BASIC and requires the following variables in the CALL statement:

CALL SORT, NUMBER%, ARRAY$ (1)

The above call is in the same form as that of the previous call, except that ARRAY$ (1) is used.

The flowchart is essentially the same as Fig. 6.1 with one proviso, the details of block 7. The flowchart, showing the amendment is given in Fig. 6.3. The listing is given in Program 6.2.

```
>LIST
   10 REM   STRING ARRAY BUBBLE SORT
   20 REM WITH VARIOUS LENGTH STRINGS
   30 NUMBER=&70:CYCLE=&72:POINTER1=&74
   40 POINTER2=&76:FLAG=&78:string1=&79
   50 string2=&7B:length1=&7D
   60 length2=&7E
```

Program 6.2. String array bubble sort.

Sort Routines

```
 70 DIM SORT 500
 80 FOR PASS=0 TO 2 STEP 2
 90 P%=SORT
100 [OPT PASS              \***************
110 LDA &0601              \GET NUMBER OF
120 STA CYCLE              \BASIC STRINGS
130 LDA &0602              \IN ARRAY AND
140 STA CYCLE+1            \STORE IN NUMBER
150 LDY #1
160 LDA (CYCLE),Y
170 STA NUMBER+1
180 DEY
190 SEC
200 LDA (CYCLE),Y          \***************
210 SBC #1                 \DECREMENT
220 STA NUMBER             \NUMBER
230 BCS OUTERLOOP
240 DEC NUMBER+1
250 .OUTERLOOP             \***************
260 LDA #0                 \INITIALISE
270 STA FLAG               \SWOP FLAG AND
280 STA CYCLE              \CYCLE TO ZERO
290 STA CYCLE+1            \***************
300 LDA &0604              \STORE START
310 STA POINTER2           \ADDRESS OF
320 LDA &0605              \$ INF BLOCK IN
330 STA POINTER2+1         \POINTER2 TEMP.
340 .INNERLOOP             \***************
350 LDA POINTER2+1         \TRANSFER
360 STA POINTER1+1         \POINTERS
370 LDA POINTER2           \POINTER1=
380 STA POINTER1           \POINTER2
390 CLC                    \***************
400 ADC #4                 \ADD 4 TO
410 STA POINTER2           \POINTER1 AND
420 BCC SKIP               \STORE IN
430 INC POINTER2+1         \POINTER2
440 .SKIP                  \***************
450 LDY #0                 \OBTAIN ADDRESS
460 LDA (POINTER1),Y       \AND LENGTH OF
470 STA string1            \EACH OF PAIR
480 LDA (POINTER2),Y       \OF STRINGS
490 STA string2
500 INY
510 LDA (POINTER1),Y
520 STA string1+1
530 LDA (POINTER2),Y
540 STA string2+1
550 LDY #3
560 LDA (POINTER1),Y
570 STA length1
```

Program 6.2. contd

```
 580 LDA (POINTER2),Y
 590 STA length2
 600 LDY #0                  \****************
 610 .COMPLOOP               \COMPARE STRINGS
 620 LDA (string2),Y         \A CHARACTER AT
 630 CMP (string1),Y         \A TIME IF
 640 BCC SWOP                \NECESSARY
 650 BNE NOSWOP
 660 INY
 670 CPY length1
 680 BEQ NOSWOP
 690 CPY length2
 700 BEQ SWOP
 710 BNE COMPLOOP
 720 \*********************************
 730 .STAGE                  \OUT OF RANGE
 740 BNE OUTERLOOP           \BRANCH PATCH
 750 \*********************************
 760 .SWOP
 770 LDY #3
 780 STY FLAG                \SET SWOP FLAG
 790 .SWOPLOOP               \****************
 800 LDA(POINTER1),Y         \SWOP STRING
 810 TAX                     \INFORMATION
 820 LDA(POINTER2),Y         \BLOCK A BYTE AT
 830 STA(POINTER1),Y         \A TIME(4 BYTES)
 840 TXA
 850 STA(POINTER2),Y
 860 DEY
 870 BPL SWOPLOOP
 880 .NOSWOP                 \****************
 890 INC CYCLE               \INCREMENT
 900 BNE SKIP2               \CYCLE
 910 INC CYCLE+1
 920 .SKIP2                  \****************
 930 LDA CYCLE               \COMPARE CYCLE
 940 CMP NUMBER              \TO NUMBER
 950 BNE INNERLOOP           \IF <> BRANCH
 960 LDA CYCLE+1             \TO INNERLOOP
 970 CMP NUMBER+1
 980 BNE INNERLOOP
 990 LDA FLAG                \IF SW.FLG CLEAR
1000 BEQ FLAGCLEAR           \BR. FLAGCLEAR
1010 LDA NUMBER              \****************
1020 SEC                     \DECREMENT
1030 SBC #1                  \NUMBER
1040 STA NUMBER
1050 BCS SKIP3
1060 DEC NUMBER+1
1070 .SKIP3
1080 LDA NUMBER              \****************
```

Program 6.2. contd

```
1090 BNE STAGE            \IF NUMBER <>0
1100 LDA NUMBER+1         \BRANCH OUTERLOOP
1110 BNE STAGE            \VIA STAGE
1120 .FLAGCLEAR
1130 RTS:]
1140 NEXT PASS
1150
1160 REM BASIC IS FOR TESTING ONLY
1170 CLS
1180 MODE4
1190 INPUT"NUMBER OF STRINGS ",NUMBER%
1200 PRINT
1210 DIM ARRAY$(NUMBER%)
1220 FOR N%=1 TO NUMBER%
1230 string$=""
1240 FOR Z%=1 TO RND(10)
1250 K$=CHR$(RND(26)+64)
1260 string$=string$+K$
1270 NEXT Z%
1280 ARRAY$(N%)=string$
1290 PRINT ARRAY$(N%)
1300 NEXT N%
1310 PRINT
1320 PRINT "SORTING"
1330 PRINT
1340 START%=TIME
1350 CALL SORT,NUMBER%,ARRAY$(1)
1360 time%=TIME-START%
1370 FOR N%=1 TO NUMBER%
1380 PRINT ARRAY$(N%)
1390 NEXT
1400 PRINT:PRINT"NUMBER=";NUMBER%
1410 PRINT
1420 PRINT"SORTING TIME= ";time%/100;" SECONDS"
```

Program 6.2. contd

All that is now required is to explain the differences between Program 6.2 and Program 6.1. In this latter routine, POINTER1 and POINTER2 are the address pointers to the String Information Blocks of the pair of strings. A further level of indirect indexed addressing is necessary to pick up the actual string characters since the String Information Block supplies only the address of where the string is stored.

Lines 460-540 pick up the start addresses of the pair of strings, using indirect indexed addressing. The addresses are stored in string1 and string2 (zero-page locations).

Lines 550-590 pick up the fourth bytes of both the String Information Block and store them in length1 and length2.

Line 600 sets the character counter to zero (Y register).

Lines 610-710 compare the ASCII codes of the pair of strings picked up by indirect indexed addressing. On comparison, as soon as the ASCII codes are found to be in descending order, the strings are immediately swopped. If the ASCII codes are found to be in ascending order, then no swop is required.

Line 660 increments the character counter.

Lines 670-680 compare the length of the first string (length1) to the character counter. If they are equal, no swop is required.

Lines 690-700 compare the length of the second string (length2) to the character counter. If they are equal, a swop is initiated.

Line 710 forces the branch to COMPLOOP which compares the next characters in the pair of strings, and so on.

Lines 730-740 are an out-of-range branch patch and, ideally, should not be there. It is due to the 128 byte displacement limit in relative addressing. This occurs in Line 1110.

Merge sort of BASIC integer array

Although the bubble sort routines given earlier are fast for small numbers of elements, the execution time increases alarmingly when in excess of about a hundred elements. To see the delay on high numbers, try running Program 6.1 with 1000 integers. You could well wait 45 seconds before the sort is completed. A far better solution is to use a merge sort algorithm. We noted earlier that the bubble sort is fairly efficient if only a small number of elements are to be sorted. We also noted that the use of a swop flag system significantly speeds up the execution of a bubble sort of a roughly ordered list. The merge sort algorithm takes advantage of both these virtues. Essentially, the array to be sorted is split up into small sets which are bubble sorted. These are merged to form larger sets which will be roughly in order. These larger sets are bubble sorted and merged to form even larger sets and so on until we are left with one large, roughly ordered list. This is finally bubble sorted, which will be efficient due to the points made earlier. A flowchart for a version of a merge sort is given in Fig. 6.4.

There is a danger of becoming intoxicated with verbosity in an attempt to explain the intricate details of a merge sort. A better grasp of the principles can be obtained by a Trace Table. In fact, any program which is difficult to follow will benefit from such an analysis. The idea is to follow the program through with arbitrary test data, keeping track of what happens to the various 'key' locations such as loop counters, etc. A Trace Table for the flowchart is given in Fig. 6.5. The unsorted array uses 8 random integers and shows how they would be sorted at various stages of the trace. Notice how the array becomes more and more ordered as each outer loop cycle is completed.

If the flowchart and trace table have been understood, Program 6.3

Sort Routines **127**

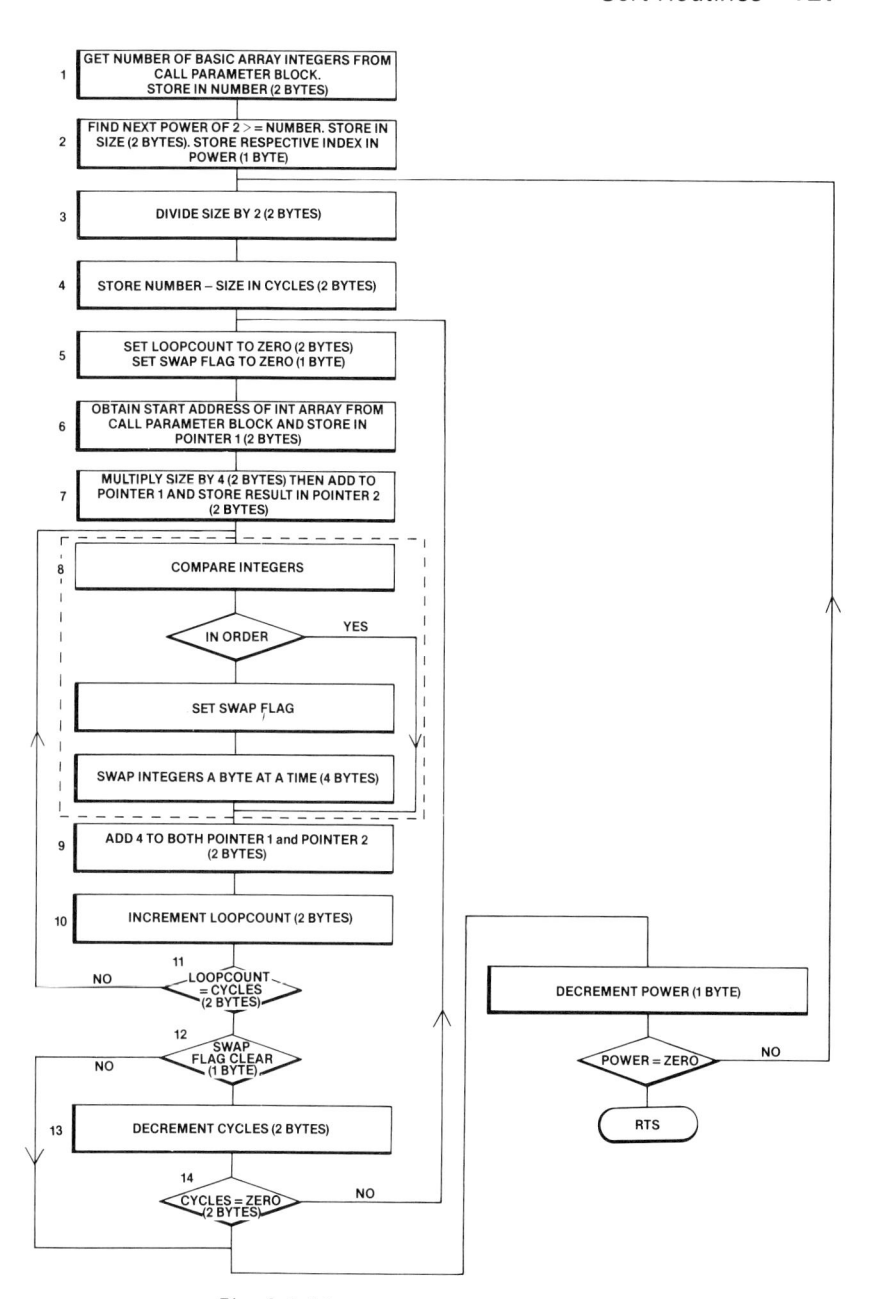

Fig. 6.4. Merge sort of an integer array.

should be reasonably easy to decipher. In this program, there is provision for sorting signed integers. An expansion of Block 8 of the flowchart (Fig. 6.4) is given in Fig. 6.6, showing the extra details required.

128 *Advanced Machine Code Techniques for The BBC Micro*

TRACE TABLE FOR A MERGE SORT

LOCATION LABELS	Value after 1st outer loop completed	Value after 2nd outer loop completed	Value after 3rd outer loop completed
NUMBER	8	8	8
POWER	2	1	0
SIZE	4	2	1
CYCLES	4	6	7

Unsorted array	Array after 1st outer loop completed	Array after 2nd outer loop completed	Array after 3rd outer loop completed
5	5	3	1
8	6	1	2
3	3	4	3
1	1	2	4
7	7	5	5
6	8	6	6
4	4	7	7
2	2	8	8

Fig. 6.5. Simple Trace Table of merge sort algorithm.

Sort Routines 129

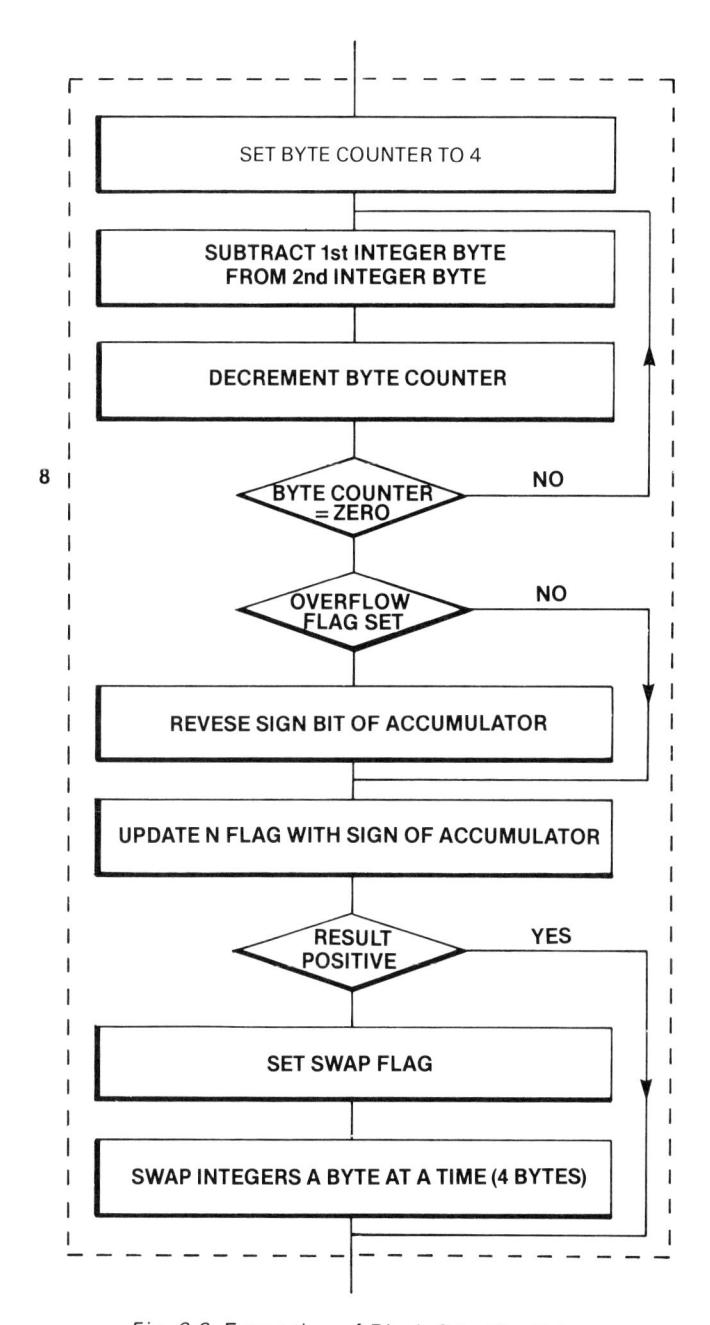

```
┌─────────────────────────────────────────┐
│         SET BYTE COUNTER TO 4           │
└─────────────────────────────────────────┘
                    │
                    ▼
┌─────────────────────────────────────────┐
│       SUBTRACT 1st INTEGER BYTE         │
│         FROM 2nd INTEGER BYTE           │
└─────────────────────────────────────────┘
                    │
                    ▼
┌─────────────────────────────────────────┐
│         DECREMENT BYTE COUNTER          │
└─────────────────────────────────────────┘
                    │
                    ▼
             ◇ BYTE COUNTER ◇ ──NO──┐
               = ZERO               │
                    │               │
                    ▼               │
             ◇ OVERFLOW ◇ ──NO──┐   │
               FLAG SET         │   │
                    │           │   │
                    ▼           │   │
┌─────────────────────────────────────────┐
│      REVESE SIGN BIT OF ACCUMULATOR     │
└─────────────────────────────────────────┘
                    │
                    ▼
┌─────────────────────────────────────────┐
│   UPDATE N FLAG WITH SIGN OF ACCUMULATOR│
└─────────────────────────────────────────┘
                    │
                    ▼
             ◇ RESULT ◇ ──YES──┐
               POSITIVE        │
                    │          │
                    ▼          │
┌─────────────────────────────────────────┐
│             SET SWAP FLAG               │
└─────────────────────────────────────────┘
                    │
                    ▼
┌─────────────────────────────────────────┐
│  SWAP INTEGERS A BYTE AT A TIME (4 BYTES)│
└─────────────────────────────────────────┘
```

Fig. 6.6. Expansion of Block 8 in Fig. 6.4.

The program breakdown of Program 6.3 is as follows:

130 *Advanced Machine Code Techniques for The BBC Micro*

```
>LIST
    10 REM MERGE SORT OF ARRAY OF
    20 REM SIGNED 32bit INTEGERS
    30 NUMBER=&70:POINTER1=&72:POWER=&74
    40 POINTER2=&75:SIZE=&77:LOOPCOUNT=&7
9:FLAG=&7B:STORE=&7C:CYCLES=&7E
    50 DIM SORT 500
    60 FOR PASS=0 TO 2 STEP 2
    70 P%=SORT
    80 [OPT PASS             \***************
    90 LDA &0601             \GET NUMBER OF
   100 STA STORE             \BASIC INTEGERS
   110 LDA &0602             \IN ARRAY AND
   120 STA STORE+1           \STORE IN NUMBER
   130 LDY #0
   140 STY SIZE+1
   150 STY POWER             \ALSO INITIALISE
   160 LDA (STORE),Y         \SIZE AND POWER
   170 STA NUMBER
   180 INY
   190 STY SIZE
   200 LDA (STORE),Y
   210 STA NUMBER+1
   220 .SIZELOOP             \***************
   230 INC POWER             \FIND NEXT POWER
   240 CLC                   \OF 2 >= NUMBER
   250 ASL SIZE              \STORE IN SIZE
   260 ROL SIZE+1
   270 SEC
   280 LDA SIZE
   290 SBC NUMBER
   300 LDA SIZE+1
   310 SBC NUMBER+1
   320 BCC SIZELOOP
   330 .OUTERLOOP            \***************
   340 CLC                   \DIVIDE SIZE
   350 LSR SIZE+1            \BY 2
   360 ROR SIZE
   370 SEC                   \***************
   380 LDA NUMBER            \SUBTRACT SIZE
   390 SBC SIZE              \FROM NUMBER
   400 STA CYCLES            \STORE IN CYCLES
   410 LDA NUMBER+1
   420 SBC SIZE+1
   430 STA CYCLES+1
   440 .MIDLOOP              \***************
   450 LDA #0                \INITIALISE
   460 STA FLAG              \SWOP FLAG AND
   470 STA LOOPCOUNT         \LOOPCOUNT
   480 STA LOOPCOUNT+1
   490 LDA &0604             \***************
```

Program 6.3. Merge sort of an array of signed 32-bit integers.

```
 500 STA POINTER1        \STORE FIRST INT
 510 LDA &0605           \ADDRESS IN
 520 STA POINTER1+1      \POINTER1
 530 LDA SIZE            \***************
 540 STA STORE           \MULTIPLY SIZE
 550 LDA SIZE+1          \BY 4 AND ADD
 560 STA STORE+1         \ADD TO POINTER1
 570 LDX #2              \STORE RESULT IN
 580 .MULT4              \POINTER2
 590 CLC
 600 ASL STORE
 610 ROL STORE+1
 620 DEX
 630 BNE MULT4
 640 CLC
 650 LDA POINTER1
 660 ADC STORE
 670 STA POINTER2
 680 LDA POINTER1+1
 690 ADC STORE+1
 700 STA POINTER2+1
 710 .INNERLOOP          \***************
 720 LDX #4              \SUBTRACT ONE
 730 LDY #0              \INTEGER FROM
 740 SEC                 \THE OTHER AND
 750 .COMPLOOP           \KEEP THE MOST
 760 LDA (POINTER2),Y    \SIGNIFICANT
 770 SBC (POINTER1),Y    \BYTE OF RESULT
 780 INY                 \IN ACCUMULATOR
 790 DEX                 \FOR SIGN BIT
 800 BNE COMPLOOP
 810 BVC NOOVERFLOW      \REVERSE SIGN
 820 EOR #&80            \BIT IF OVERFLOW
 830 .NOOVERFLOW         \OCCURS.
 840 TAX                 \UPDATE N FLAG
 850 BPL NOSWOP          \N CLEAR,NOSWOP
 860 DEY
 870 STY FLAG
 880 .SWOPLOOP           \***************
 890 LDA (POINTER1),Y    \SWOP INTEGERS
 900 TAX                 \A BYTE AT A
 910 LDA (POINTER2),Y    \TIME
 920 STA (POINTER1),Y
 930 TXA
 940 STA (POINTER2),Y
 950 DEY
 960 BPL SWOPLOOP
 970 BMI NOSWOP
 980 \-------------------------------
 990 .STAGE1             \OUT OF RANGE
1000 BNE MIDLOOP         \BRANCH PATCHES
```

Program 6.3. contd

```
1010 .STAGE2
1020 BNE OUTERLOOP
1030 \---------------------------------
1040 .NOSWOP                \***************
1050 INC LOOPCOUNT          \INCREMENT
1060 BNE SKIP               \LOOPCOUNT
1070 INC LOOPCOUNT+1
1080 .SKIP                  \***************
1090 LDA POINTER1           \ADD 4 TO
1100 CLC                    \POINTER1
1110 ADC #4
1120 STA POINTER1
1130 BCC SKIP2
1140 INC POINTER1+1
1150 .SKIP2                 \***************
1160 LDA POINTER2           \ADD 4 TO
1170 CLC                    \POINTER2
1180 ADC #4
1190 STA POINTER2
1200 BCC SKIP3
1210 INC POINTER2+1
1220 .SKIP3                 \***************
1230 LDA CYCLES             \COMPARE
1240 CMP LOOPCOUNT          \LOOPCOUNT
1250 BNE INNERLOOP          \TO CYCLE
1260 LDA CYCLES+1           \IF <> BRANCH
1270 CMP LOOPCOUNT+1        \TO INNERLOOP
1280 BNE INNERLOOP
1290 LDA FLAG               \IF SW.FLG CLEAR
1300 BEQ FLAGCLEAR          \BR. FLAGCLEAR
1310 SEC
1320 LDA CYCLES             \***************
1330 SBC #1                 \DECREMENT
1340 STA CYCLES             \CYCLES
1350 BCS SKIP4
1360 DEC CYCLES+1
1370 .SKIP4                 \***************
1380 LDA CYCLES             \IF CYCLES <>0
1390 BNE STAGE1             \THEN BRANCH
1400 LDA CYCLES+1           \TO MIDLOOP
1410 BNE STAGE1             \VIA STAGE1
1420 .FLAGCLEAR             \***************
1430 DEC POWER              \DECREMENT POWER
1440 BNE STAGE2             \IF>0 BR. STAGE2
1450 RTS:]
1460 NEXT PASS
1470
1480 REM BASIC TEST PROGRAM
1490 MODE4
1500 CLS
1510 INPUT"NUMBER OF INTEGERS ",NUMBER%
```

Program 6.3. contd

Sort Routines

```
1520 PRINT
1530 DIM ARRAY%(NUMBER%)
1540 FOR N%=1 TO NUMBER%
1550 ARRAY%(N%)=RND/1000
1560 PRINT ARRAY%(N%)
1570 NEXT
1580 PRINT
1590 PRINT "SORTING"
1600 PRINT
1610 START%=TIME
1620 CALL SORT,NUMBER%,ARRAY%(1)
1630 time%=TIME-START%
1640 FOR N%=1 TO NUMBER%
1650 PRINT ARRAY%(N%)
1660 NEXT N%
1670 PRINT
1680 PRINT"NUMBER= ";NUMBER%
1690 PRINT
1700 PRINT"SORTING TIME= ";time%/100; "
SECONDS"
```

Program 6.3. contd

Lines 90-120 obtain the address of the BASIC variable NUMBER% from the CALL parameter block. The address is placed in zero-page locations STORE (2 bytes).

Lines 130-210 pick up the data by indirect indexed addressing and store it in NUMBER (zero-page). At the same time, various locations are initialised.

Lines 220-320 are a block of code dedicated to finding the next power of 2, $>=$ the contents of NUMBER. The result is stored in SIZE (2 bytes). The corresponding power index is stored in POWER (1 byte). The op-codes ASL and ROL in conjunction are convenient for 2-byte manipulation of powers of 2.

Lines 330-360 divide SIZE by 2 by shifting right.

Lines 370-430 subtract SIZE from NUMBER and store the result in CYCLES (2 bytes).

Lines 450-480 initialise LOOPCOUNT (2 bytes) and the swop FLAG to zero.

Lines 490-520 pick up the address of the first element in the array and store it in POINTER1 (2 bytes).

Lines 530-700 are a block of code which multiplies SIZE by 4 and adds POINTER1, storing the result in POINTER2. The reason why it is multiplied by 4 is because each integer occupies four bytes. The multiplication is achieved by shifting left twice.

Line 720 sets the byte counter (X register) to 4.

Lines 730-800 subtract the two integers picked up by indirect indexed addressing, keeping the result of the most significant byte (which has the sign bit).

Line 810 checks if the V flag is set. If clear, it skips line 820.

Line 820 assumes that the V flag is set, so reverses the sign bit.

Line 840 updates the N flag to the accumulator contents. This is necessary because DEX, in line 790, corrupts the N flag. TAX is economical for this purpose since it uses only 2 cycles.

Line 850 tests the sign of the accumulator and by-passes the swop loop if positive. This ensures that if both integers are the same, no swopping occurs.

Lines 890-960 swop the integers, a byte at a time, using indirect indexed addressing.

Line 970 serves no useful purpose in the program, other than causing a by-pass of the out of range branch-patch section (lines 990-1020).

Lines 1050-1080 increment LOOPCOUNT.

Lines 1090-1220 add the usual 4 to each of POINTER1 and POINTER2.

Lines 1230-1280 compare LOOPCOUNT to CYCLES, branching to INNERLOOP if not equal.

Lines 1290-1300 test the swop flag and, if clear, branch to FLAGCLEAR.

Lines 1310-1370 decrement CYCLES.

Lines 1380-1410 compare CYCLES to zero, branching to MIDLOOP via STAGE1, the out of range branch-patch.

Lines 1430-1440 decrement POWER and compare to zero, branching to OUTERLOOP via STAGE 2.

Lines 1480-1700 handle the BASIC test routine described earlier.

Merge sort of a BASIC string array.

The overall structure of Program 6.4 is similar to Program 6.3, the only difference being the substitution of the string comparison routine (block 8 in the flowchart). This routine has already been described in detail for the bubble sort.

```
>LIST
   10 REM MERGE SORT OF STRING ARRAY
   20 REM WITH VARIOUS LENGTH STRINGS
   30 NUMBER=&70:POINTER1=&72:POWER=&74
   40 POINTER2=&75:SIZE=&77:LOOPCOUNT=&7
9:FLAG=&7B:STORE=&7C:CYCLES=&7E
   50 string1=&80:string2=&82:length1=&8
4:length2=&85
   60 DIM SORT 500
   70 FOR PASS=0 TO 2 STEP 2
   80 P%=SORT
   90 [OPT PASS          \**************
  100 LDA &0601          \GET NUMBER OF
  110 STA STORE          \BASIC STRINGS
```

Program 6.4. Merge sort of a BASIC string array.

Sort Routines 135

```
120 LDA &0602          \IN ARRAY AND
130 STA STORE+1        \STORE IN NUMBER
140 LDY #0
150 STY SIZE+1
160 STY POWER          \ALSO INITIALISE
170 LDA (STORE),Y      \SIZE AND POWER
180 STA NUMBER
190 INY
200 STY SIZE
210 LDA (STORE),Y
220 STA NUMBER+1
230 .SIZELOOP          \***************
240 INC POWER          \FIND NEXT POWER
250 CLC                \OF 2 >= NUMBER
260 ASL SIZE           \AND STORE IN
270 ROL SIZE+1         \SIZE
280 SEC
290 LDA SIZE
300 SBC NUMBER
310 LDA SIZE+1
320 SBC NUMBER+1
330 BCC SIZELOOP
340 .OUTERLOOP         \***************
350 CLC                \DIVIDE SIZE
360 LSR SIZE+1         \BY 2
370 ROR SIZE
380 SEC                \***************
390 LDA NUMBER         \SUBTRACT SIZE
400 SBC SIZE           \FROM NUMBER AND
410 STA CYCLES         \STORE IN CYCLES
420 LDA NUMBER+1
430 SBC SIZE+1
440 STA CYCLES+1
450 .MIDLOOP           \***************
460 LDA #0             \SET SWOP FLAG
470 STA FLAG           \AND LOOPCOUNT
480 STA LOOPCOUNT      \TO ZERO
490 STA LOOPCOUNT+1    \***************
500 LDA &0604          \STORE START
510 STA POINTER1       \ADDRESS OF
520 LDA &0605          \ $ INF.BLOCK IN
530 STA POINTER1+1     \POINTER1
540 LDA SIZE           \***************
550 STA STORE          \MULTIPLY SIZE
560 LDA SIZE+1         \BY 4 AND ADD TO
570 STA STORE+1        \POINTER1 STORE
580 LDX #2             \RESULT IN
590 .MULT4             \POINTER2
600 CLC
610 ASL STORE
620 ROL STORE+1
```

Program 6.4. contd

```
 630 DEX
 640 BNE MULT4
 650 CLC
 660 LDA POINTER1
 670 ADC STORE
 680 STA POINTER2
 690 LDA POINTER1+1
 700 ADC STORE+1
 710 STA POINTER2+1
 720 .INNERLOOP           \***************
 730 LDY #0               \OBTAIN ADDRESS
 740 LDA (POINTER1),Y     \AND LENGTH
 750 STA string1          \OF EACH OF
 760 LDA (POINTER2),Y     \PAIR OF STRINGS
 770 STA string2
 780 INY
 790 LDA (POINTER1),Y
 800 STA string1+1
 810 LDA (POINTER2),Y
 820 STA string2+1
 830 LDY #3
 840 LDA (POINTER1),Y
 850 STA length1
 860 LDA (POINTER2),Y
 870 STA length2
 880 LDY #0               \***************
 890 .COMPLOOP            \COMPARE STRINGS
 900 LDA (string2),Y      \A CHARACTER AT
 910 CMP (string1),Y      \A TIME IF
 920 BCC SWOP             \NECESSARY
 930 BNE NOSWOP
 940 INY
 950 CPY length1
 960 BEQ NOSWOP
 970 CPY length2
 980 BEQ SWOP
 990 BNE COMPLOOP
1000 \--------------------------------
1010 .STAGE1              \OUT OF RANGE
1020 BNE MIDLOOP          \BRANCH PATCHES
1030 .STAGE2
1040 BNE OUTERLOOP
1050 \--------------------------------
1060 .SWOP                \***************
1070 LDY #3               \SET SWOP FLAG
1080 STY FLAG
1090 .SWOPLOOP            \***************
1100 LDA (POINTER1),Y     \SWOP STRING
1110 TAX                  \INFORMATION
1120 LDA (POINTER2),Y     \BLOCK A BYTE AT
1130 STA (POINTER1),Y     \A TIME(4 BYTES)
```

Program 6.4. contd

Sort Routines 137

```
1140 TXA
1150 STA (POINTER2),Y
1160 DEY
1170 BPL SWOPLOOP
1180 .NOSWOP              \***************
1190 INC LOOPCOUNT        \INCREMENT
1200 BNE SKIP             \LOOPCOUNT
1210 INC LOOPCOUNT+1
1220 .SKIP                \***************
1230 LDA POINTER1         \ADD 4 TO
1240 CLC                  \POINTER1
1250 ADC #4
1260 STA POINTER1
1270 BCC SKIP2
1280 INC POINTER1+1
1290 .SKIP2               \***************
1300 LDA POINTER2         \ADD 4 TO
1310 CLC                  \POINTER2
1320 ADC #4
1330 STA POINTER2
1340 BCC SKIP3
1350 INC POINTER2+1
1360 .SKIP3               \***************
1370 LDA CYCLES           \COMPARE
1380 CMP LOOPCOUNT        \LOOPCOUNT TO
1390 BNE INNERLOOP        \CYCLES
1400 LDA CYCLES+1         \IF <> BRANCH
1410 CMP LOOPCOUNT+1      \TO INNERLOOP
1420 BNE INNERLOOP
1430 LDA FLAG             \IF SW.FLG CLEAR
1440 BEQ FLAGCLEAR        \BR. FLAGCLEAR
1450 SEC
1460 LDA CYCLES           \***************
1470 SBC #1               \DECREMENT
1480 STA CYCLES           \CYCLES
1490 BCS SKIP4
1500 DEC CYCLES+1
1510 .SKIP4               \***************
1520 LDA CYCLES           \IF CYCLES <>0
1530 BNE STAGE1           \THEN BRANCH
1540 LDA CYCLES+1         \TO MIDLOOP
1550 BNE STAGE1           \VIA STAGE1
1560 .FLAGCLEAR           \***************
1570 DEC POWER            \DECREMENT POWER
1580 BNE STAGE2           \IF>0 BR.STAGE2
1590 RTS:]
1600 NEXT PASS
1610
1620 REM BASIC TEST PROGRAM
1630 MODE4
1640 CLS
```

Program 6.4. contd

138 *Advanced Machine Code Techniques for The BBC Micro*

```
1650 INPUT"NUMBER OF STRINGS ",NUMBER%
1660 PRINT
1670 DIM ARRAY$(NUMBER%)
1680 FOR N%=1 TO NUMBER%
1690 string$=""
1700 FOR Z%=1 TO RND(10)
1710 K$=CHR$(RND(26)+64)
1720 string$=string$+K$
1730 NEXT Z%
1740 ARRAY$(N%)=string$
1750 PRINT ARRAY$(N%)
1760 NEXT N%
1770 PRINT
1780 PRINT "SORTING"
1790 PRINT
1800 START%=TIME
1810 CALL SORT,NUMBER%,ARRAY$(1)
1820 time%=TIME-START%
1830 FOR N%=1 TO NUMBER%
1840 PRINT ARRAY$(N%)
1850 NEXT
1860 PRINT
1870 PRINT"STRINGS= ";NUMBER%
1880 PRINT
1890 PRINT"SORTING TIME= ";time%/100; " SECONDS"
```

Program 6.4. contd

Since the overall structure is similar to the previous program, a detailed line by line analysis is unnecessary.

Merge sort of an unsigned BASIC floating point array

Programs which handle records or tables often need to sort unsigned floating point numbers (most numerical values in such programs are unsigned). It is, therefore, important to have at least an outline understanding of how floating numbers are stored by the BASIC interpreter. A floating point number consists of a *mantissa* and an *exponent*. Four bytes are allocated to the mantissa and one byte for the exponent. The most significant bit of the exponent is the sign bit and is in reverse two's complement. That is to say, a negative exponent has '0' as the sign bit; a '1' indicates a positive exponent. The reason for this rather strange practice is that the maximum possible negative exponent closely approaches zero. This means that zero can be loosely taken as the most negative exponent. Therefore less negative exponents through to positive exponents correspond to a progression of increasingly larger exponents.

From a mathematical viewpoint, a mantissa is always positive so no sign

Sort Routines

bit is required. Therefore, the sign bit in the mantissa is used to denote the sign of the entire number in conventional two's complement form.

How floating point variables are stored
Floating point variables are stored by the interpreter in a five-byte form, the details of which are below:

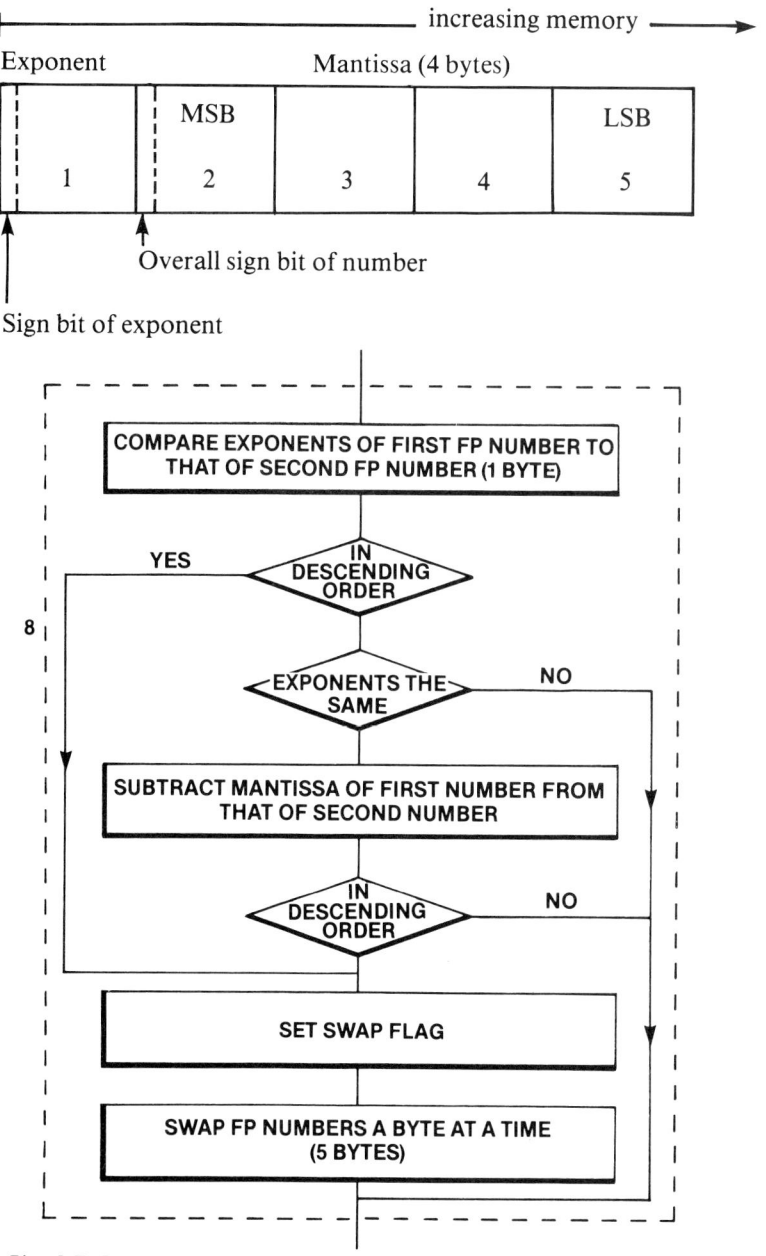

```
                              ──── increasing memory ────▶
Exponent            Mantissa (4 bytes)
┌──────┬──┬────────┬────────┬────────┬────────┐
│      │  │  MSB   │        │        │  LSB   │
│  1   │  │   2    │   3    │   4    │   5    │
└──────┴──┴────────┴────────┴────────┴────────┘
 ▲        ▲
 │        └── Overall sign bit of number
 │
 Sign bit of exponent
```

Fig. 6.7. Block 8 expansion for unsigned floating point merge sort.

Flow (Block 8):
- COMPARE EXPONENTS OF FIRST FP NUMBER TO THAT OF SECOND FP NUMBER (1 BYTE)
- IN DESCENDING ORDER? — YES → (exit)
- EXPONENTS THE SAME? — NO → (exit)
- SUBTRACT MANTISSA OF FIRST NUMBER FROM THAT OF SECOND NUMBER
- IN DESCENDING ORDER? — NO → (exit)
- SET SWAP FLAG
- SWAP FP NUMBERS A BYTE AT A TIME (5 BYTES)

Block 8 of the flowchart in Fig. 6.4 is replaced by Fig. 6.7. This is the only essential difference in the algorithm other than the addition of 5 instead of 4 to the address pointers POINTER1 and POINTER2 when appropriate. The complete listing is shown in Program 6.5. and requires the following BASIC parameters:

CALL SORT, NUMBER%, ARRAY (1)

The variables used are arbitrary but must be in the order given. The listing is liberally 'remarked' and, hopefully, should require no further explanation.

```
>LIST
   10 REM      MERGE SORT OF UNSIGNED
   20 REM      FLOATING POINT NUMBERS
   30 NUMBER=&70:POINTER1=&72:POWER=&74
   40 POINTER2=&75:SIZE=&77:LOOPCOUNT=&7
9:FLAG=&7B:STORE=&7C:CYCLES=&7E
   50 DIM SORT 500
   60 FOR PASS=0 TO 2 STEP 2
   70 P%=SORT
   80 [OPT PASS            \***************
   90 LDA &0601            \GET NUMBER OF
  100 STA STORE            \FP NUMBERS
  110 LDA &0602            \IN ARRAY AND
  120 STA STORE+1          \STORE IN NUMBER
  130 LDY #0
  140 STY SIZE+1
  150 STY POWER            \ALSO INITIALISE
  160 LDA (STORE),Y        \SIZE AND POWER
  170 STA NUMBER
  180 INY
  190 STY SIZE
  200 LDA (STORE),Y
  210 STA NUMBER+1
  220 .SIZELOOP            \***************
  230 INC POWER            \FIND NEXT POWER
  240 ASL SIZE             \OF 2 >= NUMBER
  250 ROL SIZE+1           \AND STORE IN
  260 SEC                  \SIZE
  270 LDA SIZE
  280 SBC NUMBER
  290 LDA SIZE+1
  300 SBC NUMBER+1
  310 BCC SIZELOOP
  320 .OUTERLOOP           \***************
  330 LSR SIZE+1           \DIVIDE SIZE
  340 ROR SIZE             \BY 2
  350 SEC                  \***************
  360 LDA NUMBER           \SUBTRACT SIZE
  370 SBC SIZE             \FROM NUMBER AND
  380 STA CYCLES           \STORE IN CYCLES
```

Program 6.5. Merge sort of an unsigned floating point array.

Sort Routines 141

```
390 LDA NUMBER+1
400 SBC SIZE+1
410 STA CYCLES+1
420 .MIDLOOP              \***************
430 LDA #0                \INITIALISE
440 STA FLAG              \SWOP FLAG AND
450 STA LOOPCOUNT         \LOOPCOUNT
460 STA LOOPCOUNT+1       \***************
470 LDA &0604             \STORE START
480 STA POINTER1          \ADDRESS OF
490 LDA &0605             \FP ARRAY IN
500 STA POINTER1+1        \POINTER1
510 LDA SIZE+1            \***************
520 STA STORE+1           \MULTIPLY SIZE
530 LDA SIZE              \BY 4 AND ADD
540 ASL A                 \SIZE THUS
550 ROL STORE+1           \OBTAINING AN
560 ASL A                 \EFFECTIVE
570 ROL STORE+1           \MULTIPLICATION
580 CLC                   \OF SIZE BY 5
590 ADC SIZE              \STORE RESULT
600 ADC POINTER1          \IN POINTER2
610 STA POINTER2
620 LDA STORE+1
630 ADC SIZE+1
640 ADC POINTER1+1
650 STA POINTER2+1
740 .INNERLOOP            \***************
750 LDY #0                \COMPARE
760 LDA (POINTER2),Y      \EXPONENT OF
770 CMP (POINTER1),Y      \PAIR OF FP
780 BCC SWOP              \NUMBERS
790 BNE NOSWOP
800 LDY #4                \***************
810 SEC                   \SUBTRACT
820 .COMPLOOP             \MANTISSI
830 LDA (POINTER2),Y      \A BYTE AT A
840 SBC (POINTER1),Y      \TIME KEEPING
850 DEY                   \TRACK OF THE
860 BNE COMPLOOP          \CARRY FLAG
870 BCS NOSWOP            \AT COMPLETION
880 .SWOP                 \***************
890 LDY #4                \SET SWOP FLAG
900 STY FLAG
910 .SWOPLOOP             \***************
920 LDA (POINTER1),Y      \SWOP FP NUMBERS
930 TAX                   \A BYTE AT A
940 LDA (POINTER2),Y      \TIME(5 BYTES)
950 STA (POINTER1),Y
960 TXA
970 STA (POINTER2),Y
```

Program 6.5. contd

```
 980 DEY
 990 BPL SWOPLOOP
1000 BMI NOSWOP
1010 \---------------------------------
1020 .STAGE1                \OUT OF RANGE
1030 BNE MIDLOOP            \BRANCH PATCHES
1040 .STAGE2
1050 BNE OUTERLOOP
1060 \---------------------------------
1070 .NOSWOP                \***************
1080 INC LOOPCOUNT          \INCREMENT
1090 BNE SKIP1              \LOOPCOUNT
1100 INC LOOPCOUNT+1
1110 .SKIP1                 \***************
1120 LDA POINTER1           \ADD 5 TO
1130 CLC                    \POINTER1
1140 ADC #5
1150 STA POINTER1
1160 BCC SKIP2
1170 INC POINTER1+1
1180 .SKIP2                 \***************
1190 LDA POINTER2           \ADD 5 TO
1200 CLC                    \POINTER2
1210 ADC #5
1220 STA POINTER2
1230 BCC SKIP3
1240 INC POINTER2+1
1250 .SKIP3                 \***************
1260 LDA CYCLES             \COMPARE
1270 CMP LOOPCOUNT          \LOOPCOUNT TO
1280 BNE INNERLOOP          \CYCLE
1290 LDA CYCLES+1           \IF <> BRANCH
1300 CMP LOOPCOUNT+1        \TO INNERLOOP
1310 BNE INNERLOOP
1320 LDA FLAG               \IF SW.FLG CLEAR
1330 BEQ FLAGCLEAR          \BR.FLAGCLEAR
1340 SEC
1350 LDA CYCLES             \***************
1360 SBC #1                 \DECREMENT
1370 STA CYCLES             \CYCLES
1380 BCS SKIP4
1390 DEC CYCLES+1
1400 .SKIP4                 \***************
1410 LDA CYCLES             \IF CYCLES <>0
1420 BNE STAGE1             \THEN BRANCH
1430 LDA CYCLES+1           \TO MIDLOOP
1440 BNE STAGE1             \VIA STAGE1
1450 .FLAGCLEAR             \***************
1460 DEC POWER              \DECREMENT POWER
1470 BNE STAGE2             \IF>0 BR.STAGE2
1480 RTS:]
```

Program 6.5. contd

```
1490 NEXT PASS
1500
1510 REM BASIC TEST PROGRAM
1520 MODE4
1530 CLS
1540 INPUT"NUMBER OF FP ELEMENTS ",NUMB
ER%
1550 PRINT
1560 DIM ARRAY(NUMBER%)
1570 FOR N%=1 TO NUMBER%
1580 ARRAY(N%)=ABS(RND)*1E-9
1590 PRINT ARRAY(N%)
1600 NEXT
1610 PRINT
1620 PRINT "SORTING"
1630 PRINT
1640 START%=TIME
1650 CALL SORT,NUMBER%,ARRAY(1)
1660 time%=TIME-START%
1670 FOR N%=1 TO NUMBER%
1680 PRINT ARRAY(N%)
1690 NEXT
1700 PRINT
1710 PRINT"SORTING TIME= ";time%/100; "
SECONDS"
1720 PRINT
1730 PRINT"NUMBER= ";NUMBER%
```

Program 6.5. contd

Machine code sort routines applied to BASIC multifield filing programs

There are two common methods of generating multifield records in BASIC. One is to use fields of fixed length substrings where the whole record is stored as one string array element. The other is to create a two-dimensional string array where the records occupy one dimension and the fields occupy the other. This is often referred to as the row/column file format. Both have advantages and disadvantages. The former method is more economical when storing records since only one String Information block is set up per record by the interpreter. On the other hand, the BASIC programming can be tedious and expensive on memory. The latter method makes for concise programming in BASIC but is heavy on String Information blocks (the number of fields multiplied by the number of records). It is a matter of personal preference which method is used, so a machine code merge sort routine to handle each type of record format will be given. The requirement of any routine of this type is to sort entire records according to any specified field, therefore additional calling parameters will be necessary.

Merge sort of multifield fixed-length records

The complete source code listing and BASIC test routine are given in Program 6.6. The overall structure is similar to that of previous routines with the extra coding 'remarked' on the listing. The machine code call is executed from BASIC via the call statement:

CALL SORT, NUMBER%,FIELD%,FIELDEND%,ARRAY$(1)

where:

SORT=the start address of the routine.
NUMBER%=the number of records in the array.
FIELD%=the first character position of the field in the string array element.
FIELDEND%=the last character position of the field in the string array element.
ARRAY$ (1)=the first usable element in the array.

By convention, the zero element is reserved for headings, labels, etc.

```
>LIST
   10 REM MERGE SORT OF MULTIFIELD
   20 REM FIXED LENGTH RECORDS
   30 NUMBER=&70:POINTER1=&72:POWER=&74
   40 POINTER2=&75:SIZE=&77:LOOPCOUNT=&7
9:FLAG=&7B:STORE=&7C:CYCLES=&7E
   50 string1=&80:string2=&82:FIELD=&84:
FIELDEND=&85
   60 DIM SORT 500
   70 FOR PASS=0 TO 2 STEP 2
   80 P%=SORT
   90 [OPT PASS               \**************
  100 LDA &0601               \GET NUMBER OF
  110 STA STORE               \RECORDS IN THE
  120 LDA &0602               \BASIC ARRAY AND
  130 STA STORE+1             \STORE IN NUMBER
  140 LDY #0
  150 STY SIZE+1
  160 STY POWER               \ALSO INITIALISE
  170 LDA (STORE),Y           \SIZE AND POWER
  180 STA NUMBER
  190 INY
  200 STY SIZE
  210 LDA (STORE),Y
  220 STA NUMBER+1
  230 LDA &0604               \**************
  240 STA STORE               \STORE FIELD
  250 LDA &0605               \START POSITION
  260 STA STORE+1             \IN FIELD
  270 DEY
```

Program 6.6. Merge sort of multifield fixed-length records.

Sort Routines

```
280 LDA (STORE),Y
290 STA FIELD
300 LDA &0607            \***************
310 STA STORE            \STORE FIELD
320 LDA &0608            \END POSITION
330 STA STORE+1          \IN FIELDEND
340 LDA (STORE),Y
350 STA FIELDEND
360 .SIZELOOP            \***************
370 INC POWER            \FIND NEXT POWER
380 CLC                  \OF 2 >= NUMBER
390 ASL SIZE             \AND STORE IN
400 ROL SIZE+1           \SIZE
410 SEC
420 LDA SIZE
430 SBC NUMBER
440 LDA SIZE+1
450 SBC NUMBER+1
460 BCC SIZELOOP
470 .OUTERLOOP           \***************
480 CLC                  \DIVIDE SIZE
490 LSR SIZE+1           \BY 2
500 ROR SIZE
510 SEC                  \***************
520 LDA NUMBER           \SUBTRACT SIZE
530 SBC SIZE             \FROM NUMBER AND
540 STA CYCLES           \STORE IN CYCLES
550 LDA NUMBER+1
560 SBC SIZE+1
570 STA CYCLES+1
580 .MIDLOOP             \***************
590 LDA #0               \SET SWOP FLAG
600 STA FLAG             \AND LOOPCOUNT
610 STA LOOPCOUNT        \TO ZERO
620 STA LOOPCOUNT+1      \***************
630 LDA &060A            \STORE START
640 STA POINTER1         \ADDRESS OF
650 LDA &060B            \ $ INF.BLOCK IN
660 STA POINTER1+1       \POINTER1
670 LDA SIZE             \***************
680 STA STORE            \MULTIPLY SIZE
690 LDA SIZE+1           \BY 4 AND ADD TO
700 STA STORE+1          \POINTER1 STORE
710 LDX #2               \RESULT IN
720 .MULT4               \POINTER2
730 CLC
740 ASL STORE
750 ROL STORE+1
760 DEX
770 BNE MULT4
780 CLC
```

Program 6.6. contd

```
 790 LDA POINTER1
 800 ADC STORE
 810 STA POINTER2
 820 LDA POINTER1+1
 830 ADC STORE+1
 840 STA POINTER2+1
 850 .INNERLOOP        \***************
 860 LDY #0            \OBTAIN ADDRESS
 870 LDA (POINTER1),Y  \OF EACH OF
 880 STA string1       \PAIR OF STRINGS
 890 LDA (POINTER2),Y
 900 STA string2
 910 INY
 920 LDA (POINTER1),Y
 930 STA string1+1
 940 LDA (POINTER2),Y
 950 STA string2+1
 960 LDY FIELD         \INIT.Yreg FIELD
 970 DEY
 980 .COMPLOOP         \COMPARE FIELDS
 990 LDA (string2),Y   \A CHARACTER AT
1000 CMP (string1),Y   \A TIME IF
1010 BCC SWOP          \NECESSARY
1020 BNE NOSWOP
1030 INY
1040 CPY FIELDEND
1050 BNE COMPLOOP
1060 BEQ NOSWOP
1070 \--------------------------------
1080 .STAGE1           \OUT OF RANGE
1090 BNE MIDLOOP       \BRANCH PATCHES
1100 .STAGE2
1110 BNE OUTERLOOP
1120 \--------------------------------
1130 .SWOP             \***************
1140 LDY #3            \SET SWOP FLAG
1150 STY FLAG
1160 .SWOPLOOP         \***************
1170 LDA (POINTER1),Y  \SWOP STRING
1180 TAX               \INFORMATION
1190 LDA (POINTER2),Y  \BLOCK A BYTE AT
1200 STA (POINTER1),Y  \A TIME(4 BYTES)
1210 TXA
1220 STA (POINTER2),Y
1230 DEY
1240 BPL SWOPLOOP
1250 .NOSWOP           \***************
1260 INC LOOPCOUNT     \INCREMENT
1270 BNE SKIP          \LOOPCOUNT
1280 INC LOOPCOUNT+1
1290 .SKIP             \***************
```

Program 6.6. contd

```
1300 LDA POINTER1          \ADD 4 TO
1310 CLC                    \POINTER1
1320 ADC #4
1330 STA POINTER1
1340 BCC SKIP2
1350 INC POINTER1+1
1360 .SKIP2                 \***************
1370 LDA POINTER2           \ADD 4 TO
1380 CLC                    \POINTER2
1390 ADC #4
1400 STA POINTER2
1410 BCC SKIP3
1420 INC POINTER2+1
1430 .SKIP3                 \***************
1440 LDA CYCLES             \COMPARE
1450 CMP LOOPCOUNT          \LOOPCOUNT TO
1460 BNE INNERLOOP          \CYCLES
1470 LDA CYCLES+1           \IF <> BRANCH
1480 CMP LOOPCOUNT+1        \TO INNERLOOP
1490 BNE INNERLOOP
1500 LDA FLAG               \IF SW.FLG CLEAR
1510 BEQ FLAGCLEAR          \BR. FLAGCLEAR
1520 SEC
1530 LDA CYCLES             \***************
1540 SBC #1                 \DECREMENT
1550 STA CYCLES             \CYCLES
1560 BCS SKIP4
1570 DEC CYCLES+1
1580 .SKIP4                 \***************
1590 LDA CYCLES             \IF CYCLES <>0
1600 BNE STAGE1             \THEN BRANCH
1610 LDA CYCLES+1           \TO MIDLOOP
1620 BNE STAGE1             \VIA STAGE1
1630 .FLAGCLEAR             \***************
1640 DEC POWER              \DECREMENT POWER
1650 BNE STAGE2             \IF>0 BR.STAGE2
1660 RTS:]
1670 NEXT PASS
1680
1690 REM BASIC TEST ROUTINE
1700 MODE4
1710 CLS
1720 INPUT"NUMBER OF STRINGS ",NUMBER%
1730 DIM ARRAY$(NUMBER%)
1740 FOR N%=1 TO NUMBER%
1750 string$=""
1760 FOR Z%=1 TO 10
1770 K$=CHR$(RND(26)+64)
1780 string$=string$+K$
1790 NEXT Z%
1800 ARRAY$(N%)=string$
```

Program 6.6. contd

```
1810 PRINT ARRAY$(N%)
1820 NEXT N%
1830 INPUT"GIVE FIELD START POS.   ",FIELD%
1840 INPUT"GIVE FIELD END POS.   ",FIELDEND%
1850 PRINT "SORTING"
1860 START%=TIME
1870 CALL SORT,NUMBER%,FIELD%,FIELDEND%,ARRAY$(1)
1880 time%=TIME-START%
1890 FOR N%=1 TO NUMBER%
1900 PRINT ARRAY$(N%)
1910 NEXT N%
1920 PRINT"SORTED FIELD BEGINS AT CHARACTER   ";FIELD%
1930 PRINT"SORTED FIELD ENDS WITH CHARACTER   ";FIELDEND%
1940 PRINT"NUMBER OF RECORDS= ";NUMBER%
1950 PRINT"SORTING TIME= ";time%/100;" SECONDS"
```

Program 6.6. contd

Merge sort of a two-dimensional string array

The interpreter stores the String Information blocks corresponding to multidimensional string array elements sequentially in memory. The following series shows the order in which they occur for a two-dimensional string array:

A$ (0,0), A$ (0,1), A$ (0,2), A$ (1,0), A$ (1,1), A$ (1,2) ......A$ (R,C)

If a file is DIMensioned in BASIC:

ARRAY$ (ROWNUM%, COLNUM%)

then a file ARRAY$ can be considered as containing ROWNUM% records and COLNUM% fields.

We can define a specific field of a specific record by:

ARRAY$ (RECORD%, FIELD%)

If we call the sort routine with

CALL SORT, ROWNUM%, COLNUM%, FIELD%, ARRAY(1,0)

all the necessary parameters required to sort all the records by field are passed. The complete source code listing and BASIC test routine are shown in Program 6.7.

Since each String Information block occupies four bytes and there are COLNUM%+1 fields to each record, the sort routine will need to calculate the number of bytes necessary before swopping the SI blocks corresponding to each record. This is performed by lines 380 to 480 and the result is stored in NUMBYTE (1 byte).

The by now familar SI block address pointers POINTER1 and POINTER2 refer to the zeroth dimension of COLNUM% so an offset needs to be calculated by the routine to point to the required sort field element SI block in the COLNUM% dimension (remember that 4 bytes offset is required for each). This is performed by lines 490 to 560 and the result is stored in offset (1 byte). Using indirect indexed addressing, the offset accesses the required field SI block position. Plainly, we will need to add NUMBYTE instead of 4 to the previous SI block address pointers in order to access the next record. Apart from these differences, the overall structure is similar to that previously described.

The routine can sort records with up to a maximum of 128/4=32 fields (not much of a handicap in practice). Program 6.7 has been well-tried and tested in a practical filing system and will sort a computer full or records in less than a second.

```
>LIST
    10 REM MERGE SORT OF A TWO
    20 REM DIMENSIONAL STRING ARRAY
    30 REM row/column record format
    40 REM sorting entire record (row)
    50 REM according to any specified
    60 REM field (column)
    70 NUMBER=&70:POINTER1=&72:POWER=&74
    80 POINTER2=&75:SIZE=&77:LOOPCOUNT=&7
9:FLAG=&7B:STORE=&7C:CYCLES=&7E
    90 string1=&80:string2=&82:length1=&8
4:length2=&85:NUMBYTE=&86:offset=&87
   100 DIM SORT 500
   110 FOR PASS=0 TO 2 STEP 2
   120 P%=SORT
   130 [OPT PASS             \***************
   140 LDA &0601              \GET NUMBER OF
   150 STA STORE              \BASIC STRINGS
   160 LDA &0602              \IN ARRAY AND
   170 STA STORE+1            \STORE IN NUMBER
   180 LDY #0
   190 STY SIZE+1
   200 STY POWER              \ALSO INITIALISE
   210 LDA (STORE),Y          \SIZE AND POWER
   220   STA NUMBER
   230 INY
   240 STY SIZE
   250 LDA (STORE),Y
```

Program 6.7. Merge sort of a two-dimensional string array.

```
260 STA NUMBER+1
270 .SIZELOOP             \***************
280 INC POWER             \FIND NEXT POWER
290 CLC                   \OF 2 >= NUMBER
300 ASL SIZE              \AND STORE IN
310 ROL SIZE+1            \SIZE
320 SEC
330 LDA SIZE
340 SBC NUMBER
350 LDA SIZE+1
360 SBC NUMBER+1
370 BCC SIZELOOP
380 LDA &0604             \***************
390 STA STORE             \GET NUMBER OF
400 LDA &0605             \FIELDS IN
410 STA STORE+1           \RECORD THEN
420 LDY #0                \ADD 1 AND
430 LDA (STORE),Y         \MULTIPLY BY 4
440 CLC                   \STORE RESULT
450 ADC #1                \IN NUMBYTE
460 ASL A
470 ASL A
480 STA NUMBYTE           \***************
490 LDA &0607             \GET SORT FIELD
500 STA STORE             \NUMBER THEN
510 LDA &0608             \MULTIPLY BY 4
520 STA STORE+1           \STORE RESULT IN
530 LDA (STORE),Y         \offset
540 ASL A
550 ASL A
560 STA offset
570 .OUTERLOOP            \***************
580 CLC                   \DIVIDE SIZE
590 LSR SIZE+1            \BY 2
600 ROR SIZE
610 SEC                   \***************
620 LDA NUMBER            \SUBTRACT SIZE
630 SBC SIZE              \FROM NUMBER AND
640 STA CYCLES            \STORE IN CYCLES
650 LDA NUMBER+1
660 SBC SIZE+1
670 STA CYCLES+1
680 .MIDLOOP              \***************
690 LDA #0                \SET SWOP FLAG
700 STA FLAG              \AND LOOPCOUNT
710 STA LOOPCOUNT         \TO ZERO
720 STA LOOPCOUNT+1       \***************
730 LDA &060A             \STORE START
740 STA POINTER1          \ADDRESS OF
750 LDA &060B             \ $ INF.BLOCK IN
760 STA POINTER1+1        \POINTER1
```

Program 6.7. contd

```
 770 LDA #0              \***************
 780 STA STORE           \MULTIPLY SIZE
 790 STA STORE+1         \BY NUMBYTE
 800 LDX NUMBYTE         \AND ADD TO
 810 .MULTLOOP           \POINTER1
 820 CLC                 \STORE RESULT IN
 830 LDA STORE           \POINTER2
 840 ADC SIZE
 850 STA STORE
 860 LDA STORE+1
 870 ADC SIZE+1
 880 STA STORE+1
 890 DEX
 900 BNE MULTLOOP
 910 CLC
 920 LDA POINTER1
 930 ADC STORE
 940 STA POINTER2
 950 LDA POINTER1+1
 960 ADC STORE+1
 970 STA POINTER2+1
 980 .INNERLOOP          \***************
 990 LDY offset          \OBTAIN ADDRESS
1000 LDA (POINTER1),Y    \AND LENGTH
1010 STA string1         \OF EACH OF
1020 LDA (POINTER2),Y    \PAIR OF STRINGS
1030 STA string2
1040 INY
1050 LDA (POINTER1),Y
1060 STA string1+1
1070 LDA (POINTER2),Y
1080 STA string2+1
1090 INY
1100 INY
1110 LDA (POINTER1),Y
1120 STA length1
1130 LDA (POINTER2),Y
1140 STA length2
1150 LDY #0              \***************
1160 .COMPLOOP           \COMPARE STRINGS
1170 LDA (string2),Y     \A CHARACTER AT
1180 CMP (string1),Y     \A TIME IF
1190 BCC SWOP            \NECESSARY
1200 BNE NOSWOP
1210 INY
1220 CPY length1
1230 BEQ NOSWOP
1240 CPY length2
1250 BEQ SWOP
1260 BNE COMPLOOP
1270 \--------------------------------
```

Program 6.7. contd

152 Advanced Machine Code Techniques for The BBC Micro

```
1280 .STAGE1              \OUT OF RANGE
1290 BNE MIDLOOP          \BRANCH PATCHES
1300 .STAGE2
1310 BNE OUTERLOOP
1320 \--------------------------------
1330 .SWOP                \INITIALISE BYTE
1340 LDY NUMBYTE          \COUNTER TO
1350 DEY                  \NUMBYTE
1360 STY FLAG             \SET SWOP FLAG
1370 .SWOPLOOP            \***************
1380 LDA (POINTER1),Y     \SWOP STRING
1390 TAX                  \INFORMATION
1400 LDA (POINTER2),Y     \BLOCKS A BYTE
1410 STA (POINTER1),Y     \AT A TIME TILL
1420 TXA                  \COMPLETE RECORD
1430 STA (POINTER2),Y     \IS SWOPPED
1440 DEY
1450 BPL SWOPLOOP
1460 .NOSWOP              \***************
1470 INC LOOPCOUNT        \INCREMENT
1480 BNE SKIP             \LOOPCOUNT
1490 INC LOOPCOUNT+1
1500 .SKIP                \***************
1510 LDA POINTER1         \ADD NUMBYTE TO
1520 CLC                  \POINTER1
1530 ADC NUMBYTE
1540 STA POINTER1
1550 BCC SKIP2
1560 INC POINTER1+1
1570 .SKIP2               \***************
1580 LDA POINTER2         \ADD NUMBYTE TO
1590 CLC                  \POINTER2
1600 ADC NUMBYTE
1610 STA POINTER2
1620 BCC SKIP3
1630 INC POINTER2+1
1640 .SKIP3               \***************
1650 LDA CYCLES           \COMPARE
1660 CMP LOOPCOUNT        \LOOPCOUNT TO
1670 BNE INNERLOOP        \CYCLES
1680 LDA CYCLES+1         \IF <> BRANCH
1690 CMP LOOPCOUNT+1      \TO INNERLOOP
1700 BNE INNERLOOP
1710 LDA FLAG             \IF SW.FLG CLEAR
1720 BEQ FLAGCLEAR        \BR. FLAGCLEAR
1730 SEC
1740 LDA CYCLES           \***************
1750 SBC #1               \DECREMENT
1760 STA CYCLES           \CYCLES
1770 BCS SKIP4
1780 DEC CYCLES+1
```

Program 6.7. contd

Sort Routines 153

```
1790 .SKIP4                \***************
1800 LDA CYCLES            \IF CYCLES <>O
1810 BNE STAGE1            \THEN BRANCH
1820 LDA´CYCLES+1          \TO MIDLOOP
1830 BNE STAGE1            \VIA´STAGE1
1840 .FLAGCLEAR            \***************
1850 DEC POWER             \DECREMENT POWER
1860 BNE STAGE2            \IF>O BR.STAGE2
1870 RTS:]
1880 NEXT PASS
1890
1900 REM BASIC TEST ROUTINE
1910 MODE4
1920 CLS
1930 INPUT"NUMBER OF RECORDS ",ROWNUM%
1940 INPUT"NUMBER OF COLUMNS ",COLNUM%
1950 INPUT"SORT WHICH FIELD   ",FIELD%
1960 PRINT
1970 DIM ARRAY$(ROWNUM%,COLNUM%)
1980 FOR R%=1 TO ROWNUM%
1990 FOR C%=0 TO COLNUM%-1
2000 string$=""
2010 FOR Z%=1 TO RND(10)
2020 K$=CHR$(RND(26)+64)
2030 string$=string$+K$
2040 NEXT Z%
2050 ARRAY$(R%,C%)=string$
2060 PRINT ARRAY$(R%,C%)
2070 NEXT C%
2080 PRINT
2090 NEXT R%
2100 PRINT "SORTING"
2110 PRINT
2120 START%=TIME
2130 CALL SORT,ROWNUM%,COLNUM%,FIELD%,A
RRAY$(1,0)
2140 time%=TIME-START%
2150 FOR R%=1 TO ROWNUM%
2160 FOR C%=0 TO COLNUM%-1
2170 PRINT ARRAY$(R%,C%)
2180 NEXT C%
2190 PRINT
2200 NEXT R%
2210 PRINT
2220 PRINT"RECORDS= ";ROWNUM%
2230 PRINT
2240 PRINT"SORTING TIME= ";time%/100; "
SECONDS"
```

Program 6.7. contd

Table of sorting times

As a guide to the execution times you can expect from the sorting routines, a comprehensive table is given below for various array sizes.

Table 6.1: Table of sorting times.

Unsigned integer bubble sort

Number of elements	100	300	1000	2000	3000
Time (secs) reverse order	0.7	5.7	64	253	567
Time (secs) random (average)	0.5	4.3	47	187	418

String bubble sort

Number of elements	100	300	1000
Time (secs) random length strings	0.5	4.3	50

Signed integer merge sort

Number of elements	100	300	1000	2000	3000
Time (secs) reverse order	0.09	0.3	1.4	3	5
Time (secs) random (average)	0.3	1.2	8.5	22	47

String merge sort

Number of elements	100	300	1000
Time (secs) random length strings	0.2	1.2	8.5

Unsigned floating point merge sort

Number of elements	100	300	1000	2000
Time (secs) random (average)	0.2	1.2	8.0	24

Multi-field fixed length records

Number of records	100	200	300
Time (secs) random	0.2	0.7	1.2

Multi-field unlimited length records (2-dimensional array)

Number of records	100	200	300
Time (secs) 3-field records	0.3	1.2	1.7

Summary

1. BASIC and machine code mix well in the BBC system.
2. There is little point in using machine code just for its own sake. Use BASIC for routine tasks which are not time-critical and slip into machine code for those that are.
3. The standardised unit of computer speed is the 'mip', meaning millions (of machine code instructions) per second. The BBC machine has an average speed of 0.5 mips.
4. A speed of 0.5 mips is good for personal microcomputers but slow in comparison with mainframes. Some can achieve speeds of 100 mips.
5. Sorting data into numerical or alphabetical order occupies about 30% of computer time in the commercial and scientific fields.
6. The bubble sort is simple and effective providing the number of items to be sorted is moderate (not > 100).
7. Integer array variables occupy 4 bytes. Bit 7 of the highest order byte is used for distinguishing sign.
8. String arrays are handled by a four-byte String Information Block which gives string length, maximum length and start address of the array.
9. For sorting large arrays of data items, the bubble method is slow. A much faster sort is obtained by the 'merge' method.
10. The merge sort still uses bubble techniques but first splits up the array into small sets. The sorted sets are then progressively merged into larger sets until a single sorted set remains.

Self test

6.1 Name at least five factors which you consider might influence the processing power of a computer.

6.2 Develop a comprehensive merge sort program which will sort signed integers, strings or floating point arrays as specified by a CALL statement.

6.3 Develop a comprehensive bubble sort program which will sort signed integers. strings or unsigned floating point numbers.

6.4 Develop a routine which will sort signed floating point numbers.

6.5 Develop a bubble sort routine which will sort signed integers.

Chapter Seven
Using Subroutines, Macros and Look-up Tables

User subroutines

Machine code programs which are called from, and intended to return to, BASIC via RTS are essentially subroutines. However, it is a common requirement for the machine code program itself to use subroutines, either user-designed or one of the many resident subroutines embedded within the operating system. Subroutines designed by the user are called by JSR followed by an operand, either an absolute machine address (not recommended) or a destination label. As in BASIC, machine code subroutines can be nested one within the other. Enthusiasm for high nesting levels should not be carried to excess or the stack could overflow. Each unreturned JSR uses up two stack locations, storing the two-byte return address in the Program Counter. No provision is made in the 6502 for saving the other registers. It is up to the programmer to make provisions for protecting valuable register data from corruption by the subroutine. Subroutines are best avoided altogether within loops which are time-critical. Each JSR squanders 6 clock cycles and RTS another six. It is far better to splice the code within the main program, even if it means writing the same segment of code several times.

Resident subroutines

Acorn strongly advise that programs affecting the input/output devices (screen, keyboard, printer, etc.) do so via the appropriate resident subroutines. Circumvention, by writing your own, is not dangerous but the program may not work if a second processor is added. This need not be an effective deterrent. You may never consider owning the second processor. You may feel that the advantages of writing your own input/output routines outweigh other considerations. There are certain speed advantages to be gained by using direct screen addressing techniques. Some fascinating (often bizarre) graphic displays can be produced. Objects can be persuaded to move across the screen with far less, in fact almost imperceptible, flicker. However, it should be realised that writing your own code for screen animation is not going to be easy. The resident subroutines are excellent but we should bear in mind that design constraints are inevitable during the development of general purpose software. In the case of the BBC system, additional constraints are imposed by the problem of maintaining compatibility with the Tube. It comes down in the end to a question of personal choice whether you regard or disregard Acorn's warning. The choice is simple: use the resident subroutines and feel safe, or bow to the spirit of adventure and experiment with your own. The designers of the BBC operating system have bent over backwards to provide free access to most of the ROM's internal anatomy. It would be hard to find a competitive machine which offers more scope for experimentation.

It would be pointless at this stage to plod wearily through the entire repertoire of operating system calls. The complete list appears in the User Guide but, for convenience, has been repeated in slightly different form in Appendix B.

The practical programs that appear throughout this chapter should be useful for insertion as subroutines in BASIC programs employing graphics and sound.

Vectors and indirection

One term which crops up when reading literature on operating system calls is *vector* so it is important to be certain of its meaning:

> A vector is a word (normally 2 bytes) in memory which contains the address of a particular routine.

Detailed specifications of routines might include something like:

OSRDCH: Calling address=&FFE0 : Indirected through &0210

The word 'indirected' can be read as 'internally redirected' and, in the above case, refers to the vector in address &0210. Thus, although we would call OSRDCH at &FFE0, the code at that address is not OSRDCH but simply information where OSRDCH can be found.

Why all this apparently needless treasure trail? The answer lies in flexibility. There are three possibilities for the machine code programmer:

(1) Intercept the standard operating system call by simply changing the vector (changing the address in &0210 in the above example). Calling OSRDCH now at address &FFE0 would call up a different routine, written by the user.

Using Subroutines, Macros and Look-up Tables 159

```
>LIST
   10 REM READ TEXT CURSOR POSITION
   20 REM USING AN OSBYTE CALL
   30 MODE6
   40 DIM START 256
   50 OSBYTE=&FFF4
   60 XPOS=&70:YPOS=&71
   70 FOR PASS=0 TO 2 STEP 2
   80 P%=START
   90 [OPT PASS
  100 LDA #&86      \READ CURSOR POSITION
  110 JSR OSBYTE
  120 STX XPOS      \STORE X AND Y REG'S
  130 STY YPOS      \IN ZERO PAGE LOC'S
  140 RTS:]
  150 NEXT PASS
  160 REM RANDOMISE CURSOR POSITION
  170 VDU31,RND(24),RND(24)
  180 CALL START
  190 PRINT"XPOS=";?XPOS;" YPOS=";?YPOS;
```
Program 7.1. Read text cursor position.

(2) Intercept as before but using some preliminary code at the vectored address to modify the normal call. The original routine could then be re-entered.

(3) Operating system ROMs can be updated or modified without affecting the original call. All that needs to be changed are the contents of the vector.

```
>LIST
   10 REM TYPING PRACTICE PROGRAM
   20 MODE6
   30 DIM START 256
   40 OSASCI=&FFE3:OSRDCH=&FFE0
   50 OSNEWL=&FFE7:OSWRCH=&FFEE
   60 FOR PASS=0 TO 3 STEP 3
   70 P%=START
   80 [OPT PASS
   90 LDA #12
  100 JSR OSWRCH    \CLEAR SCREEN
  110 .BEGIN
  120 JSR OSRDCH    \ACC=ASCII(KEY HIT)
  130 CMP #ASC("*") \COMP TO "*" ASCII
  140 BEQ FINISH    \BR. FINISH IF =
  150 JSR OSASCI    \SEND TO SCREEN
  160 BNE BEGIN     \BR. BEGIN IF <>
  170 .FINISH
  180 LDA #7        \ACC=ASCII FOR BELL
  190 JSR OSWRCH    \OUTPUT ACCUMULATOR
  200 JSR OSNEWL    \EXIT WITH NEW LINE
  210 RTS:]
  220 NEXT PASS
  230 CALL START
```
Program 7.2. Typing practice.

160 *Advanced Machine Code Techniques for The BBC Micro*

Not all the system calls are indirected. Some of those that are include OSWRCH, OSRDCH, OSCLI, OSBYTE, OSWORD. Nearly all the vectors are situated in page 2 although there are a few which can extend into page &0D when using ROM paging. Note carefully that page &0D is often referred to as the 'user subroutine area'.

Three examples, using the simpler routines are given, with outline explanation, in the three following programs. Program 7.1 reads the current text cursor position using OSBYTE. Program 7.2 is a simple typing practice program using OSASCI, OSRDCH, OSNEWL and OSWRCH. To exit the program, enter *.

Using OSWORD

Program 7.3 is an example using the sound generators with envelope

```
>LIST
    10 REM USING THE SOUND GENERATORS
    20 REM WITH ENVELOPE SHAPING
    30 REM (LASER GUN TYPE NOISE)
    40
    50 P%=&1E00
    60 FOR item=1 TO 22
    70 READ D$
    80 D=EVAL(D$)
    90 ?P%=D:P%=P%+1
   100 NEXT item
   110
   120 DATA 1,0,1,0,200,0,3,0
   130 DATA 1,1,0,-4,0,0,50,0,42,&F0,&FE,
&FE,126,94
   140
   150 OSWORD=&FFF1
   160 FOR PASS=0 TO 2 STEP 2
   170 P%=&1D00
   180
   190 [OPT PASS
   200 LDA #8         \CALL OSWORD WITH 8
   210 LDX #&08       \IN THE ACCUMULATOR
   220 LDY #&1E       \AND ENV PARA BLOCK
   230 JSR OSWORD     \ADDRESS IN X AND Y
   240
   250 LDA #7         \CALL OSWORD WITH 7
   260 LDX #&00       \IN THE ACCUMULATOR
   270 LDY #&1E       \AND SOUND PARA BLOCK
   280 JSR OSWORD     \ADDRESS IN X AND Y
   290
   300 RTS:]
   310 NEXT PASS
   320 CALL &1D00
```

Program 7.3. Using the sound generator with envelope shaping.

shaping via a pair of OSWORD calls. Lines 50 to 130 set up the respective parameter block data at &1E00 (an arbitrary address). The sound parameter block data is given in line 120 and the envelope parameter block data in line 130. The data given produce a laser 'zapping' sound, used extensively in many 'shoot out of the sky' types of game.

Readers will no doubt be aware that this is the assembler equivalent of the SOUND and ENVELOPE statements used in BASIC. Notice that two bytes are used for each of the four SOUND parameters which are channel, envelope number, pitch and duration. The high-bytes are usually zero, except for the volume/envelope number parameter which can take a negative value, thus requiring &FF as the high-byte. On the other hand, the 14 envelope parameter block data items are all single-byte entities.

As a point of interest, alternative data for an explosion, gun shot and bonus signal are given below.

Explosion data:
120 DATA 0,0,1,0,6,0,5,0
130 DATA 1,10,0,0,0,0,0,0,42,&F0,0,&FE,126,94

Gun shot data:
120 DATA 0,0,1,0,5,0,4,0
130 DATA 1,10,0,0,0,0,0,0,126,−16,0,−16,126,94

Bonus signal data:
120 DATA 1,0,1,0,200,0,50,0
130 DATA 1,1,0,−20,0,0,10,0,0,0,0,−127,126,0

Perhaps the most useful to the machine code programmer is OSWRCH so it deserves more detailed treatment. Any examples given assume that symbolic operands used, such as OSWRCH itself, have been prior-assigned in BASIC. Such names are of mnemonic value only. They are not recognised by the operating system until equated to a specific machine address, in this case, &FFFE.

Using OSWRCH

> OSWRCH writes the ASCII character code in the accumulator to 'the currently selected' output device.

The term 'currently selected' refers to either the screen, printer or RS423 interface. The default condition is to screen and printer only. Other combinations can be achieved by a prior call to OSBYTE (see later).

The way OSWRCH works is as follows:

(a) Calling address &FFEE (indirected via &020E).
(b) The A,X and Y registers have their contents preserved.

(c) The C,N,V and Z flags are undefined.

Example 1: LDA #72
           JSR OSWRCH \Prints"H"on the screen
Example 2: LDA ASC("H")
           JSR OSWRCH

Relating OSWRCH to VDU codes

However, OSWRCH is capable of much more than is suggested above. This is due to the cunning use of the 32 control codes which extend through the ASCII range 0 to 31. This code band was left vague when ASCII was launched way back in primeval times. It was felt that a degree of latitude was desirable at the bottom end to allow for individual hardware design. All the graphics facilities available in BASIC can be obtained in machine code by means of OSWRCH. Page 378 of the User Guide lists the VDU code summary. VDU statements can, amongst other things, control screen colour, define graphics windows and various x,y plotting operations. All these can be achieved in machine code by the use of OSWRCH. Columns 1 and 2 on Page 378 of the User Guide are the decimal and hex ASCII control codes. Column 3 relates to the CTRL keys, and column 4 is more or less useless. Column 5 – 'Bytes extra' – is particularly important for our purpose. All the codes have to place the appropriate ASCII code in the accumulator before using JSR OSWRCH. Some, however, require extra trips to OSWRCH, depending on the number of 'extra bytes'. Codes which demand '0' extra bytes are 'one-trip' excursions. Examples are:

```
LDA  #2            \Equivalent to VDU 2
JSR  OSWRCH        \Enable printer
```

```
LDA  #16           \Equivalent to VDU 16
JSR  OSWRCH        \Clear graphics area
```

```
LDA  #12           \Equivalent to VDU 12
JSR  OSWRCH        \Clear text area
```

VDU equivalents begin to be a little unruly when there are 'extra' bytes. Each extra byte involves the setting of another number in the accumulator and, of course, another trip to OSWRCH. Examples are:

Using Subroutines, Macros and Look-up Tables   163

```
LDA #17    \VDU 17,2
JSR OSWRCH   \Define text colour 2
LDA #2
JSR OSWRCH

LDA #22    \VDU 22,5
JSR OSWRCH   \Set Mode 5
LDA #5
JSR OSWRCH

LDA #25    \VDU 25,0,100;500;
JSR OSWRCH   \PLOT K,x,y
LDA #0    \K=0 (move relative to
JSR OSWRCH   \last point)
LDA #100   \x=100 (low byte)
JSR OSWRCH
LDA #0    \x=0 (high byte)
JSR OSWRCH
LDA #244   \y=244 (low byte)
JSR OSWRCH
LDA #1    \y=256 (high byte)
JSR OSWRCH
```

Users of BBC BASIC will be aware that VDU statements can be chained together. For example,

VDU 22,2 followed by VDU 24,0;0;1279;767;
can be written more economically as
VDU 22,2,24,0;0;1279;767;

Although OSWRCH can indeed simulate any VDU statement, there is no point in denying that its use, particularly when chaining lengthy examples, is tedious. In short, it appears to be a weary and ponderous task. Consider for a moment the tedium of typing in scores of LDAs and JSR OSWRCHs involved in drawing a complex graphics screen. The end listing could eventually resemble a toilet roll. We need a routine where the computer does most of the work for us. There are two main methods of performing this task: one is to use a BASIC procedure acting as a macro; the other is to create a look-up table of data bytes that can be accessed by indexed addressing. The chain of VDU parameters could then be parcelled up neatly within DATA statements and then assembled into equivalent source code.

The macro approach

First, the macro method will be described. The routine is given in

Program 7.4 and is universal whichever BASIC ROM happens to be installed. However, a simpler version for those with a BASIC II ROM is given in Program 7.5. This modification is due to the introduction of the EQUS pseudo op-code.

To be useful, the macro should have the following qualities:

(1) It should utilise decimal or hex data.
(2) It should handle single- or double-byte data automatically.
(3) It should assemble single-byte labelled locations.
(4) It should handle positive and negative data elements whether single- or double-byte in length.

Referring to Program 7.4, an example list of VDU chains is put into DATA statements in lines 470 and 480. The data sets the text and graphics windows and constructs a yellow square on a blue backcloth in MODE 2. Where a two-byte VDU entity is required by the operating system (that is, a number followed by a ';' rather than a ',') the DATA element must be followed by a '@' so that the routine can differentiate between the two. Notice that negative decimal two-byte data can be used which is especially useful in relative plotting. Armed with this routine, a graphics screen can be planned out in BASIC and quickly changed to an assembly language version. The example also shows how labelled locations can be incorporated. The macro can be used once or many times during an assembly program by coming out into BASIC and typing PROCvdu(N) where N is the sequential number of DATA elements you require to incorporate at that particular time. It is essential, however, to restore the DATA pointer at the start of each pass of the assembler (line 290).

```
>LIST
   10 REM CONDITIONAL ASSEMBLY PROGRAM
   20 REM FOR CHAINING VDU PARAMETERS
   30 GOTO240
   40
   50 DEFPROCvdu(N)
   60 LOCAL D,D$,B,byte,lbyte
   70 FOR item=1 TO N
   80 READ D$
   90 IF RIGHT$(D$,1)="@" THEN B=2 ELSE B=1
  100 D=EVAL(D$)
  110 IF ASC(D$)>64 THEN [OPT PASS:LDA D:JSR OSWRCH:]:GOTO150
  120 IF D<0 THEN D=(ABS(D) EOR &FFFF)+1
  130 byte=D MOD 256:PROCform
  140 IF B=2 THEN byte=D DIV 256:PROCform
  150 NEXT item
  160 ENDPROC
```

Program 7.4. Macro assembly of VDU parameters.

Using Subroutines, Macros and Look-up Tables **165**

```
170
180 DEFPROCform
190 IF byte<>lbyte THEN [OPT PASS:LDA #byte:]
200 [OPT PASS:JSR OSWRCH:]
210 lbyte=byte
220 ENDPROC
230
240 OSWRCH=&FFEE
250 BCOL=&70:SQCOL=&71
260 DIM START 256
270 FOR PASS=0 TO 3 STEP 3
280 P%=START
290 RESTORE
300
310 [OPT PASS
320 LDA #3        \SET SQUARE COLOUR
330 STA SQCOL
340 LDA #&84      \SET BACKGROUND COLOUR
350 STA BCOL
360 ]
370 PROCvdu(39)
380 [OPT PASS
390  \ ANY SOURCE CODE
400 RTS:]
410
420 NEXT PASS
430 CALL START
440
450 REM DATA IS A LIST OF VDU CHAINS
460 REM YELLOW SQUARE/BLUE BACKGROUND
470 DATA 22,2,28,0,3,19,1,24,0@,0@,127
9@,767@,18,0,BCOL,16
480 DATA 18,0,SQCOL,25,4,500@,500@,25,
1,200@,0@,25,81,0@,-200@,25,1,-200@,0@,2
5,81,0@,200@
```

Program 7.4. contd

Program 7.4 takes advantage of the concept of *conditional assembly*. In this case, a conditional test is made to see if the next byte of data is the same as the byte preceding it. If this is so then a LDA #byte will not be required (since the data byte will already be in the accumulator).

The operation of the program is as follows:
The routine reads in each DATA element and tests for the '@' character termination, setting the variable B to the number of bytes as appropriate. Line 100 uses EVAL rather than VAL to evaluate the data string (D$) and places the result into the variable D. This line is necessary when the following situations occur in D$.

(1) A '&' precedes a number, indicating hexadecimal.

166 *Advanced Machine Code Techniques for The BBC Micro*

(2) A labelled location is encountered, in which case the assigned location address is put into the variable D, assuming, of course, it has been previously defined.

(3) The temporary '@' character is ignored (it has outgrown its usefulness).

Line 110 tests whether D$ contains numeric or alpha data. If the data is alpha – that is, a labelled location – then the accumulator is loaded with the assigned address since, in this case, we do not want immediate addressing.

Line 120 checks if D is negative so that a two-byte two's complement form can be generated. Line 130 forms the low-byte and line 140 forms the high-byte if required. PROCform handles conditional assembly using immediate addressing.

With the upgraded BASIC II ROM installed, the above program can still be used but a more convenient version is given in Program 7.5. The difference is that we need not leave the assembler to use the macro. The pseudo op-code EQUS can place a string, where positioned, within a program. If we use the function FNvdu(N) which returns a null string (we do not want a string returned) then all the goings on of the macro will be performed without the complication of leaving the assembler!

This type of modification can be employed in similar programs where procedures are encountered on breaking out of the assembler. For the sake of standardisation, the method is not used in further examples since large numbers of BBC Micro's have BASIC I installed.

```
>LIST
   10 REM CONDITIONAL ASSEMBLY PROGRAM
   20 REM FOR CHAINING VDU PARAMETERS
   30 GOTO240
   40
   50 DEF FNvdu(N)
   60 LOCAL D,D$,B,byte,item,lbyte
   70 FOR item=1 TO N
   80 READ D$
   90 IF RIGHT$(D$,1)="@" THEN B=2 ELSE
B=1
   100 D=EVAL(D$)
   110 IF ASC(D$)>64 THEN [OPT PASS:LDA D
:JSR OSWRCH:]:GOTO150
   120 IF D<0 THEN D=(ABS(D) EOR &FFFF)+1
   130 byte=D MOD 256:PROCform
   140 IF B=2 THEN byte=D DIV 256:PROCfor
m
   150 NEXT item
   160 =""
   170
   180 DEFPROCform
   190 IF byte<>lbyte THEN [OPT PASS:LDA
#byte:]
```

Program 7.5. Macro assembly of VDU parameters (BASIC II onwards).

Using Subroutines, Macros and Look-up Tables   167

```
 200 [OPT PASS:JSR OSWRCH:]
 210 lbyte=byte
 220 ENDPROC
 230
 240 OSWRCH=&FFEE
 250 BCOL=&70:SQCOL=&71
 260 DIM START 256
 270 FOR PASS=0 TO 3 STEP 3
 280 P%=START
 290 RESTORE
 300
 310 [OPT PASS
 320 LDA #3        \SET SQUARE COLOUR
 330 STA SQCOL
 340 LDA #&84      \SET BACKGROUND COLOUR
 350 STA BCOL
 360 EQUS FNvdu(39)
 370 RTS:]
 380
 390 NEXT PASS
 400 CALL START
 410
 420 REM EXAMPLE LIST OF OSWRCH CHAINS
 430 REM YELLOW SQUARE/BLUE BACKGROUND
 440 DATA 22,2,28,0,3,19,1,24,0@,0@,127
9@,767@,18,0,BCOL,16
 450 DATA 18,0,SQCOL,25,4,500@,500@,25,
1,200@,0@,25,81,0@,-200@,25,1,-200@,0@,2
5,81,0@,200@
```

Program 7.5. contd

The look-up table approach

Another approach to this problem is by using a look-up table. Program 7.6 shows the essential differences. For a start, conditional assembly is not used as in the previous example and the use of labelled locations has been dropped. The DATA elements in the BASIC routine are split up into the relevant single bytes and stored as a look-up table from the location labelled 'data' onwards. The short piece of code at lines 230 to 290 can be placed anywhere within the source program to access this table sequentially. The term 'look-up' is used since any element can be looked up by setting the index register to the required offset from the table base address. It is conventional to place data tables such as this at the end of a program. The previous example has the edge on speed but this method is more economical in the use of memory locations.

Program 7.7 is an example of the type of moving graphics available by using the macro approach. The program sets up a graphics screen in mode 2

168 *Advanced Machine Code Techniques for The BBC Micro*

```
>LIST
   10 REM USING DATA TABLES FOR
   20 REM CHAINING VDU PARAMETERS
   30 GOTO160
   40
   50 DEFPROCdatatable(N)
   60 FOR item=1 TO N
   70 READ D$
   80 IF RIGHT$(D$,1)="@" THEN B=2 ELSE
B=1
   90 D=EVAL(D$)
  100 IF D<0 THEN D=(ABS(D) EOR &FFFF)+1
  110 ?P%=D MOD 256:P%=P%+1
  120 IF B=2 THEN ?P%=D DIV 256:P%=P%+1
  130 NEXT item
  140 ENDPROC
  150
  160 OSWRCH=&FFEE
  170 DIM START 500
  180 FOR PASS=0 TO 3 STEP 3
  190 P%=START
  200 RESTORE
  210
  220 [OPT PASS
  230 LDY #0           \LOOP OUTPUTS ALL
  240 .LOOP            \DATA ITEMS STORED
  250 LDA data,Y       \FROM data ONWARDS
  260 JSR OSWRCH       \BY PROCdatatable
  270 INY              \AND CAN BE PLACED
  280 CPY #53          \ANYWHERE WITHIN
  290 BNE LOOP         \SOURCE CODE PROG.
  300 BEQ FINISH
  310 .data
  320 ]PROCdatatable(39)
  330 [OPT PASS
  340 .FINISH
  350 RTS:]
  360
  370 NEXT PASS
  380 CALL START
  390
  400 REM DATA IS A LIST OF VDU CHAINS
  410 REM YELLOW SQUARE/BLUE BACKGROUND
  420 DATA 22,2,28,0,3,19,1,24,0@,0@,127
9@,767@,18,0,132,16
  430 DATA 18,0,3,25,4,500@,500@,25,1,20
0@,0@,25,81,0@,-200@,25,1,-200@,0@,25,81
,0@,200@
```

Program 7.6. Using data tables for chaining VDU parameters.

and produces the ubiquitous bouncing ball, by now the standard apprenticeship exercise in the use of animated graphics. The macro is used

Using Subroutines, Macros and Look-up Tables 169

at line 310 to set up the screen and again at line 980 to form the subroutine BALL.

Any Moving OBject (MOB) must have an associated velocity. In simple cases this is little more than an increment added to the object's previous position so as to calculate its next position on the screen. An acceleration, incidentally, can be mimicked (position-wise) by adding a further steadily increasing increment as new positions are calculated. When the object reaches a boundary, the velocity (increment) must reverse sign if it is to remain on the screen. This is straightforward to program in BASIC. In machine code, however, the object's position on the screen is a two-byte number. You could be forgiven for thinking that the increment need only be a single-byte number because of its normally small value. However, this is not so. Numbers differing in byte length cannot be added if they are of mixed sign, therefore we must also have a two-byte increment.

```
>LIST
   10 REM BOUNCING BALL EXAMPLE
   20 GOTO 230
   30
   40 DEFPROCvdu(N)
   50 LOCAL D,D$,B,byte,item,lbyte
   60 FOR item=1 TO N
   70 READ D$
   80 IF RIGHT$(D$,1)="@" THEN B=2 ELSE B=1
   90 D=EVAL(D$)
  100 IF ASC(D$)>64 THEN [OPT PASS:LDA D:JSR OSWRCH:]:GOTO 140
  110 IF D<0 THEN D=(ABS(D) EOR &FFFF)+1
  120 byte=D MOD 256:PROCform
  130 IF B=2 THEN byte=D DIV 256:PROCform
  140 NEXT item
  150 ENDPROC
  160
  170 DEFPROCform
  180 IF byte<>lbyte THEN [OPT PASS:LDA #byte:]
  190 [OPT PASS:JSR OSWRCH:]
  200 lbyte=byte
  210 ENDPROC
  220
  230 OSWRCH=&FFEE:OSBYTE=&FFF4
  240 X=&70:Y=&72:XINC=&74:YINC=&76
  250 BCOL=&78
  260 DIM START 1000
  270 FOR PASS=0 TO 3 STEP 3
  280 P%=START
  290 RESTORE
```

Program 7.7. the ubiquitous bouncing ball.

```
300 REM SET UP SCREEN
310 PROCvdu(16)
320 DATA 22,2,28,0,3,19,1,24,0@,0@,127
9@,767@,18,0,132,16
330
340 [OPT PASS
350 LDA #0         \INITIALISE X,Y,XINC
360 STA X          \AND YINC
370 STA Y
380 STA XINC+1
390 STA YINC+1
400 STA X+1
410 STA Y+1
420 LDA #8
430 STA XINC
440 STA YINC
450
460 .LOOP
470 LDA #&13       \WAIT FOR FIELD SYNC
480 JSR OSBYTE
490 LDA #4         \PLACE BALL ON SCREEN
500 STA BCOL       \IN FOREGROUND COLOUR
510 JSR BALL
520 LDA X          \ADD XINC TO X
530 CLC            \(2 BYTES)
540 ADC XINC
550 STA X
560 LDA X+1
570 ADC XINC+1
580 STA X+1
590 LDA Y          \ADD YINC TO Y
600 CLC            \(2 BYTES)
610 ADC YINC
620 STA Y
630 LDA Y+1
640 ADC YINC+1
650 STA Y+1
660 LDA #7         \DELETE BALL WITH
670 STA BCOL       \BACKGROUND COLOUR
680 JSR BALL
690 LDA Y+1        \CHECK Y ON SCREEN
700 CMP #3
710 BCC YONSCR
720 LDA YINC       \FIND 2's COMPLIMENT
730 EOR #&FF       \OF YINC (2 BYTES)
740 STA YINC
750 LDA YINC+1
760 EOR #&FF
770 STA YINC+1
780 INC YINC
790 BNE YONSCR
```

Program 7.7. contd

Using Subroutines, Macros and Look-up Tables 171

```
 800 INC YINC+1
 810 .YONSCR
 820 LDA X+1        \CHECK X ON SCREEN
 830 CMP #5
 840 BCC XONSCR
 850 LDA XINC       \FIND 2's COMPLIMENT
 860 EOR #&FF       \OF XINC (2 BYTES)
 870 STA XINC
 880 LDA XINC+1
 890 EOR #&FF
 900 STA XINC+1
 910 INC XINC
 920 BNE XONSCR
 930 INC XINC+1
 940 .XONSCR
 950 JMP LOOP
 960
 970 .BALL
 980 ]PROCvdu(13)
 990 DATA 18,0,BCOL,25,4,X,X+1,Y,Y+1,25
,1,0@,-8@
1000 [RTS:]
1010
1020 NEXT PASS
1030 CALL START
1040 END
```

Program 7.7. contd

The program is liberally remarked but one area worthy of further comment is where the on-screen position checks are made. Referring to the case of the Y screen boundary checks in lines 690 to 710, the CMP instruction sets the carry flag if M<=A and clears it if M>A. In this case, the CMP #3 instruction in line 700 will set the carry flag if the accumulator contents Y+1 >= 3. This will occur when the accumulator contents are between 3 and 255 inclusive (&3 and &FF). Consequently, the carry flag will be clear when the high byte of the screen position Y+1 takes a value of 0,1, or 2 which are legitimate screen positions. The end result of the conditional branch in line 710 is that XINC (2 bytes) is only reversed in sign (two's complement) when the carry flag is set. Therefore, only one comparison is required to test for both the top and bottom screen boundaries. The screen boundary tests in the other dimension are conducted in a similar fashion.

Summary

1. High levels of subroutines nesting can overflow the stack.
2. Each unreturned JSR uses two stack locations.

3. Each JSR uses 6 clock cycles and RTS another 6, so a JSR within a loop can squander time.
4. Resident subroutines, within the ROM operating system, are plentiful and easy to use in machine code programs.
5. Where the screen display is involved, there are speed advantages to be gained by using direct screen addressing. However, the program may not work through the Tube with the second processor. If you never buy one, this won't matter anyway.
6. A vector is a two-byte word in memory which is the address of a routine.
7. Some resident subroutines have vectored addresses. Changing the contents of the vector allows interception to a different routine.
8. Most vectored addresses are in page 2.
9. Graphic facilities are handled by OSWRCH at address &FFEE, indirected via &020E.
10. The sound generators and envelope shaping are handled by OSWORD.
11. Input data is handled by OSRDCH at address &FFE0, indirected via &0210.
12. Although the assembler does not offer macro facilities, they can be simulated by temporary transfer from assembly code to a BASIC procedure.
13. If the new BASIC II ROM is installed, the EQUS structure can be used within the assembler for simulating macros and other functions.

Self test

7.1 Use the macro procedure to draw a large red square on a yellow background in MODE 2.
7.2 Use the look-up table method to draw a yellow triangle on a blue background.
7.3 Program the sound generator to play a scale in F# major.
7.4 Add a keyboard controllable bat routine to intercept the ball in Program 7.7.
7.5 Employ the user-definable character method for plotting the ball in Program 7.7.

Chapter Eight
Direct Screen Addressing and Hardware Scrolling

Direct screen addressing overview

Addressing screen locations directly has some advantages over using operating system subroutines such as OSWRCH. Faster and smoother moving graphics can be devised. The disadvantage of directly addressing screen locations (incompatibility with the Tube) has been emphasised before. When using direct screen addressing, the extra work involved in programming is considerable. The screen can no longer be considered as a convenient rectangle of plot points with X, Y coordinates. Instead, the screen is considered as a block of memory locations, laid out in a form similar to the screen layout map for MODE 2 shown in Fig. 8.1. In practice, the most commonly used mode for this method of programming is MODE 2 since the full sixteen colours are available to the user with a reasonably high resolution of 160*256 pixels. It is not practicable in a book of this size to discuss all MODES so direct screen addressing in this chapter will refer entirely to a MODE 2 screen.

The programs in this chapter should be helpful when writing games or educational material, particularly those which involve animation. They show how faster and smoother graphic displays appear when use is made of machine code routines called from BASIC.

In MODE 2, each screen memory location which is written to will light up two pixels. If we are happy with a minimum movement of two pixels at a time in an animated sequence then the whole process simplifies to shifting bytes around in the screen memory area shown in Fig. 8.1. Any of the sixteen colours can be selected for each pixel by setting appropriate bits within the byte written to screen memory. Figure 8.2 shows how this is done and the relationship to pixels lit on the screen.

Each pixel is represented by a nibble (4 bits) in a somewhat staggered format as shown. All that is needed is to set each nibble to the required colour code. These are the standard colour numbers as used in BASIC (0 to 15). If only one pixel is required to be lit then the other can be set to the relevant background colour, usually all zeros (default black). To reinforce

174 *Advanced Machine Code Techniques for The BBC Micro*

3000	3008		3278
3001	3009		3279
3002	300A		327A
3003	300B		327B
⋮	⋮		⋮
3007	300F		327F

3280	⋮
⋮	⋮
7B07	

7D80	7D88		7FF8
7D81	7D89		7FF9
7D82	7D8A		7FFA
7D83	7D8B		7FFB
⋮	⋮		⋮
7D87	7D8F		7FFF

Fig. 8.1. The MODE 2 screen map.

Left hand pixel bits

| L_3 | R_3 | L_2 | R_2 | L_1 | R_1 | L_0 | R_0 |

Right hand pixel bits

| 0 | 0 | 0 | 0 | 0 | 1 | 1 | 1 |

Bit setting example

Red Yellow

Pixel pair lit on screen

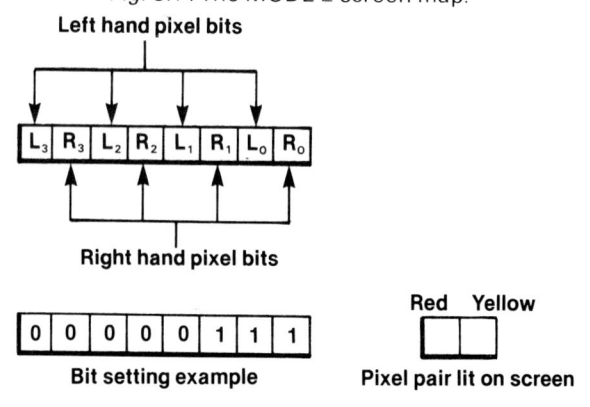

Fig. 8.2. How a MODE 2 screen byte is set up.

Direct Screen Addressing and Hardware Scrolling 175

the point, try the following simple routine and experiment with the value loaded into the accumulator in line 40:

```
10 MODE 2
20 P%=&0D00
30 [
40 LDA #7      \Load byte
50 STA &7FF0   \Light up pixel pair
60 RTS:]
70 CLS
80 CALL &0D00
```

The routine lights up a red pixel to the left of a yellow pixel at the bottom right-hand corner of the screen. The byte loaded in line 40 consists of the code for red (1 binary) and the code for yellow (11 binary). These amalgamated in the form shown in Fig. 8.2 produce a byte 0000 0111.

As an example of how fast direct screen addressing can be, a screen fill routine is given in Program 8.1. This program sets the whole screen to red by writing a byte of 0000 0011 to each screen location. Blocks of 128 bytes are sent to the screen memory by indirect indexed addressing. The reason for this will become apparent later when we start to whip UFOs and things around the screen.

```
>LIST
   10 REM FILLING A COLOUR SCREEN  ,
   20 REM DIRECT SCREEN LOCATIONS MODE 2
   30 OSWRCH=&FFEE
   40 LOC=&70
   50 DIM START 256
   60 FOR PASS=0 TO 2 STEP 2
   70 P%=START
   80 [OPT PASS
   90 LDA #&16      \SET UP MODE2
  100 JSR OSWRCH
  110 LDA #2
  120 JSR OSWRCH
  130 LDA #&00      \SET LOC TO SCREEN
  140 STA LOC       \START ADDRESS
  150 LDA #&30      \(2 BYTES)
  160 STA LOC+1
  170 .BEGIN
  180 LDA #3
  190 LDY #&7F
  200 .LOOP
  210 STA (LOC),Y
  220 DEY
  230 BPL LOOP
  240 CLC
  250 LDA LOC       \ADD 128 TO LOC
```

Program 8.1. Filling a colour screen.

176 *Advanced Machine Code Techniques for The BBC Micro*

```
260 ADC #&80
270 STA LOC
280 BCC SKIP
290 INC LOC+1
300 .SKIP
310 CMP #&00      \COMPARE LOC TO END
320 BNE BEGIN    \ADDRESS OF SCREEN
330 LDA LOC+1    \IF NOT THE SAME
340 CMP #&80     \BRANCH TO BEGIN
350 BNE BEGIN
360 RTS:]
370 NEXT PASS
380 CALL START
```

Colour animation by addressing direct screen locations

In this section, a simple animated sequence will be described which moves a 32 pixel red rectangle from the top to the bottom of the screen smoothly and without any perceptible flicker. The routine is artificially slowed down by waiting for the field synchronisation pulse. If this is not done the rectangle flies across the screen so fast that the TV system cannot reproduce it. This is not a problem in a large practical game, since many other objects will be moved in between. However, timing plays an important part in animation if pleasing results are to be obtained.

The labelled address LOC is set to the screen start address in MODE 2, which is &3000 taking 2 bytes of zero page memory. After waiting for the frame synchronisation pulse, the red rectangle is placed on the screen with indirect indexed addressing, scooping up the arbitrary 16 bytes necessary to form the image. Since in this case we want a red rectangle, the accumulator is set to &03. The image is then deleted in a similar manner but this time the accumulator contains the code for black (&00). The value 8 is then added to the locations LOC to calculate the next image position. The reason for this is to move the image by two pixels to the right. Reference to the MODE 2 screen map in Fig. 8.1 will help here. After checking that the calculated position is still on the screen, the cycle is restarted. Program 8.2 shows how single colour objects can be moved over the screen.

```
>LIST
   10 REM COLOUR ANIMATION BY ADDRESSING
   20 REM DIRECT SCREEN LOCATIONS MODE 2
   30 OSWRCH=&FFEE:OSBYTE=&FFF4
   40 LOC=&70:COL=&72
   50 DIM START 500
   60 FOR PASS=0 TO 2 STEP 2
   70 P%=START
```

Program 8.2. Single colour MOBs.

Direct Screen Addressing and Hardware Scrolling **177**

```
 80 [OPT PASS
 90 LDA #&16        \SET UP MODE2
100 JSR OSWRCH
110 LDA #2
120 JSR OSWRCH
130 LDA #&00        \SET LOC TO SCREEN
140 STA LOC         \START ADDRESS
150 LDA #&30        \(2 BYTES)
160 STA LOC+1
170 .BEGIN
180 LDA #3          \SET BOTH PIXEL
190 STA COL         \COLOURS TO RED.
200 JSR OBJECT
210 LDA #&13        \WAIT FOR FIELD SYNC
220 JSR OSBYTE
230 LDA #0          \SET BOTH PIXEL
240 STA COL         \COLOURS TO BLACK
250 JSR OBJECT      \(BACKGROUND COLOUR)
260 CLC
270 LDA LOC         \ADD 8 TO LOC
280 ADC #&8
290 STA LOC
300 BCC SKIP
310 INC LOC+1
320 .SKIP
330 CMP #&00        \COMPARE LOC TO END
340 BNE BEGIN       \ADDRESS OF SCREEN
350 LDA LOC+1       \IF NOT THE SAME
360 CMP #&80        \BRANCH TO BEGIN
370 BNE BEGIN
380 BEQ FINISH
390 .OBJECT         \PLACE OBJECT ON
400 LDY #&0F        \SCREEN (16 BYTES)
410 LDA COL         \(32 PIXELS)
420 .LOOP
430 STA (LOC),Y
440 DEY
450 BPL LOOP
460 RTS
470 .FINISH
480 RTS:]
490 NEXT PASS
500 CALL START
```

Program 8.2. contd

Multi-colour MOBs

The use of user-defined characters has one drawback – only single colour characters can be defined. The standard way to get over this is overprinting with another character of chosen colour, thus building up the required multicolour object. This can be a time-consuming process even in assembly language. The problem does not arise with direct screen addressing. Program 8.3 shows the essential details.

```
>LIST
   10 REM MULTICOLOUR ANIMATION BY
   20 REM ADDRESSING DIRECT SCREEN
   30 REM LOCATIONS IN MODE2
   40 GOTO140
   50
   60 DEFPROCdatatable(N)
   70 FOR item=1 TO N
   80 READ D$
   90 D=EVAL(D$)
  100 ?P%=D:P%=P%+1
  110 NEXT item
  120 ENDPROC
  130
  140 OSWRCH=&FFEE:OSBYTE=&FFF4
  150 LOC=&70
  160 DIM START 500
  170 FOR PASS=0 TO 2 STEP 2
  180 P%=START
  190 RESTORE
  200 [OPT PASS
  210 LDA #&16       \SET UP MODE2
  220 JSR OSWRCH
  230 LDA #2
  240 JSR OSWRCH
  250 LDA #&00       \SET LOC TO SCREEN
  260 STA LOC        \START ADDRESS
  270 LDA #&30       \(2 BYTES)
  280 STA LOC+1
  290
  300 .BEGIN
  310 LDY #&1F       \PLACE OBJECT ON
  320 .LOOP2         \SCREEN DEFINED
  330 LDA data,Y     \BY data
  340 STA (LOC),Y
  350 DEY
  360 BPL LOOP2
  370 LDA #&13       \WAIT FOR FIELD SYNC
  380 JSR OSBYTE
  390 LDA #0         \DELETE OBJECT ON
  400 LDY #&1F       \SCREEN BY BLANKING
  410 .LOOP1         \IN BACKGROUND
  420 STA (LOC),Y    \COLOUR (BLACK)
  430 DEY
  440 BPL LOOP1
  450 CLC
```

Program 8.3. A UFO as an example of a multi-colour MOB.

Direct Screen Addressing and Hardware Scrolling

```
460 LDA LOC         \ADD 8 TO LOC
470 ADC #&8
480 STA LOC
490 BCC SKIP
500 INC LOC+1
510 .SKIP
520 LDA LOC         \COMPARE LOC TO END
530 BNE BEGIN       \ADDRESS OF SCREEN
540 LDA LOC+1       \IF NOT THE SAME
550 CMP #&80        \BRANCH TO BEGIN
560 BNE BEGIN
570 BEQ FINISH
580
590 .data
600 ]PROCdatatable(32)
610 DATA 0,0,0,1,3,3,3,0,&40,1,3,3,9,3
,3,2,&80,2,3,3,3,6,3,3,1,0,0,0,2,3,3,3,0
620
630 [OPT PASS
640 .FINISH
650 RTS:]
660 NEXT PASS
670 CALL START
```

Program 8.3. contd

The program differs from the previous one in that a look-up table is used to form the object's colours. The data consists of 32 sequential bytes (64 pixels) which are 'looked up' in a method similar to that described in Chapter 7. Notice that this program is less complex, since only single byte data is handled by the BASIC procedure. Do not forget the even simpler method with BASIC II (or later versions) involving EQUS.

The object itself can be planned out on grid paper with up to 128 consecutive bytes, since BPL is used in the loop loading sequence.

Address coordinates

The method described previously is, by virtue of speed, preferred for small MOBs travelling in a horizontal direction. However, the movement in the vertical direction leaves a lot to be desired. Movement by 8 pixels at a time is not very satisfactory! Furthermore, the height of the MOB is restricted to 8 pixels. The standard method of overcoming these problems is to employ a routine which translates address coordinates (80*256) to absolute screen addresses so that discontinuities in the memory map in the X and Y directions are avoided. The MODE 2 screen map consists of a matrix of 80 bytes (2 pixels a byte) in the X direction and 256 bytes in the Y direction making 80*256=20K bytes in all. If we are satisfied with two-pixel movement in the horizontal direction as before, the concept of address coordinates can be envisaged. The screen memory map given earlier is set out in blocks of eight sequential addresses. The difference between equivalent positions in any adjacent block of 8 in the Y direction is &280 or 640 decimal. Similarly in the X direction the difference is 8. Therefore the equation to calculate a unique screen address from an XY address coordinate is given by:

Screen address = &3000 + 8X + 640(Y DIV 8) + (Y MOD 8)

where, &3000 is the screen start address; 8X is the X contribution because there are 8 address locations difference between adjacent X coordinates; 640 (Y DIV 8) specifies the block of eight containing the Y coordinate; and Y MOD 8 specifies the position in that block of 8.

The above equation is not suited to machine coding in its present form. We need to rearrange the equation so that all multipliers are, as far as possible, in exact powers of 2. Any multiplication or division then simplifies to shifting bits left or right respectively. This can be conveniently achieved as follows:

&3000 + 8X + 640(Y DIV 8) + (Y MOD 8) = &3000 + 8X + 80(8 (Y DIV 8)) + (Y MOD 8)

Let Y1=8(Y DIV 8)
= &3000 + 8X + 80Y1 + (Y MOD 8)
= &3000 + 8X + 16Y1 + 64Y1 + (Y MOD 8)

The coding of the above is now relatively easy. All (Y DIV 8) means is shift Y right 3 times, thus losing the 3 least significant bits. Multiplying by 8, giving 8(Y DIV 8), is then achieved by shifting the result left 3 times. The net result of all this is just to lose the 3 least significant bits. They have fallen off the end.

A simpler way of arriving at the same result is to mask out the 3 least significant bits of Y with AND#&FE. Similarly, all (Y MOD8) means is to recover the bits we lost in the previous operation by masking out the 5 most significant bits of Y with AND #&7. The expression 8X is achieved by shifting X left 3 times. Two bytes will be required to accommodate the result on the last two shifts.

The 64Y1 expression can be arrived at by shifting Y1 left six times. However, if you can imagine a two-byte result, shifting Y1 right twice and storing it as the high-byte of the result will be the exact equivalent. The low-byte of the result can be set to all zeros.

Two further shifts right of the 64Y1 result will divide by 4, giving 16Y1. However, we must rotate the carry into the low-byte of the result on the last shift right. The LSR and ROR instructions, respectively, are needed.

Adding the whole lot together gives the required screen address. Program 8.4 (lines 1080 to 1380) shows one way of coding the above.

Direct Screen Addressing and Hardware Scrolling 181

```
>LIST
   10 REM MOVING MULTICOLOURED OBJECTS
   20 REM AN IMPROVED METHOD FOR MODE 2
   30 REM USING 80*256 BYTE COORDINATES
   40 GOTO140
   50
   60 DEF FNdatatable(N)
   70 FOR item=1 TO N
   80 READ D$
   90 D=EVAL("&"+D$)
  100 ?P%=D:P%=P%+1
  110 NEXT item
  120 =PASS
  130
  140 OSWRCH=&FFEE:OSBYTE=&FFF4
  150 XCOORD=&70:YCOORD=&71:width=&72:he
ight=&73:wcount=&74:LOC=&75
  160 STORE=&77:data=&79:Yreg=&7B
  170 table1=&7C:table2=&7E
  180 XCOORD1=&80:YCOORD1=&81
  190 XCOORD2=&82:YCOORD2=&83
  200 DIM START 1000
  210 FOR PASS=0 TO 2 STEP 2
  220 P%=START
  230 RESTORE
  240 [OPT PASS
  250
  260 LDA #&16       \SET UP MODE2
  270 JSR OSWRCH
  280 LDA #2
  290 JSR OSWRCH
  300 LDA #(shape1 MOD 256) \STORE SHAPE
  310 STA table1              \TABLE
  320 LDA #(shape1 DIV 256) \ADDRESSES
  330 STA table1+1
  340 LDA #(shape2 MOD 256)
  350 STA table2
  360 LDA #(shape2 DIV 256)
  370 STA table2+1
  380 LDA #0
  390 STA XCOORD1    \INITIALISE BYTE
  400 STA YCOORD1    \COORDINATES OF
  410 LDA #34        \SHAPES
  420 STA XCOORD2
  430 LDA #200
  440 STA YCOORD2
  450
  460 .LOOP
  470 INC XCOORD1    \UPDATE NEW SHAPE
  480 INC YCOORD1    \COORDINATES
  490 DEC YCOORD2
```

Program 8.4. Moving more than one shape.

182 *Advanced Machine Code Techniques for The BBC Micro*

```
 500 JSR SCREEN
 510 LDA YCOORD2
 520 CMP #80
 530 BNE LOOP
 540 BEQ START
 550
 560 .SCREEN
 570 LDA table1        \STORE ADDRESS OF
 580 STA data          \FIRST SHAPE TABLE
 590 LDA table1+1      \IN data
 600 STA data+1
 610 LDA #&13          \WAIT FOR FIELD SYNC
 620 JSR OSBYTE
 630 LDX XCOORD1       \CALL draw SUBROUT'E
 640 LDY YCOORD1       \WITH PARAMETERS IN
 650 JSR draw          \X AND Y REG'S
 660 LDA table2
 670 STA data          \STORE ADDRESS OF
 680 LDA table2+1      \SECOND SHAPE TABLE
 690 STA data+1        \IN data
 700 LDX XCOORD2
 710 LDY YCOORD2       \CALL draw SUBROUT'E
 720 JSR draw          \AS ABOVE
 730 RTS
 740
 750 .draw
 760 STX XCOORD        \STORE PARAMETERS
 770 STY YCOORD        \PASSED
 780 LDY #0
 790 LDA (data),Y      \STORE SHAPE'S
 800 STA height        \HEIGHT AND WIDTH
 810 INY               \PARAMETERS OBTAINED
 820 LDA (data),Y      \FROM DATA TABLE
 830 STA width
 840 LDX #2            \X SAVES Y (TEMP)
 850 .newrow
 860 LDA #0            \CLEAR Yreg STORE
 870 STA Yreg
 880 LDA width         \RELOAD wcount
 890 STA wcount
 900 JSR CALCADDRESS   \CALC SCREEN ADDr
 910 .newcolumn
 920 TXA               \TRANSFER X TO Y
 930 TAY
 940 LDA (data),Y      \PLACE ROWS OF DATA
 950 LDY Yreg          \INTO SCREEN
 960 STA (LOC),Y       \MEMORY UNTIL
 970 TYA               \SHAPE IS COMPLETED
 980 ADC #8
 990 STA Yreg          \Yreg SAVES Y (TEMP)
1000 INX
```

Program 8.4. contd

Direct Screen Addressing and Hardware Scrolling 183

```
1010 DEC wcount
1020 BNE newcolumn
1030 INC YCOORD
1040 DEC height
1050 BNE newrow
1060 RTS
1070
1080 .CALCADDRESS
1090 LDA #0         \CLEAR LOCATIONS
1100 STA STORE+1
1110 STA LOC
1120 LDA XCOORD     \CALC. 8*X
1130 ASL A
1140 ASL A
1150 ROL STORE+1
1160 ASL A
1170 ROL STORE+1
1180 STA STORE
1190 LDA YCOORD     \CALC Y1=8*(YDIV8)
1200 AND #&F8
1210 LSR A          \CALC 64*Y1
1220 LSR A
1230 STA LOC+1
1240 LSR A          \CALC 16*Y1
1250 LSR A
1260 ROR LOC        \also clears carry
1270 ADC LOC+1      \CALC 80*Y1
1280 TAY
1290 LDA YCOORD
1300 AND #7         \CALC  Y MOD 8
1310 ADC LOC
1320 ADC STORE      \CALCULATE
1330 STA LOC        \CUMMULATIVE RESULT
1340 TYA            \FOR SCREEN ADDRESS
1350 ADC STORE+1
1360 ADC #&30
1370 STA LOC+1
1380 RTS
1390
1400 .shape1
1410 OPT FNdatatable(86)
1420 .shape2
1430 OPT FNdatatable(62)
1440 RTS:]
1450 NEXT PASS
1460 CALL START
1470
1480 REM THIS IS THE shape1 DATA
1490 DATA E,6
1500 DATA 0,0,0,0,0,0
1510 DATA 0,0,0,0,0,0
```

Program 8.4. contd

```
1520 DATA 0,0,4F,8F,0,0
1530 DATA 0,0,1,2,0,0
1540 DATA 0,0,1,2,0,0
1550 DATA 0,0,3,3,0,0
1560 DATA 0,1,3,3,2,0
1570 DATA 0,3,9,6,3,0
1580 DATA 0,3,3,3,3,0
1590 DATA 0,3,3,3,3,0
1600 DATA 0,3,3,3,3,0
1610 DATA 0,0,2,1,0,0
1620 DATA 0,0,0,0,0,0
1630 DATA 0,0,0,0,0,0
1640
1650 REM THIS IS THE shape2 DATA
1660 DATA A,6
1670 DATA 0,0,0,0,0,0
1680 DATA 0,0,0,0,0,0
1690 DATA 0,0,1,2,0,0
1700 DATA 0,0,3,3,0,0
1710 DATA 0,1,3,3,2,0
1720 DATA 0,3,9,6,3,0
1730 DATA 0,3,3,3,3,0
1740 DATA 0,0,2,1,0,0
1750 DATA 0,0,0,0,0,0
1760 DATA 0,0,0,0,0,0
```

Program 8.4. contd

Moving more than one shape

The above program independently moves two shapes on the screen by accessing two separate data tables with a common draw routine. The shapes are built up, a data byte at a time, by the subroutine 'draw'. This subroutine constructs a shape in a row by row fashion until completely drawn. The shape's height and width in bytes must be first read in from the data table. Line 1490 contains this data. The subroutine places the requested shape on the screen by invoking the CALCADDRESS routine prior to placing each data byte of a new row into screen memory. There is no need to call CALCADDRESS for adjacent bytes in a row since simply adding 8 to the previous address gives the address of the next byte in the row. Two loops are needed for this and the routine is given in lines 750 to 1060. The relevant data tables are at the foot of the program but note yet another way of incorporating data into a machine code program. The OPT statement has FNdatable(86) following it. Providing the datatable function returns PASS, all BASIC lines in the function are executed without 'officially' leaving the assembler.

A border of background colour, one byte wide in the horizontal and two bytes in the vertical direction, is useful. This ensures that all the bits and pieces remaining from the last drawn position are automatically erased which ever direction the shape is moving. On initialisation, the addresses of the supplied shape tables must be stored so that the subroutine SCREEN can specify which shape to draw. The X and Y address coordinates are then passed over to the draw subroutine in the X and Y registers respectively. Lines 560 to 730 are responsible for this. Lines 460 to 540 complete the program by incrementing the various coordinates of shape1 and shape2 to update the next drawing positions. The overall structure of the program is such that more shapes can easily be added.

A study of Program 8.4 (and its remarks) will reveal a few of the essential techniques for producing action video games.

Hardware scrolling by programming the 6845 CRTC

Hardware scrolling has many uses but ones that immediately spring to mind are applications such as word processing and producing moving landscapes in games programs.

The 6845 CRTC controller has eighteen internal registers of which only two are of interest to us in this chapter. These are registers 12 and 13 which together, high-byte and low-byte respectively, are known as the Displayed Screen Start Address Register. By re-specifying the displayed screen start address, we can scroll in any direction (wrap around) as long as the register contains a 'legal' screen memory location for the particular MODE used. The software must ensure that this does not happen or some unpredictable results will occur! In MODES 0, 1, 2, 3 the 6845 CRTC controller generates 80 characters a line where as in MODES 4, 5, 6 there are 40. These are not characters as seen on the screen, however. In MODE 2, for instance, a CRTC character is only a quarter of a displayed character. The CRTC, then, sees a MODE 2 screen as 80*32=&0A00 characters. It is important to remember that the screen address, sent to the displayed screen start register, must be the actual screen memory location divided by 8. This arises from the CRTC dealing with characters consisting of 256/32=8 output scan lines in MODE 2. From now on we will be concentrating exclusively on MODE 2 graphics screens for the reasons outlined at the beginning of the chapter. There is an added advantage in that each CRTC character sideways scroll represents only two pixels' displacement, producing a very smooth movement.

Sideways scrolling

To scroll the screen one CRTC character to the left, the screen start address register must be incremented. Decrementing the register, on the other hand, will scroll the screen one character to the right. There are two ways of achieving this in assembly language. The first is to use the assembler equivalent of the BASIC VDU 23 command; the other is to address directly the memory-mapped area SHEILA (256 bytes starting from &FE00). Incidentally, all the BBC Micro's internal hardware registers are accessible at these locations.

First, the operating system subroutine method will be described. The necessary VDU 23 commands to enable sideways scrolling are as follows, if SCR is the screen address low-byte and SCR+1 is the high-byte:

```
VDU 23;12,SCR;0;0;0
VDU 23;13,SCR+1;0;0;0
```

Only the first of the two lines above is necessary if the screen is to be sideways scrolled left by less than 256 characters since the actual screen start address in MODE 2 is &3000. The equivalent address, as required by displayed screen start address register, is &3000/8=&0600. Thus, SCR+1 will be constant at &06 for 256 bytes or scrolls. The VDU 23 commands can be conveniently coded in assembly language by our macro developed in Chapter 7 along with a simple test graphics screen. Program 8.5 shows this method, the object being to create a continuous sideways scroll to the left.

```
>LIST
    10 REM SIDEWAYS SCROLLING USING THE
    20 REM OPERATING SYSTEM SUBROUTINES
    30 GOTO240
    40
    50 DEFPROCvdu(N)
    60 LOCAL D,D$,B,byte,item,lbyte
    70 FOR item=1 TO N
    80 READ D$
    90 IF RIGHT$(D$,1)="@" THEN B=2 ELSE B=1
   100 D=EVAL(D$)
   110 IF ASC(D$)>64 THEN [OPT PASS:LDA D
:JSR OSWRCH:]:GOTO150
   120 IF D<0 THEN D=(ABS(D) EOR &FFFF)+1
   130 byte=D MOD 256:PROCform
   140 IF B=2 THEN byte=D DIV 256:PROCform
   150 NEXT item
   160 ENDPROC
   170
   180 DEFPROCform
   190 IF byte<>lbyte THEN [OPT PASS:LDA
#byte:]
   200 [OPT PASS:JSR OSWRCH:]
   210 lbyte=byte
   220 ENDPROC
   230
```

Program 8.5. Continuous sideways scrolling using operating system subroutines.

Direct Screen Addressing and Hardware Scrolling 187

```
 240 OSWRCH=&FFEE:OSBYTE=&FFF4
 250 SCR=&70
 260 DIM START 1000
 270 FOR PASS=0 TO 3 STEP 3
 280 P%=START
 290 RESTORE
 300 PROCvdu(29)
 310 REM SET UP TEST GRAPHICS SCREEN
 320 DATA 22,2,18,0,132,16,18,0,3,25,4,
500@,500@,25,1,200@,0@,25,81,0@,-200@,25
,1,-200@,0@,25,81,0@,200@
 330
 340 [OPT PASS
 350 .BEGIN
 360 LDA #&00        \SET SCR (2 BYTES) TO
 370 STA SCR         \SCREEN START ADDRESS
 380 LDA #&06        \AS SEEN BY THE CRTC
 390 STA SCR+1
 400 .SCROLL
 410 LDA #&13        \WAIT FOR FIELD SYNC
 420 JSR OSBYTE
 430 ]
 440 PROCvdu(7)
 450 [OPT PASS
 460 LDA SCR
 470 BNE OVER
 480 ]PROCvdu(7)
 490 [OPT PASS
 500 .OVER
 510 INC SCR         \INCREMENT SCR
 520 BNE SKIP        \(2 BYTES)
 530 INC SCR+1
 540 .SKIP
 550 LDA SCR         \CHECK IF SCREEN END
 560 BNE SCROLL      \ADDRESS AS SEEN BY
 570 LDA SCR+1       \CRTC IS EXCEEDED
 580 CMP #&10        \(MEM DIV 8)
 590 BNE SCROLL
 600 BEQ BEGIN       \IF SO RESTART CYCLE
 610 RTS:]
 620 NEXT PASS
 630 CALL START
 640
 650 REM DATA TO SET UP 6845 CRTC REG'S
 660 DATA 23@,13,SCR,0,0@,0@,0
 670 DATA 23@,12,SCR+1,0,0@,0@,0
```

Program 8.5. contd

When executed, the first thing to notice is that, when an object scrolls off left-hand side of the screen, it will reappear a character line higher at the right-hand side. The exception is at the top left of the screen where it will

188　*Advanced Machine Code Techniques for The BBC Micro*

reappear at the bottom right. To achieve a true sideways scroll, all the 'current' bytes on the right-hand side of the screen will need to be moved down a character line in memory (wrap around). We say 'current', because the screen addresses corresponding to any fixed position on the screen will change as each hardware scroll is executed. Another option is continuously to generate a landscape strip a byte wide at the current memory locations corresponding to the screen' extreme right-hand side, thus overprinting the above results. All this, however, will be regarded as an exercise. Experimenting with the programs can be a help here by placing markers at various known addresses and watching their progressions on the screen when scrolled. For example, the following could be inserted into Program 8.5:

```
LDA #3 \red marker(one byte wide)
STA &3000\at default screen addr.
```

An annoying flash occasionally occurs when register 12 is updated every 256 scrolls. This is due to the time lag in setting register 12 after register 13 or vice versa. Even waiting for the field synchronisation pulse has little effect on this. The problem can be overcome by directly addressing the 6845 CRTC. The corresponding routine is shown in Program 8.6.

```
>LIST
   10 REM PROGRAMMING THE 6845 CRTC
   20 REM SIDEWAYS SCROLLING BY DIRECTLY
   30 REM ADDRESSING SHEILA LOCATIONS
   40 GOTO250
   50
   60 DEFPROCvdu(N)
   70 LOCAL D,D$,B,byte,item,lbyte
   80 FOR item=1 TO N
   90 READ D$
  100 IF RIGHT$(D$,1)="@" THEN B=2 ELSE B=1
  110 D=EVAL(D$)
  120 IF ASC(D$)>64 THEN [OPT PASS:LDA D:JSR OSWRCH:]:GOTO160
  130 IF D<0 THEN D=(ABS(D) EOR &FFFF)+1
  140 byte=D MOD 256:PROCform
  150 IF B=2 THEN byte=D DIV 256:PROCform
  160 NEXT item
  170 ENDPROC
  180
  190 DEFPROCform
  200 IF byte<>lbyte THEN [OPT PASS:LDA #byte:]
  210 [OPT PASS:JSR OSWRCH:]
```

Program 8.6. Sideways scrolling by directly addressing SHEILA locations.

Direct Screen Addressing and Hardware Scrolling

```
 220 lbyte=byte
 230 ENDPROC
 240
 250 OSWRCH=&FFEE:OSBYTE=&FFF4
 260 SCR=&70
 270 DIM START 1000
 280 FOR PASS=0 TO 3 STEP 3
 290 P%=START
 300 RESTORE
 310
 320 REM SET UP A TEST GRAPHICS SCREEN
 330 PROCvdu(29)
 340 DATA 22,2,18,0,132,16,18,0,3,25,4,
500@,500@,25,1,200@,0@,25,81,0@,-200@,25
,1,-200@,0@,25,81,0@,200@
 350
 360 [OPT PASS
 370 .BEGIN
 380 LDA #&00      \SET SCR (2 BYTES) TO
 390 STA SCR       \SCREEN START ADDRESS
 400 LDA #&06      \AS SEEN BY THE CRTC
 410 STA SCR+1
 420 .SCROLL
 430 LDA #&13      \WAIT FOR FIELD SYNC
 440 JSR OSBYTE
 450 LDA #&0D      \SEND (R13) ADDRESS
 460 STA &FE00     \TO ADDRESS REGISTER
 470 LDA SCR
 480 STA &FE01     \SEND SCR TO (R13)
 490 BNE OVER
 500 LDA #&0C
 510 STA &FE00     \SEND (R12) ADDRESS
 520 LDA SCR+1
 530 STA &FE01     \SEND SCR+1 TO (R12)
 540 .OVER
 550 INC SCR
 560 BNE SKIP      \INCREMENT SCR
 570 INC SCR+1     \(2 BYTES)
 580 .SKIP
 590 LDA SCR       \CHECK IF SCREEN END
 600 BNE SCROLL    \ADDRESS AS SEEN BY
 610 LDA SCR+1     \CRTC IS EXCEEDED
 620 CMP #&10      \(MEM DIV 8)
 630 BNE SCROLL
 640 BEQ BEGIN     \IF SO RESTART CYCLE
 650 RTS:]
 660 NEXT PASS
 670 CALL START
```

Program 8.6. contd

The 6845 CRTC registers can be accessed directly by storing the required register address (or number) in the 6845 address register at SHEILA location &00 (that is, &FE00). The selected register can then be read from or written to at SHEILA address &01. This is fairly straightforward and details are documented on the listing.

Vertical scrolling

Vertical scrolling involves no new principles other than adding 80 each time, the number of 6845 CRTC characters in a line, to the current screen start address. The listing is shown in Program 8.7 with the necessary details. Notice that, in this case, the high-byte of the screen start address register is set each time within the loop since the extra code needed to by-pass it would be counter-productive.

```
>LIST
   10 REM PROGRAMMING THE 6845 CRTC
   20 REM VERTICAL SCROLLING BY DIRECTLY
   30 REM ADDRESSING SHEILA LOCATIONS
   40 GOTO250
   50
   60 DEFPROCvdu(N)
   70 LOCAL D,D$,B,byte,lbyte
   80 FOR item=1 TO N
   90 READ D$
  100 IF RIGHT$(D$,1)="@" THEN B=2 ELSE B=1
  110 D=EVAL(D$)
  120 IF ASC(D$)>64 THEN [OPT PASS:LDA D
:JSR OSWRCH:]:GOTO160
  130 IF D<0 THEN D=(ABS(D) EOR &FFFF)+1
  140 byte=D MOD 256:PROCform
  150 IF B=2 THEN byte=D DIV 256:PROCfor
m
  160 NEXT item
  170 ENDPROC
  180
  190 DEFPROCform
  200 IF byte<>lbyte THEN [OPT PASS:LDA
#byte:]
  210 [OPT PASS:JSR OSWRCH:]
  220 lbyte=byte
  230 ENDPROC
  240
  250 OSWRCH=&FFEE:OSBYTE=&FFF4
  260 SCR=&70
  270 DIM START 1000
  280 FOR PASS=0 TO 3 STEP 3
```

Program 8.7. Vertical scrolling of a MODE 2 graphics screen.

Direct Screen Addressing and Hardware Scrolling 191

```
 290 P%=START
 300 RESTORE
 310
 320 REM SET UP A TEST GRAPHICS SCREEN
 330 PROCvdu(29)
 340 DATA 22,2,18,0,132,16,18,0,3,25,4,
500@,500@,25,1,200@,0@,25,81,0@,-200@,25
,1,-200@,0@,25,81,0@,200@
 350
 360 [OPT PASS
 370 .BEGIN
 380 LDA #&00     \SET SCR (2 BYTES) TO
 390 STA SCR      \SCREEN START ADDRESS
 400 LDA #&06     \AS SEEN BY THE CRTC
 410 STA SCR+1
 420 .SCROLL
 430 LDA #&13     \WAIT FOR FIELD SYNC
 440 JSR OSBYTE
 450 LDA #&0D     \SEND (R13) ADDRESS
 460 STA &FE00    \TO ADDRESS REGISTER
 470 LDA SCR
 480 STA &FE01    \SEND SCR TO (R13)
 490 LDA #&0C
 500 STA &FE00    \SEND (R12) ADDRESS
 510 LDA SCR+1
 520 STA &FE01    \SEND SCR+1 TO (R12)
 530 CLC
 540 LDA SCR      \ADD 80 CHARACTER
 550 ADC #&50     \POSITIONS AS SEEN BY
 560 STA SCR      \CRTC(2 BYTES)
 570 BCC SKIP
 580 INC SCR+1
 590 .SKIP
 600 LDA SCR      \CHECK IF SCREEN END
 610 BNE SCROLL   \ADDRESS AS SEEN BY
 620 LDA SCR+1    \CRTC IS EXCEEDED
 630 CMP #&10     \(MEM DIV 8)
 640 BNE SCROLL
 650 BEQ BEGIN    \IF SO RESTART CYCLE
 660 RTS:]
 670 NEXT PASS
 680 CALL START
```

Program 8.7. contd

Summary

1. Machine code graphics can be smoother and faster if direct screen addressing is used.
2. Mode 2 is popular for coloured graphics because of the 16 variations.
3. In Mode 2, each screen memory location handles two pixels.

4. Movement of objects on the screen can be reduced to shifting bytes around in memory. This allows a dynamic resolution of two pixels per byte in Mode 2.
5. The bit pattern within the byte determines the pixel colour.
6. Each pixel within the byte occupies 4 bits (a nibble) so a single pixel blob of colour is achieved by setting the other nibble to background colour.
7. Mode 2 screen locations extend from &3000 (top left) to &7FFF (bottom right).
8. Direct screen addressing is often fast enough to beat the field synchronisation pulses so a 'wait until pulse' trap is often required.
9. Moving multicolour objects (MOBs), can be programmed by user-defined characters but overprinting with another colour is time-consuming and causes flickering. This problem does not arise with direct screen addressing.
10. MOB colours can be achieved by look-up tables.
11. Hardware scrolling can be achieved by direct action on the 6845 CRTC controller. Registers 12 and 13 in the controller contain the start address of the displayed screen. They are within the SHEILA address band.
12. Sideways scrolling to the left can be achieved by incrementing, and to the right by decrementing, the start address register.
13. Vertical scrolling is achieved by adding 80 to, or subtracting 80 from, the start address register. This is because there are 80 CRTC characters per line in Mode 2.

Self test

8.1 Adapt Program 8.5 to scroll the screen to the right.
8.2 Adapt Program 8.7 to scroll the screen downwards.
8.3 Adapt Program 8.4 to move three MOBs independently.
8.4 Design a MOB of your own which traverses the screen horizontally.

Chapter Nine

Interrupt Techniques and the User Port

The anatomy of the user port

Superficially, the user port is a 20-pin socket situated at the rear of the machine. It is rather neglected, only a minority of owners putting it to use. There are several reasons for this lack of interest. In the first place, its use demands at least a smattering of electronic knowledge and perhaps some dexterity with a soldering iron. For some reason (snobbery, perhaps?), many reviewers and critics mention the soldering iron with a slight air of patronage. This is a pity because once the craze for games begins to wear thin (hopefully not too far distant in time.), practical work, combining computer interests with home-made electronic gadgetry can open up exciting new possibilities. Another reason for the neglect may be a failure to appreciate the sophistication built into the 6522 VIA. This powerful chip provides the versatility and power of the port. The 20-pin socket is only the visible interface. To put the port into perspective, it should be considered as a component of the VIA, the full complement being as follows:

(a) Sixteen memory-mapped registers.
(b) Two 16-bit timers (also under software control).
(c) A serial port.
(d) Two 8-bit parallel ports, referred to as the A and B sides, each with two handshake control lines.

Apart from one of the 8-bit parallel ports (Side A, which is dedicated to forming the Centronics printer interface), all the above facilities are freely available to the user.

Both the user port and the RS423 are undedicated links to the outside world but the user port is the more complex and, unlike the RS423, obeys no established protocol. Although there are twenty pins in the socket, only ten carry information. The rest are either unused or earth return and +5 V lines. The pin connections are shown in Fig. 9.1. In this chapter there will follow examples of routines rather than programs. They should help you to experiment with the user port so as to control external machinery, robotic projects etc.

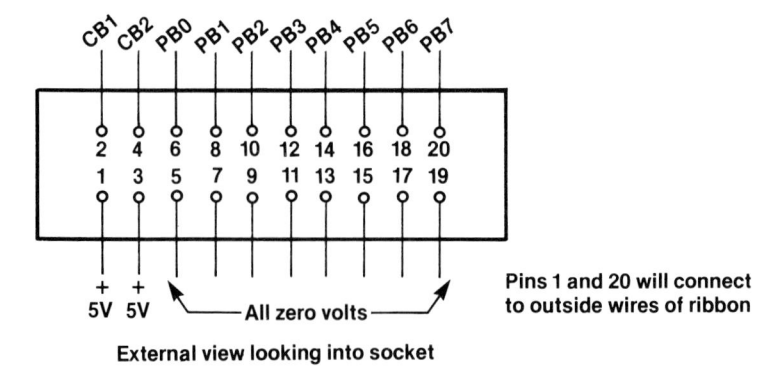

194 *Advanced Machine Code Techniques for The BBC Micro*

Fig. 9.1. Pin connections on the user port.

Never use gash wiring when you are experimenting. Resist the temptation to make both connections to the pins with croc clips or twisted wire. Croc clips are a boon in 'heavy' engineering hook-ups but getting them to stick on to the delicate pins of computer plugs (without shorting other pins) requires patience, dexterity and luck. Luck is not an acceptable commodity where the user port is concerned. Damage to the port can feed back through the entire VIA and consequently damage the health of the printer interface. The correct thing to do, before even contemplating experimentation, is to purchase the correct ribbon cable and socket which mates with the user port plug. The cable and plug can be bought a little more cheaply as separate items. The plug is of the type known as an 'Insulation Displacement Connector' (IDC for short). All you need is a vice to squeeze the plug directly onto the ribbon cable, the insulation is automatically pierced and good contact made during the vice pressure. No solder and no wire strippers are needed! However, if you are at all squeamish, or don't have a vice (mechanical that is), you can buy the ribbon cable with the plug already attached.

Before the connection is made to the plug on the user port you should do something to the other end, the free end of the cable. Don't just leave it flopping about with bare wires sticking out. Connect them, even if only temporarily, to some form of positive terminal. This can be a multipin connector strip soldered directly to the cable wires. Alternatively, if you intend to embark on long experimental orgies, it is wise to invest in one of those boards containing rows of tiny sockets into which you can push components and wires directly. The best solution of all (although requiring more outlay) is to invest in one of the more ambitious contraptions on the market, providing on-board power supplies. For what it's worth, we have used a Proto-board (trademark) for some years. It provides just about everything needed for safe experimentation. ICs, even the 40-pin species, resistors, capacitors, LEDs and wire connecting links can all be pushed directly into any of the hundreds of tiny holes. The net result is a gadget which allows quite complex circuitry to be assembled quickly without suffering second degree burns on the finger tips. Power supply bus bars run round the edges, supplied from a 1.0 amp/5V power supply and a pair of +/-15 volt lines, ideal for supplying op-amp chips needed in hybrid systems.

Although a +5V supply is provided to the port, it should be used with great care. Remember, the power comes from the long-suffering switched mode power supply which already is reasonably well-occupied, particularly if it has to supply a single drive disk. Another useful purchase which quickly becomes invaluable is one of the 'logic probes'. The power supply for the probes is taken (via croc clips this time) from the 5 volt computer supply or, preferably, from the Proto-board. The probe can be placed on any point of the circuit and will indicate whether it is in the HIGH (logic 1) or LOW (logic 0). The nature of the indication will vary according to the make but will normally be the colour of a LED lamp.

Notice from Fig. 9.1 that each signal line has its own independent earth line. All these earths are already electrically connected together inside the computer and will, in most cases, be similarly connected at the user device end of the ribbon cable. A signal line, and its own separate earth line running next to it behave together as a 'transmission line' with an impedance of the order of 600 ohms. This technique helps to guard against 'cross talk' between wires and stray interference induced electromagnetically. The transmission line concept, however, borders on the tongue-in-cheek because no attempt is made to terminate the lines with a matched load – a necessary practice according to established theory. However, the ribbon cable connection is quite satisfactory, providing it is not too long. A couple of metres is probably the safe limit.

The 6522 VIA registers

Before discussing these, the overall disposition of the user port lines should be understood. Figure 9.2 is the effective diagram.

The eight data lines are labelled PB0 to PB7. Each one can be separately programmed as either an input or an output by setting appropriate bits in a direction register (see later). When programmed as outputs, they deliver the usual TTL logic levels but are also capable of delivering 1mA at 1.5V. It is therefore possible to drive silicon transistor pairs in the Darlington configuration. (ie. two transistors connected in series to achieve gain multiplication). Since a Darlington can have exceptionally high current gains, it is possible to switch loads approaching, say, 0.5 amp directly. PB7 has a unique feature. It can be programmed to receive the output of T1, one of the interval timers on the chip. PB6 is also unique when programmed as an input. It is possible for the other timer (T2) to count the number of pulses arriving at the input of PB6.

196 *Advanced Machine Code Techniques for The BBC Micro*

The handshake (control) lines are CB1 and CB2. These can act as interrupt inputs or as handshake outputs.

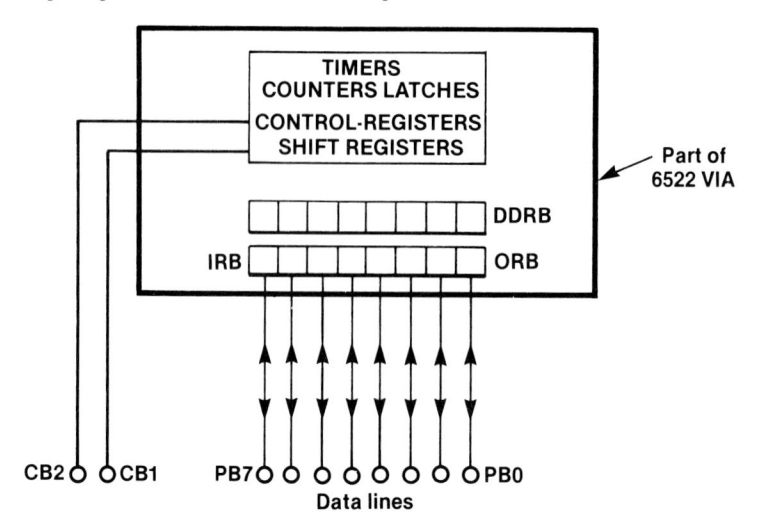

Fig. 9.2. The electrical appearance of the user port.

The VIA internal registers

The VIA responsible for the user port occupies 16 consecutive addresses in the SHEILA band, starting at &FE60. The following table shows the addresses in the form of an offset to &FE60. Thus, if the offset number for a particular register is given as 3, then its absolute address is &FE63. It is better to think of the address of any individual register as consisting of the base address (&FE60) plus the offset number of the register. for example, the address base+5 is tidier than writing this as &FE65. Table 9.1 shows the location of the registers in the VIA.

Table 9.1 The VIA addresses.

Register offset no.	Designation	Function
0	ORB or IRB	Output or input register B
1	ORA or IRA	Output or input register A
2	DDRB	Data direction register B
3	DDRA	Data direction register A
4	T1C-L	T1 low-byte latch or T1 low-byte counter
5	T1C-H	T1 high-byte counter

Table 9.1. contd

Register offset No.	Designation	Function
6	T1L-L	T1 low-byte latch
7	T1L-H	T1 high-byte latch
8	T2C-L	T2 low-byte latch or T2 low-byte counter
9	T2C-H	T2 high-byte counter
10	SR	Shift register
11	ACR	Auxiliary Control Register
12	PCR	Peripheral Control register
13	IFR	Interrupt Flag Register
14	IER	Interrupt Enable Register
15	ORA/IRA	Identical to offset 1 but no handshake.

Registers 1 and 3 will normally be left unused because, as stated previously, they are dedicated to the parallel printer interface. This still leaves fourteen registers left to grapple with. To understand them all is a formidable task. It would be demoralising to plod methodically through them in register order. Far better to attack the most commonly used ones first, the DDRB and the ORB.

DDRB (Data Direction Register B)

This is addressed at &FE62 (Base+2). The binary pattern initialised in DDR defines which of the lines PB0-PB7 will behave as outputs and which as inputs. The rule for direction in this register is as follows;

> A '1' defines the corresponding pin as an output and a '0' defines an input.

Here are some examples:

```
LDA #&FF \all data lines outputs
STA DDRB

LDA #&0F \PB0-PB3 outputs
STA DDRB \PB4-PB7 inputs
```

ORB or IRB (Output Register B or Input Register B)

DDRB defines the directivity of the data lines only; it does not define their actual logic states. For example, just because we have a 1 in bit 7 of the DDRB, it does not mean PB7 will be in the '1' state. Only the contents of ORB or IRB control the logic states on the data lines. Thus, when a data line

198 *Advanced Machine Code Techniques for The BBC Micro*

is programmed as an output, the corresponding bit set into DDRB decides the logic on the data line. On the other hand, if a line is programmed as an input, the logic state received from a device on that line is entered into the Input Register (IRB). If a line is programmed as an input, then any attempt to write into that line via ORB is ignored.

Example 1:
```
LDA #&FF   \All data lines outputs
STA DDRB
LDA #&03   \Set PB0 and PB1 to 1
STA ORB    \rest at 0
```
Example 2:
```
LDA #0     \All data lines inputs
STA DDRB
LDA IRB    \Read input reg. into A
```
Example 3:
```
LDA #&F0   \PB4-PB7 outputs,
STA DDRB   \rest inputs
LDA #&FF   \Attempt to write 1
STA ORB    \in all lines
```

Example 3 illustrates the point made earlier that any attempt to write into lines programmed as inputs will fail. Although we have written &FF in the instruction, only the higher order nibble will directly affect ORB. The bits in the output register corresponding to PB0-PB3 will depend on the peripheral input logic. It is assumed in these examples that DDRB and ORB have been assigned to &FE62 and &FE60 respectively.

There are two variations of input behaviour depending on whether 'latching' is enabled or disabled. If latching is disabled, the level present at an input (the relevant PB pin) is read into IRB. If the latch is enabled, the level read into IRB is that which existed after the 'last active transition' arriving on CB1 (when a pulse of the correct phasing and shape hit CB1 input). In other words, if the conditions existing *now* are required, then latch must be in the disabled condition. We only enable latching if we require CB1 to act as a data-valid signal and we wish to ignore levels arriving after the latching. The latch enabling is carried out on bit 1 of the Auxiliary Control Register (ACR). If this bit is 1, the input latch on IRB is enabled. If 0, it is disabled. The ACR (addressed at base+&B) controls many other functions, so it is essential that programming bit 1 is carried out in such a way that the remaining bits are left undisturbed. This is where the logic instructions ORA and AND become useful (refer back to Chapter 3).

To enable the input latch, study the following:

```
LDA ACR    \Obtain the ACR
ORA #&02   \OR it with 0000 0010
STA ACR    \Bit-1 in ACR is now 1
```

To disable the latch:

```
LDA ACR     \Obtain ACR
AND #&FD    \AND with 1111 1101
STA ACR     \Bit-1 in ACR now 0
```

The two control lines

The control lines CB1 and CB2 can be used for a wide range of control functions apart from initiating interrupt action.

We are concerned at this point only with the VIA registers which are involved either entirely or partly with these control lines. They will also be used for defining the kind of signal we wish to intitiate the interrupt. These and other registers in the VIA must be understood first. Any gadget we construct (or buy) which is going to initiate interrupts will emit an electrical pulse of fixed characteristics. The pulse (or electrical level) will, of course, have to conform to TTL protocol but, even so, there are many possible variants. For example, the initiating signal may be simply the drop in voltage from HIGH to LOW (a so-called negative-going edge) or it may be from LOW to HIGH (a positive-going edge). It may even be a narrow downward-going or an upward-going spike. The VIA is brilliantly designed to cater for many possible input conditions. Registers can be initialised to accept, as an active interrupt, one of the above signal patterns but ignore the others. You may also remember that if an interrupt request is made, it will be refused if the I bit in the Processor Status Register is 1.

PCR (Peripheral Control Register)

The two control, or 'handshake', lines CB1 and CB2 have other functions

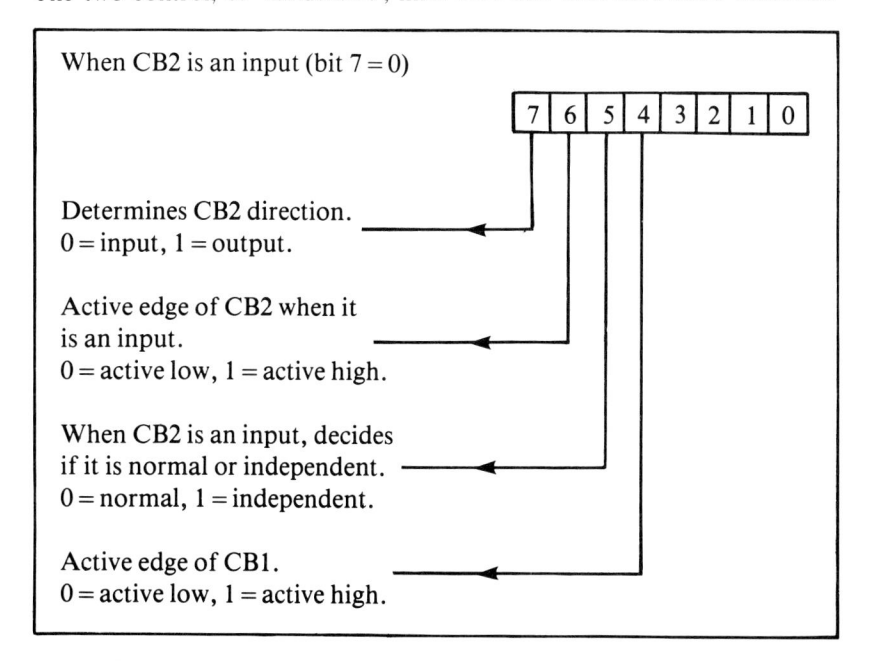

When CB2 is an input (bit 7 = 0)

| 7 | 6 | 5 | 4 | 3 | 2 | 1 | 0 |

Determines CB2 direction.
0 = input, 1 = output.

Active edge of CB2 when it
is an input.
0 = active low, 1 = active high.

When CB2 is an input, decides
if it is normal or independent.
0 = normal, 1 = independent.

Active edge of CB1.
0 = active low, 1 = active high.

besides interrupt. CB1 is always an input but CB2 can be an input or an output. Although the PCR is an 8-bit register, we shall only treat the left-hand four (bits 4 to 7) because the other half is identical and dedicated to the parallel printer interface. It is also a fraction easier to understand if the bit pattern is first restricted to the case when CB2 is an input.

When mention is made of the 'active edge', it refers to the setting of the appropriate flag in another register (IFR). That is to say, the only indication that an acceptable pulse has appeared on CB1 or CB2 input is the setting of the appropriate flag.

The terms 'normal' and 'independent', apply only to CB2 and, even then, only when it is an input. These terms concern the conditions under which the CB2 flag is reset after it has been set. in the normal mode, the flag remains set until a READ or WRITE instruction on the data registers, ORB or IRB is activated (for example, an LDA or STA). In the independent mode, once a flag is set, READ or WRITE does not reset it. The normal mode is designed for handshaking operations between computer and peripheral. The independent mode is useful for actions not directly involving computer interraction.

Behaviour of CB2 when it is an output

CB2 becomes an output if bit 7 of the PCR is set to 1. Clearly, the significance of bits 6 and 5 is then completely different as can be seen from the following:

(a) Let bit 5=0 and bit 6=0. This configures the so-called handshake mode. CB2 goes LOW by a write operation on ORB and goes HIGH again on an active transition of the CB1 input signal.

(b) Let bit 5=1 and bit 6=0. This is the pulse output mode. A negative-going pulse (goes from HIGH down to LOW then back again) is emitted following a write operation on ORB. Ideal for gadgetry which is activated by a negative-going pulse. Just do a dummy write to ORB with an STA ORB. If the pulse is in the wrong direction for the gadget, it is a simple matter to interpose an inverter.

(c) Let bit 6=1. This is the so-called manual mode because both levels output on CB2 must be directly programmed. The level on CB2 depends on bit 5. If bit 5 is 0, CB2 remains LOW. If bit 5 is 1, then CB2 is HIGH. In other words, providing bit 6 remains at 1,CB2 mirrors the state of bit 5.

Before continuing with the next register, some consolidation examples may help to decipher all this terrible complexity. If you find the above just a bit too much, don't despair, yet! Just study the following and console yourself with the fact that the control of sophisticated and versatile equipment (and the VIA is certainly within this catagory) can never be easy.

(1) To configure a simple 8-bit input port, with CB1 and CB2 not used:

Interrupt Techniques and the User Port 201

```
LDA #0
STA DDRB   \make all 8 lines inputs
```

This would be useful for reading a set of push-buttons. Once configured as above, IRB could be read into the accumulator for processing.

(2) A simple 8-bit output port, with CB1 and CB2 not used:

```
LDA #&FF
STA DDRB   \make all 8 lines outputs
```

This is used for switching LEDs, etc.

(3) An output port with CB1 to be active high input and CB2 to be active high input in independent mode:

```
LDA #&FF   \Make all lines outputs
STA DDRB
LDA #&70   \set 0111 in left half
STA PCR
```

Note that the right-hand four bits in the PCR (the A side of the VIA dedicated to the printer) have been tentatively reset to 0. This is not always a safe procedure because the printer is controlled by the operating system and should not be altered. The safe way, in the general case, would be to use masking techniques. For example:

```
LDA #&FF
STA DDRB
LDA PCR    \Bring out PCR
AND #&0F   \Clear left, keep right
ORA #&70   \0111 in left; leave right
STA PCR    \replace modified PCR
```

(4) PB0-PB4 to be inputs, PB5-PB7 to be outputs. CB1 to be active low input; CB2 to be a negative-going pulse on a WRITE to the ORB:

```
LDA #&E0   \1110 0000 in DDRB
STA DDRB
LDA #&A0   \1010 in left half
STA PCR    \of PCR
```

The previous remarks regarding the printer interface still apply but the extra coding, if considered important, would be the same as before.

(5) All data lines to be inputs. CB1 active high input. CB2 an output in the manual mode commencing with CB2 LOW.

```
LDA #0
STA DDRB
LDA #&D0   \1101 0000 IN PCR
STA PCR
```

The general concepts of interrupt techniques have been discussed in Chapter 1. You will remember that it is possible for a signal, which could arrive from an external device, to set in motion a chain of events. Such events (if allowed to progress) interrupt the present program then bring into play an interrupt service routine. On completion of this routine, the original program is rejoined at the point from which it was interrupted. If all goes well, the interruption and the rejoining goes smoothly. However, there are many pitfalls to overcome and much to be learned before 'things do go well'.

As might be expected, the computer itself contributes little towards the task. Apart from recognising the existence of an interrupt, most of the pre-preparation is the programmer's responsibility. The concept of an interrupt is based on unpredictability. The computer never knows when it is going to be interrupted so precautions must be taken to ensure that the interrupt service routine contains provisions for preserving the contents of all registers (on the stack is a good a place as any) before corrupting them with the new routine data. Before the return from interrupt (RTI) the original register data must be returned. Apart from the loss in time, the original program should not even be aware of the interruption. With regard to the question of time, there is a well-established rule in the BBC machine. It is unwise for interrupt routines to last longer than 2 milliseconds.

The routine is deemed to start at the instant the request is granted and lasts until the recognition of RTI. The operating system periodically requests interrupt to service the screen, keyboard and other routine background tasks, hence the above warning. However, 2 milliseconds is a long time. The clock is 2 MHz so it is still possible to squeeze in about 500 machine code instructions, even if they each take an average of 4 clock cycles.

The IFR (Interrupt Flag Register)

When a signal arrives on CB1 or CB2 (if it is an input) it sets an appropriate flag to 1 in the IFR. The significance of each bit in the IFR is as follows:

Interrupt Techniques and the User Port

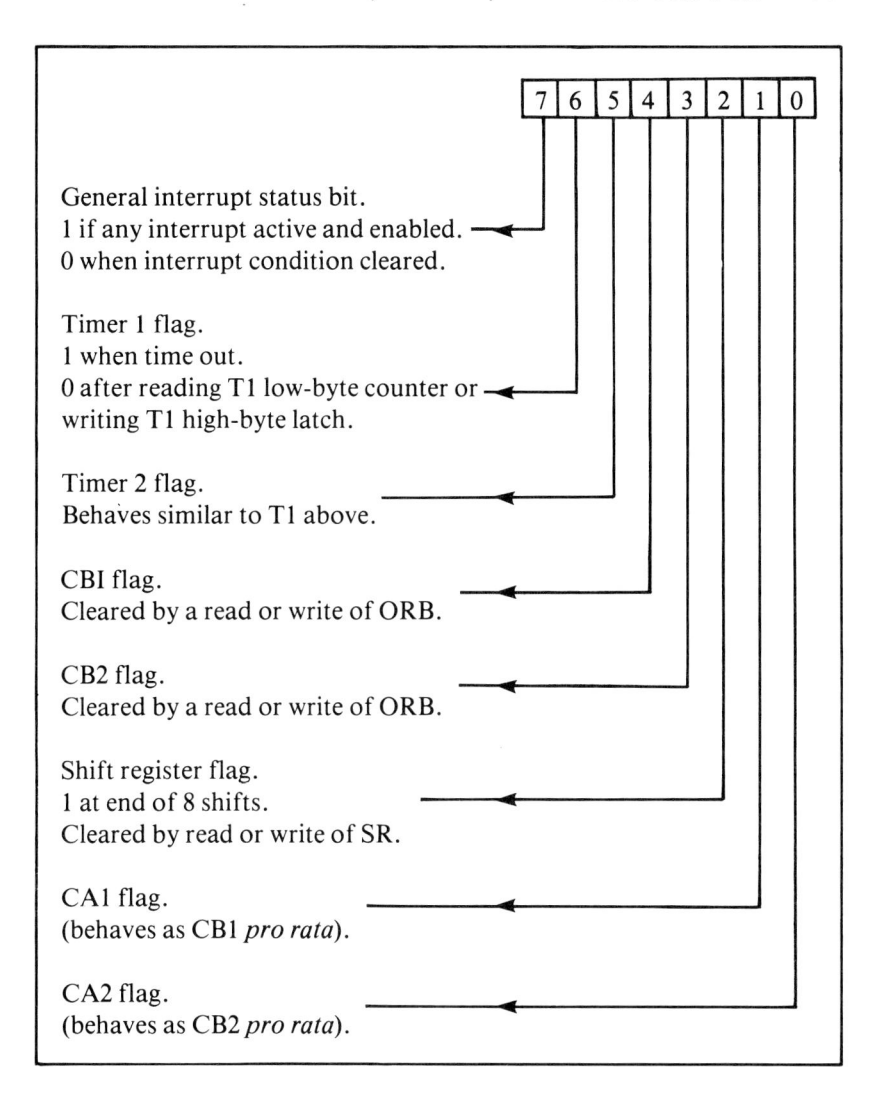

```
                                      7 6 5 4 3 2 1 0
```

General interrupt status bit.
1 if any interrupt active and enabled.
0 when interrupt condition cleared.

Timer 1 flag.
1 when time out.
0 after reading T1 low-byte counter or
writing T1 high-byte latch.

Timer 2 flag.
Behaves similar to T1 above.

CB1 flag.
Cleared by a read or write of ORB.

CB2 flag.
Cleared by a read or write of ORB.

Shift register flag.
1 at end of 8 shifts.
Cleared by read or write of SR.

CA1 flag.
(behaves as CB1 *pro rata*).

CA2 flag.
(behaves as CB2 *pro rata*).

It is possible, and sometimes desirable, to clear directly one or more of the flags in the IFR. This is done (rather strangely) by writing '1's into the flag positions to be cleared. Direct clearing in this manner will normally be required when the CB1 or CB2 inputs are being used for purposes other than 6502 involvement – in particular, when using the manual mode (refer back to PCR). Here are some examples in direct clearing:

(1) Clear CB2 flag

```
LDA #&08  \0000 1000
STA IFR
```

(2) Clear CB1 and T2 flags

```
LDA #&30  \0011 0000
STA IFR
```

(3) Clear all flags

```
LDA #&FF  \1111 1111
STA IFR
```

Bit 7 is the general interrupt status and is the only flag which cannot be reset (or set) directly. Therefore, the 1 in bit 7 position above is really of no consequence.

The IER (Interrup Enable Register)

The bits in this register correspond exactly as described for the previous register (IFR). It represents a last ditch stand between the various interrupt request sources and the 6502 IRQ input pin. For example, there may have been an active signal arriving on, say, CB1. This will have set the CB1 flag in the IFR. However, there may already be another flag or flags set. The 6502 can only accept one interrupt at a time so there is clearly a need for higher status register which can be programmed to select which flag is to be recognised (enabled). This is the role of the IER. It operates as follows:

Bits 0-6:
1 = enable
0 = enable

Bit 7:
Like bit 7 in the IFR, this bit is special.
When bit 7 = 0: Each 1 in a bit position is cleared (disabled).
When bit 7 = 1: Each 1 in a bit position enables that bit.
(Zeros in bit positions are left unchanged)

We found this quite terrible to understand. Here are some examples which we hope will help you:

(1) *Enable CB1 interrupt and disable all others*:

```
LDA #&6F  \0110 1111
STA IER   \Bit-7=0 so '1's disabled
LDA #&90  \1001 0000
STA IER   \Bit-7=1 so bit-4 enabled
```

Note that the second pattern is the logical complement of the first. This is not a coincidence.

(2) *Enable Timer 1, disable the rest and then clear the T1 flag bit in the IFR.*

```
LDA #&3F \Disable all others
STA IER
LDA #&C0 \1100 0000 to enable T1
STA IER
STA IFR  \Reset T1 flag in IFR
```

Note the logical complement again.

Organising a system in which only one device is expected to request interrupts is not too dificult. We can see from the above that the trouble starts when there are many devices, all requesting interrupt at the same time. Whatever machinations we employ down at the VIA end, they will always be subservient to the I bit in the 6502. If this is at 1, nothing can barge into the existing program except, of course, via the NMI input which should be treated as sacrosanct anyway. It is worth repeating the 6502 instructions directly concerned with interrupt control:

SEI will set the I bit, preventing interrupts.
CLI will clear the I bit.
BRK will set the B bit, save the Program Counter and the Status Register on the stack, set the I bit and load the contents of addresses &FFFE and &FFFF into the Program Counter.
RTI restores the Status Register and the Program Counter from the stack. Unlike RTS, it does not add 1 to the return address.

The timers and counters

It is always possible to generate delays (time intervals) by loading one or more of the 6502 instruction registers with the desired delay number and counting down to zero. This is not always satisfactory because it ties up the computer. To provide for independent delays and various other pulse-counting operations, the VIA is equipped with a variety of timers, counters and latches. They are useful for generating interrupts at regular intervals, triggering external devices or simulating a real-time environment. The two timers, T1 and T2, are essentially 16-bit counters. Each counter occupies two consecutive addresses (low and high byte) but T1, the more complex of the two, has an associated 16-bit latch, consequently occupying a further two addresses. Before treating the timers in detail, it is useful to begin with an overview of the possibilities on offer.

(1) They may be read or written into as six memory locations, four for T1 and two for T2. (See the VIA addresses given earlier in this chapter.)
(2) Their respective operation modes are governed by bits 5,6 and 7 of the Auxiliary Control Register (this is treated later).
(3) Their status, at any time during the counting phase, is obtainable by

examining bits 5 and 6 in the IFR. By 'status' we mean whether or not the programmed interval has ended (time out).

(4) To generate a single time interval, a timer is loaded with the number of clock pulses required (to generate that interval).

(5) Pulses arriving on PB6 can be counted until they compare with a previously loaded number (T2 only). The normal use of PB6 as one of the eight data lines is, of course, suspended.

(6) T1 can be used to provide continuous time intervals. The time interval between pulses will depend on a previously loaded number.

(7) A single, or continuous series of pulses can be produced on PB7; the pulse width will be dependent on a previously loaded number. In this mode, PB7 will not be available as a normal data line.

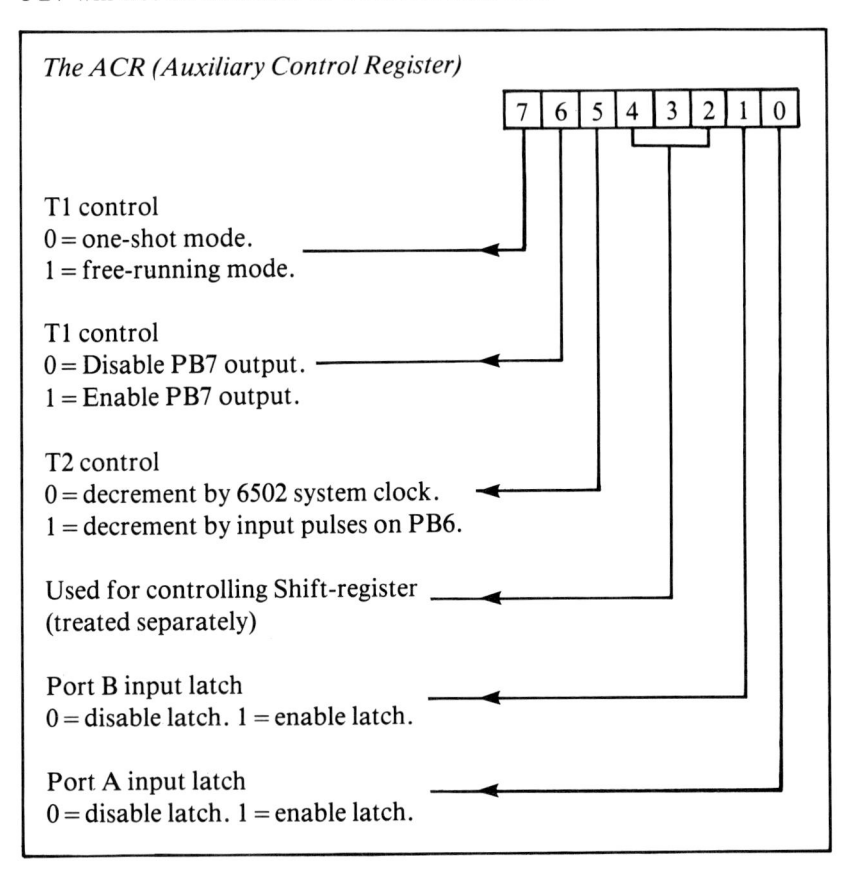

The ACR (Auxiliary Control Register)

| 7 | 6 | 5 | 4 | 3 | 2 | 1 | 0 |

T1 control
0 = one-shot mode.
1 = free-running mode.

T1 control
0 = Disable PB7 output.
1 = Enable PB7 output.

T2 control
0 = decrement by 6502 system clock.
1 = decrement by input pulses on PB6.

Used for controlling Shift-register (treated separately)

Port B input latch
0 = disable latch. 1 = enable latch.

Port A input latch
0 = disable latch. 1 = enable latch.

Timer T2 details

It is clear from the above overview that T2 is more simple than T1. It can only generate simple time intervals or count pulses arriving on PB6.

The low-byte address of T2 is used to write or read the low-order byte of the delay number. The T2 interrupt flag is automatically cleared on a read action. The high-byte address is used to write or read the high-byte of the number. Writing to this address completes the timer loading, clears the T2 interrupt flag and starts the timing operation. On completion of the timing interval, the T2 interrupt flag is set (bit 5 of IFR). Here are some examples:

(1). *To program a delay time, equivalent to 2048 clock pulses:*

```
LDA #0      \Ensure bit-5=0 for system
STA ACR     \clock mode
STA T2Lowbyte \Clear low-byte
LDA #&08
STA T2Highbyte \This starts count
LDA #&20    \0010 0000 mask for bit-5
.BACK BIT IFR \Performs AND mask
BEQ BACK    \Bit-5 not yet set
LDA T2Lowbyte \Dummy read clears f
```

(2) *To cause delay until 100 pulses have been counted from an external source on PB6:*

```
LDA #0
STA DDRB    \Make data lines inputs
LDA #&20    \0010 0000
STA ACR     \Make bit-5=0,pulse count
LDA #&64    \Prepare for 100 pulses
STA T2Lowbyte
LDA #0
T2 Highbyte \ This starts count
LDA #&20    \0010 0000 mask for bit-5
.BACK BIT IFR \Performs AND mask
BEQ BACK    \ Bit-5 not yet set
LDA T2Lowbyte \Dummy read clears f
```

Since these two examples have used the BIT test you may find it necessary to refer back to chapter 3.

Timer T1 details

This timer has a 16-bit latch as well as the normal 16-bit counter. It is also possible to generate an output on PB7. There are four different operating modes, depending on bits 6 and 7 in the ACR. The choice is single-shot or free-running mode (bit 6) and enable or disable PB7 output (bit 7).
Bit 7=0 will disable PB7 output. Bit 7=1 will enable PB7 output.
Bit 6=0 is one-shot mode. Bit 6=1 is free-running mode.

The addressing details and the start and finish of timing are virtually the same as described under T2 apart from the different addresses and bit 6, instead of bit 5, for the interrupt flag in the IFR. The free-running mode is made possible by the provision of a separate 16-bit latch in the usual low-byte (T1L), high-byte (T1H) form. These occupy two separate addresses. It is possible, therefore, to read or write into the latches without affecting the associated timer count. In the free-running mode, the number in the latches is automatically re-entered into the timer again and the count restarted. This makes it possible to generate a wave form of any mark to space ratio on PB7. This is because the logic level (HIGH or LOW) on PB7 remains fixed within a timing interval but inverts to the opposite state during the next interval and so on. Some examples of T1 operations are now given.

(1) To produce a wave form of unity mark to space ratio from PB7 which carries on indefinitely. The pulse width is to be equivalent to 1024 clock cycles.

```
LDA #&FF \Make data lines outputs
STA DDRB
LDA #&C0 \1100 0000(bit6,7 set to 1

STA ACR \Free-running moDe in T1
LDA #0
STA T1L \Clear T1 low byte latch
LDA #&04 \&04=1024 dec in high byte

STA T1H \Starts waveform action
```

Note carefully that no loop is necessary in the the above coding to produce repetitive action because of the automatic re-entering of the latch into the timers. The above coding merely triggers off the action and the computer is then free to carry on with other work. This can be a boon when designing complex control devices fed from the user port. It is useful to remember that the flag in the IFR is still a valid signal if the completion of each timing interval is significant to the rest of the program. It could, of course, be made to initiate an interrupt service routine.

(2) To produce an output on PB7 after 64535 clock pulses.

```
LDA #0 \Set T1 in one-shot mode
STA ACR
LDA #&FF
STA T1L \&FF in T1 low byte latch
STA T1H \This starts timing
LDA #&40 \0100 0000 mask for bit-6
.BACK BIT IFR
BEQ BACK \Flag not yet set
LDA T1L \Dummy read to clear f
```

The SR (Shift Register)

This will not be one of the commonly used registers. It is more suitable for serial data transmission, whereas the user port is oriented towards parallel. However, in the interests of continuity, the following information is given on the facilities available. As previously stated, bits 2,3 and 4 in the ACR determine the behaviour of the SR so it is sufficient to limit the discussion to the eight permutations of the three bits.

ACR Bits	Effect on Shift Register
000	Disable SR
001	Shift in at Counter 2 rate
010	Shift in at system clock rate
011	Shift in at external clock rate
100	Free running output at Counter 2 rate
101	Shift out at Counter 2 rate
110	Shift out at system clock rate
111	Shift out at external clock rate

Summary of the user port and its functions

Any chapter attempting to explain a device as complex as the user port is an ordeal for the writer and an even worse ordeal for anyone trying to make sense of it afterwards! A brief summary is therefore justified.

1. The 16 registers within the 6522 VIA chip are addressed within the band &FE60 to &FEFF.
2. The chip handles the parallel printer interface on the 'A side' and the user port on the 'B side'.
3. Any of the eight data lines, PB0 to PB7, can be inputs or outputs depending on the bit pattern set into the DDRB. PB6 and PB7 have qualities unique to the rest.
4. Output states on the lines depend on writing to ORB. Input states (which can be either direct or latched, depending on bit 1 of the ACR) can be read from IRB. ORB and IRB share the same address. Trying to write to an input is a sterile exercise.
5. Lines CB1 (always an input) and CB2 are for control purposes. They can be used for handshaking data transfers to or from the eight data lines or for any other purpose thought desirable. Either of them can be used to set 'interrupt flags' in the IFR. The setting of a flag, however, need not actually initiate an interrupt.

6. The CB2 direction depends on bit 7 of the PCR.
7. CB1 and CB2 can be programmed (by the PCR) to accept either a falling or rising edge of a pulse. CB2 can also have its flag in IFR reset 'normally' (by a read of IRB or a write to ORB) or 'independently'.
8. Two flags in the IFR act as event signals for CB1 and CB2. They are reset automatically on a read of IRB or a write to ORB. They can also be directly cleared by writing '1's into the flag bits (yes '1'!). Bit 7 of the IFR is immune to attempts directly to set or reset. It is a general signal to indicate if any flags at all are at 1.
9. The timers T1 and T2 are associated with low- and high-byte counters. Numbers placed in the counters determine the time intervals. The count starts and the previous flag (in the IFR) cleared when the high-byte is loaded. The flag is set after the count number loaded has decreased to zero.
10. There are many possible modes of timer operation, determined by bits 5,6 and 7 in the ACR.
11. T2 is the simplest of the two. It can generate a delay of N clock pulses, terminated by a flag, or count input pulses arriving on PB6 input.
12. T1 can be used to provide various continuous waveforms on PB7 output, independent of continuing computer support. It can also provide simple delays.
13. A programmable Shift Register is available, mainly for organising serial data activities.

This completes the treatment of the user port. Although it is under some control from the central processor (6502), it is clearly capable of carrying out some operations almost under its own volition. This is why the treatment has, so far, made little reference to the operating system. The coding examples given have been in isolation but it is hoped they will at least point the way. It is worth emphasising again that the flags are often referred to (rather misleadingly) as 'interrupt flags'. They can cause interrupt (if you let them) only by enabling the appropriate bit in the IER. Many interesting projects designed for attachment to the user port can be handled quite successfully without involving interrupt action. Nevertheless, this is no excuse for not attempting simple interrupt routines. The essential thing is to keep them simple, in fact very simple, during the learning period. It is better to get used to handling *internally* generated interrupts before progressing to their initiation from the user port.

Internally generated interrupts

The BBC operating system is unique in the way it exposes (almost indecently) its hidden workings to the ordinary user. Not only does it expose them, it almost demands they are made use of. One example of this

Interrupt Techniques and the User Port 211

is the list of FX14 calls at the top of page 426 of the User Guide, which is given more detailed treatment on page 465. FX calls become OSBYTE calls when in machine code. Thus, if we wish to take advantage of these calls, we ensure that the accumulator contains 14 before calling OSBYTE at &FFF4. There are seven dynamic conditions, any of which can be chosen to initiate an interrupt, as set out in Table 9.2.

Table 9.2 OSBYTE Event Interrupt Table.
Note: Place 14 in A and Event Number in X before calling &FFEE

Event number (number in X)	Enable event causing interrupt
0	Output buffer empty
1	Input buffer full
2	Character entering input buffer
3	A/D conversion complete
4	Start of vertical sync pulse
5	Interval timer crossing zero
6	Escape key pressed

A table, similar to the above, applies to disabling interrupts, except that A must contain 13 instead of 14 before calling OSBYTE.

The interrupts service routine, initiated by any of the above events, depends on the user and guidelines will be given later. However, the first problem is how to prepare the operating system to accept the routine and, what is more important, how to instruct the operating system to jump to it and return. The steps to ensure smooth linkage can be carried out in the following order:

(1) Load A and X then JSR OSBYTE (&FFEE), as selected from the Event Table above.
(2) Load the low- and high-byte starting address of your service routine in the indirection vector locations at &0220 and &0221 respectively. These addresses can be confirmed from page 465 of the User Guide.

Program 9.1 is a skeleton program to illustrate the above steps. To keep everything simple, the service routine is a simple jump to OSWRCH which prints the letter 'Z' whenever the ESCAPE key is pressed.

Lines 100 to 180 prepare everything for a smooth transition to the service routine. Lines 190 to 230 give the example service routine. The event enabled is code 6 in the Event Table, so lines 110 and 111 load 6 in X and 14 in A, prior to calling OSBYTE. This sets in motion an interrupt to 'SERVICE' whenever the ESCAPE key is pressed. Lines 140 to 170 are responsible for placing the starting address of 'SERVICE' in the page two vectors &0220/1

212 *Advanced Machine Code Techniques for The BBC Micro*

```
 10 REM SIMPLE EVENT INTERRUPT
 20 DIM ITEST 100
 30 OSBYTE=&FFF4:OSWRCH=&FFEE
 40 REM ----------------------
 50 FOR PASS=0 TO 3 STEP 3
 60 P%=ITEST
 70 REM ----------------------
 80 [
 90 OPT PASS
100 .PREPARE
110 LDX #6 \Enable ESCAPE event
120 LDA #14
130 JSR OSBYTE
140 LDA #Service MOD 256
150 STA &220 \Low byte interrupt vector
160 LDA #Service DIV 256
170 STA &221 \High byte interrupt vector
180 RTS
190 .Service
200 PHA:TXA:PHA:TYA:PHA:PHP
210 LDA #90
220 JSR OSWRCH
230 PLP:PLA:TAY:PLA:TAX:PLA
240 RTS
250 ]
260 REM ----------------------
270 NEXT
```

Program 9.1. Simple interrupt on event code 6.

which the operating system reserves for user-supplied interrupt routines. Since the program uses dynamic storage space allocated by the DIM statement at the top, it is not possible to know in advance the absolute addresses of 'SERVICE'. This is why lines 140 and 160 take advantage of the MOD and DIV instructions. These sort out the addresses in the form of low- and high-byte.

'Service' starts, as all interrupt routines should start, with saving all the registers on the stack. This is done by line 200 and it is well to note carefully the order of stacking. The example routine is a simple call to OSWRCH to write the character 'Z'. Line 230 restores, in reverse order, the registers to their previous values.

RUN the program first and examine the assembly out, particularly the addresses for the start of 'SERVICE' which was generated by the DIM statement.

Then enter CALL PREPARE. The interrupt routine is now activated. This can be verified by pressing ESCAPE several times and noting the 'Z'. This routine is permanent (until BREAK) and will appear to remain as part of the operating system. For example, type NEW to get rid of the BASIC program and type in a few lines of another program, say, a simple

Interrupt Techniques and the User Port 213

FOR/NEXT loop. Whenever ESCAPE key is pressed, the letter 'Z' will still appear.

To counter possible 'so what?' criticism, we must admit that Program 9.1 is not expected to be of the slightest use, apart from pointing the way to event interrupt handling. To have included a complex program as a service routine would have clouded the essential issues. Any coding you choose can be substituted in the space occupied by lines 210 and 220 (you can always RENUMBER 10,100) to get more line space.) Also, you can change the event code 6 in line 110 to experiment with other events. Try it with Event 4 in A so that 'SERVICE' interrupts whenever a vertical sync pulse appears (which is very often!). The screen fills up with Zs until you BREAK.

Peripheral initiated interrupts

Once the general form of Program 9.1 is understood, it is comparatively simple to transfer the idea from Event interrupts to peripheral interrupts. The peripheral is, of course, the user port. You will remember that an active transition at the input of either CB1 or CB2 (when it is an input) can set a flag in the IFR. If the corresponding bit in the IER is set to 1, the VIA sends the signal up the IRQ line and, providing the I bit in the process status register is 0, a full-blooded interrupt situation is established. The only difference in general principle in handling this kind of interrupt is the interrupt vector. It is no longer &0220/1. Page 466 of the User Guide names the vector as IRQ2V which is situated at &0206.

Summary

1. The user port is the 'B' half of the VIA. This is an interface to the outside world, providing a set of 8 data lines (PB0 to PB7) and 2 control lines (CB1 and CB2).
2. The port also supplies a five volt positive supply rail and an earth rail for each of the data and control lines.
3. There are 16 programmable registers in the VIA, occupying addresses &FE60 to &FE6F in the SHEILA band.
4. The bits within DDRB determine the direction of the 8 data lines. Data lines to be outputs must have '1's, lines to be inputs must have '0's, in the respective bit positions.
5. ORB and IRB are the output and input registers for the 8 data lines.
6. Data lines, programmed as inputs by DDRB, are unaffected by attempts to WRITE directly into them.
7. Input data can be latched or unlatched, depending on whether bit 1 in the ACR is 1 or 0 respectively.

8. CB1 is always an input but CB2 can be programmed as an input or as an output.
9. Bits 4 to 7 in the PCR are concerned with the behaviour of CB1 and CB2. Bits 0 to 3 are concerned with the A side of the VIA dedicated to the Centronics printer.
10. The IFR indicates to the programmer, by means of flags, that an active signal has been detected at CB1 and/or CB2 input. It also has flags for detecting time out conditions on the timers T1, T2 and the completion of 8 shifts from the shift register SR.
11. IER is closely associated with IFR on a bit by bit level. A set flag in IFR can only cause an interrupt request on the IRQ line if the corresponding bit in IER is at 1.
12. The timers T1 and T2 are 16-bit counters, T1 having an associated latch.
13. Delays can be achieved, or interrupts generated, at regular intervals by loading starting numbers into the high- and low-bytes of the counters.
14. PB7 can receive the output of the timers. PB6 can accept input pulses which can be compared with a number present in T2.
15. It is possible to produce a waveform of arbitrary mark to space ratio at the output of PB7.

Self test

9.1 What is the absolute hexadecimal address of the IFR?
9.2 What is the absolute hexadecimal address of T2 high-byte counter?
9.3 State the required hexadecimal contents of DDRB if all lines except PB5 are to be outputs.
9.4 Which of the two control lines can never be an output.
9.5 Assume the CB1 flag in the IFR is set. What additional status bits in the system must be set, or reset, before an actual interrupt occurs?
9.6 How do you enable the input latch on port B.

Appendix A
Binary and Logic

Binary

- Unless otherwise stated, numbers will be assumed to be decimal. Hex numbers are prefixed by &.
- To aid comprehension, strings of bits may be split into groups of four, but the space between groups is artificial.
- 'X' is used for 'don't care' bits and can mean 1 or 0.
- To 'flip' a bit means to change it from 1 to 0 or vice versa.

Unsigned binary system

Computer languages, whether entered in high level, assembly coding, or hexadecimal, are incomprehensible to the machine. All information is converted by the resident operating system to binary bits (1s and 0s).

All number systems, including the familiar decimal, rely on the relative position of digits to indicate their 'worth'. Each binary digit in a byte is twice the value of the bit to its right. In pure unsigned binary, the value of each binary 1 is shown below in both decimal equivalents and powers of two:

128	64	32	16	8	4	2	1		2^7	2^6	2^5	2^4	2^3	2^2	2^1	2^0
1	1	1	1	1	1	1	1	or	1	1	1	1	1	1	1	1

Examples:

    1000 1001 = 137
    1001 1111 = 159
    1111 1111 = 255

Sometimes, the following tip is useful:

A string of all 1s = $2^n - 1$, where n=number of bits in the string.
Examples:

    1111 = $2^4 - 1$ = 15
    1111 1111 1111 1111 = $2^{16} - 1$ = 65535

It is advisable, but not essential, to memorise powers of two up to the first sixteen bit positions. It is convenient to consider them divided into low-byte and high-byte as follows:

Powers of 2

High-byte	Low-byte
15 14 13 12 11 10 9 8	7 6 5 4 3 2 1 0 n
(32768) (16384) (8192) (4096) (2048) (1024) (512) (256)	(128) (64) (32) (16) (8) (4) (2) (1) 2^n

Any binary number in the high-byte position is always 256 times its low-byte value. For example: 0000 1001 would be worth 9 if low-byte, but 256*9 = 2304 if high-byte. Remember, the 6502 always stores 16-bit data in consecutive memory addresses, low-byte first.

Hexadecimal notation (hex)
Hex uses the 16 characters 0,1,2,3,4,5,6,7,8,9,A,B,C,D,E,F to describe a nibble (4 bits):

0000=0 0001=1 0010=2 0011=3
0100=4 0101=5 0110=6 0111=7
1000=8 1001=9 1010=A 1011=B
1100=C 1101=D 1110=E 1111=F

Two hex characters describe a byte. Some examples follow:

1111 0011 = F3   0001 1011 = 1B   1100 1101 = CD   0000 0001 = 01
1111 1111 1111 1111 = FFFF   1000 1100 1010 0111 = 8CA7

Hex arithmetic
Hex is based on powers of 16 so any character, depending on its position, must be multiplied by the appropriate power of 16 as follows:

$16^3 = 4096$ $16^2 = 256$ $16^1 = 16$ $16^0 = 1$

Using H for hex character: 4096   256   16   1
                              H   H   H   H

Examples:

&0032=(3*16)+2=50   &00FC=(15*16)+12 = 252
&00FF=(15*16)+15=255
&203E=(2*4096)+(3*16)+14=8254
&1111=4096+256+16+1=4369

Signed binary and two's complement

In order to represent both positive and negative numbers in a byte, the msb (bit 7) is reserved as the 'sign' bit.

The sign bit is 1 for negative and 0 for positive numbers. For example:

0XXX XXXX is positive and 1XXX XXXX is negative.

A negative number is said to be the *two's complement* of the equivalent positive and vice versa. There are two ways of obtaining the two's complement of a binary number:

(1) First flip all the bits and then add one. Ignore any carry out from msb end.
(2) Starting from msb, copy up to and including the first '1' then flip the remaining bits.

Examples:

	Number		Two's complement	
(+7)	0000 0111		1111 1001	(−7)
(+1)	0000 0001		1111 1111	(−1)
(−2)	1111 1110		0000 0010	(+2)

Method 1 can lead to errors when adding the 1, so method 2 is safer. The two's complement of decimal numbers is found by subtracting from 256.

Example: −1 = 1−256 = 255 = 1111 1111.

The two's complement of hex numbers is found by subtracting from &FF and adding 1.

Example: −3 = &FF−3 = &FC+1 = &FD

The largest positive number in a byte is +127 = 0111 1111 = &7F.
The largest negative number is −128 = 1000 0000 = &80.

Notes:
(a) The larger the negative number, the more binary 0s appear. In two's complement, everything is reversed, including the relative status of 1s and 0s.
(b) There are 128 positive and 128 negative numbers. The fact that zero is a positive number is the reason why there appears to be one more negative than positive (−128,+127).

Binary coded decimal (BCD)

Decimal numbers are awkward when expressed in binary, simply because base 10 and base 2 don't mix well. BCD is a code which sacrifices efficiency for decimal compatibility. A byte is divided into two 4-bit groups (nibbles). Each nibble is coded for numbers from 0 to 9, as follows:

BCD	Decimal
0000	0
0001	1
0010	2
0011	3
0100	4
0101	5
0110	6
0111	7
1000	8
1001	9

The six groups from 1010 to 1111, which are used for the characters A to F in hex, are *illegal* in BCD. A single byte can hold decimal numbers in BCD form only in the range, 0 to 99.

Examples: 0001 0011=13   0000 0111=07   1001 1001=99

The *efficiency* of a code = (number of combinations used)/total combinations).

In pure binary, all combinations are used, so the efficiency is 100%. In BCD, only 10 combinations are used out of a total of 16 possible, so the efficiency is 10/16=63% approximately. When the efficiency within a byte is calculated, the loss in information content is worse, 100/256 which is not quite 40%.

Because of the inefficiency of BCD, its use is limited. However, a large proportion of digital instrumentation delivers, or expects to receive, information in BCD form. The 6502 microprocessor obligingly processes BCD arithmetic if the D flag in the processor register is set to 1. However, it is up to the programmer to ensure that the data entering the arithmetic area is free from illegal groups.

Logic

Logic levels and TTL
Logic chips contain circuits which respond to, or deliver, one of two possible voltage levels. A certain family of chips (known as TTL) has set a common standard (see Fig. A.1). All members of the TTL family (there are over 300 different chips), have type numbers beginning with 74 or 74LS. The LS prefix denotes Low-power Shockty and although similar in logic function they consume less current and are faster. LS is now recommended for general use in favour of the traditional 'standard' TTL.

Binary and Logic 219

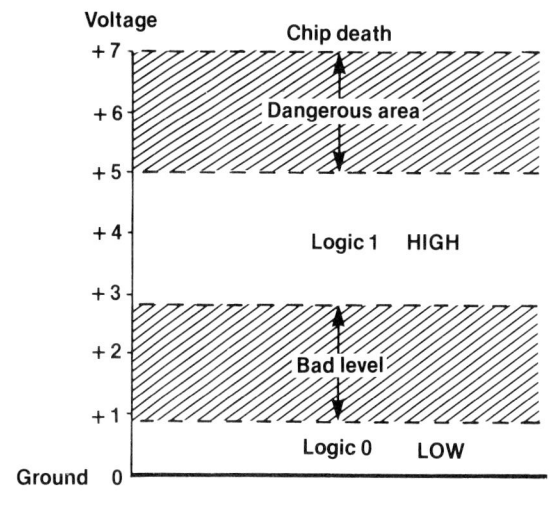

Fig. A.1. TTL logic levels.

Logic 1 (also known as a HIGH) = any voltage within the range +2.8 V to 5 V.

Logic 0 (also known as a LOW) = any voltage within the range 0 V to +0.8 V.

Any voltage in between is called a 'bad level' and will lead to indeterminate results. Bad levels are usually caused by an output over load *pulling up* or *dragging down* the voltage. Testing for HIGHs and LOWs at various points in the system can be done with a voltmeter although one of the various makes of 'logic probe' displaying either a red or green light is more convenient and less hazardous.

Logic gates

A gate is essentially a logic-operated switch with one output and one or more inputs. The combination of logic voltages on the inputs determines the output state. Although the function of a gate can be described in words, a truth table – with all possible input combinations – is concise and unequivocal. Figure A.2 shows the six common gates in their most popular diagrammatic form, together with the corresponding truth tables. The inverter is not worth a truth table.

Notes on Fig. A.2:
- *The AND gate:* output 1 only if all inputs 1.
- *The OR gate:* output 1 only if one or more inputs are 1.
- *The NAND gate:* output 0 only if all inputs are 1.
- *The NOR gate:* output 0 only if one or more inputs are 1.
- *The INVERTER:* output is reverse of input.
- *The EXCLUSIVE OR:* output 1 only if inputs are different.

220 Advanced Machine Code Techniques for The BBC Micro

A	B	S
0	0	0
0	1	0
1	0	0
1	1	1

AND

A	B	S
0	0	0
0	1	1
1	0	1
1	1	1

OR

A	B	S
0	0	1
0	1	1
1	0	1
1	1	0

NAND

A	B	S
0	0	1
0	1	0
1	0	0
1	1	0

NOR

INVERTER   Alternative INVERTER symbol

A	B	S
0	0	0
0	1	1
1	0	1
1	1	0

EXCLUSIVE OR

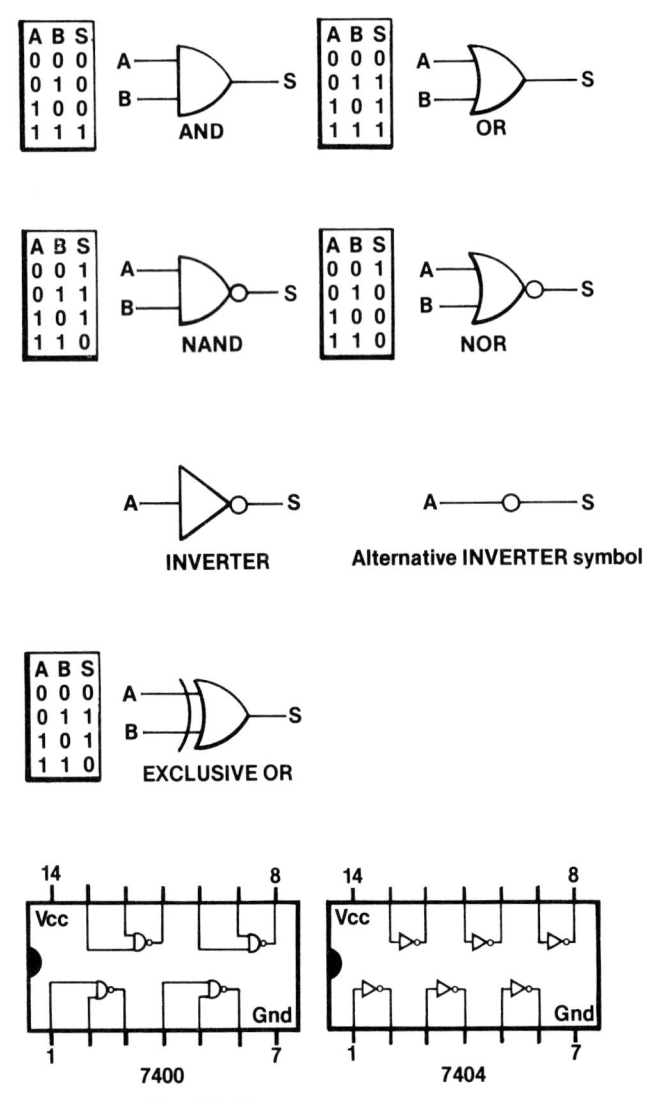

7400   7404

Fig. A.2. The six primitive gates.

Examination of the truth table reveals that it is similar to the OR but 'exludes' the bottom AND line.

Although only two inputs are shown at each gate in Fig. A.2, the TTL family include gates with as many as eight inputs. The two common chips are the 7400 quad NAND and the 7404 hex inverter. The pin connections for these appear in Fig. A.2. The power supply to the chips is marked VCC (+5V) and Gnd (0 V) pin marked Vcc. Chip pin-out diagrams are always drawn looking down on to the top of the chip.

Active levels and negation

More complex chips such as decoders, buffers, counters, etc., do not always recognise a 1 or HIGH state as being in some way superior to a 0 or LOW state. Any input terminal which is immune to a 1 but activated by 0 is said to be active-LOW. Such terminals are indicated either by (a) a bar over the terminal label such as $\overline{C}$ or $\overline{clock}$ (the bar is a Boolean symbol for negation – for example, $\overline{A}$ is the opposite state to A) or (b) a small circle or 'bubble'.

Dominance of NAND and INVERTER gates

TTL logic is based on the NAND and INVERTER, the other three gates tend to be under-used and therefore not so readily available. There are three reasons for their dominance:

(1) Many of the more complex chips are gated on by a LOW rather than a HIGH in order to minimise standby current.
(2) The internal circuitry of TTL gates is such that NAND and inverter functions arise more naturally and require less components.
(3) Combinations of NAND and INVERTER can be arranged to simulate AND and OR gates. An AND is an inverted output NAND. An OR is a NAND with all inputs inverted. Even the INVERTER is not strictly essential because a NAND, with all inputs strapped or held permanently at 1, behaves as an INVERTER.

Use of gates

Traditionally, the study of logic has leant heavily on a branch of mathematics known as Boolean Algebra. It is both a useful shorthand and a powerful tool in the mathematical analysis of logic. Boolean is still useful but, for the home enthusiast, the availability of complex integrated circuits has lessened the need to design and construct systems from an assortment of gates, so time spent on studying the special algebra may not always be justified.

The main use (now) for logic gates is to 'glue' together the more complex chips which may be incompatible in some way. For instance, one chip may deliver a 1 where a 0 is needed, meriting an inverter in between. Another possibility is the need to enable a chip only if 'something' else is at 1. Figure A.3 shows some of the switching arrangements using gates.

Figure A.3(a) shows an AND gate simulating a series switch in the data path. A serial data stream entering can only pass through the switch if the control C is HIGH.

If a NAND gate is used, as in Fig. A.3(b), an inverter is needed. Without the inverter, the serial data stream would still pass if C is held HIGH but would be in inverted form (called the 'one's or logical complement').

Figure A.3(c) shows how it is possible to enable a chip providing both A and B inputs are held HIGH. Note that the example chip is marked $\overline{CE}$ (not chip enable) which is convenient for the LOW output from the NAND.

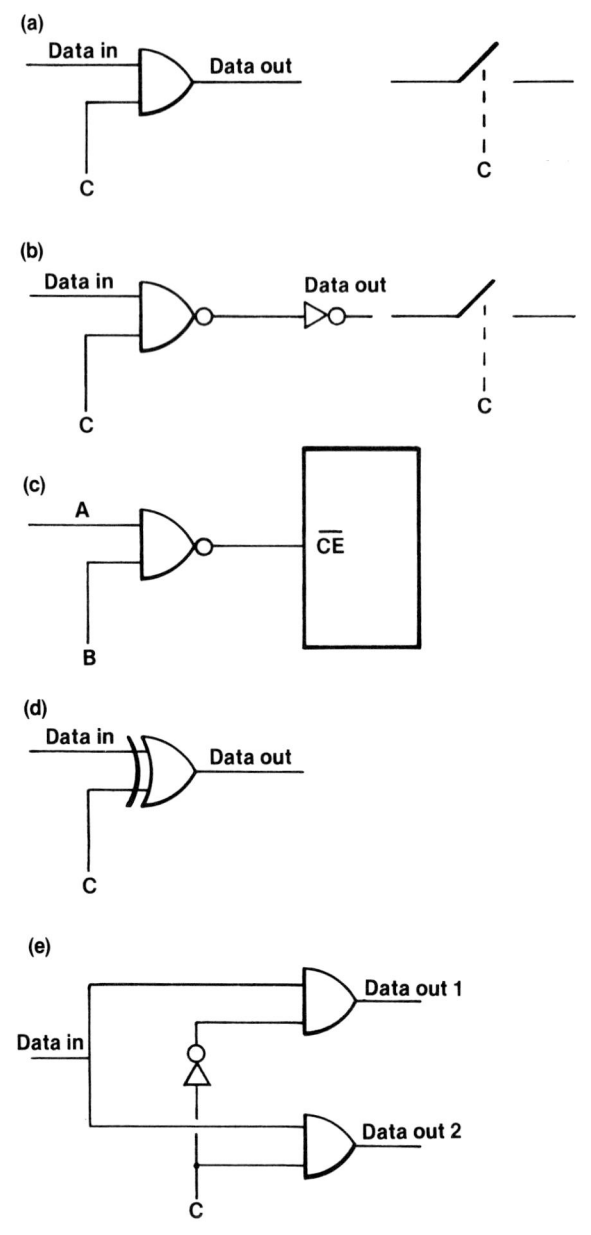

Fig. A.3. Uses of simple gates.

Remember that the bar over the CE label is an alternative to the bubble.

The exclusive-OR gate in Fig. A.3(d) provides an easy way of controlling the phase of the output data. If the control C is held LOW, the output data stream is a replica of the input. If C is held HIGH, the output data is an inverted version of the input.

Figure A.3(e) is a simulation of a single pole, double throw switch whereby the serial data stream can be diverted to either data out 1 or data out 2, depending on the state of the control C. If C is held HIGH, the data emerges from the bottom gate but from the top gate if held LOW. Inverters would be needed at the outputs if NANDs were used instead of ANDs.

Flip-flops

Logic gates deliver an output state, depending on the present input conditions. They are combinatorial devices, acting in real time and capable of analysis by simple Boolean algebra. Flip-flops are in an entirely different class because their present state depends on some event (usually a logic pulse) which occurred in the past. From this, it should be easy to conclude that flip-flops have the ability to memorise. But they can't memorise much. In fact, one flip-flop can only store a single bit so we would need eight of them to store one byte of data. A flip-flop which is storing a 1 is said to be set; if it is storing a 0, it is said to be reset. The four varieties of flip-flop in common use are shown in Fig. A.4.

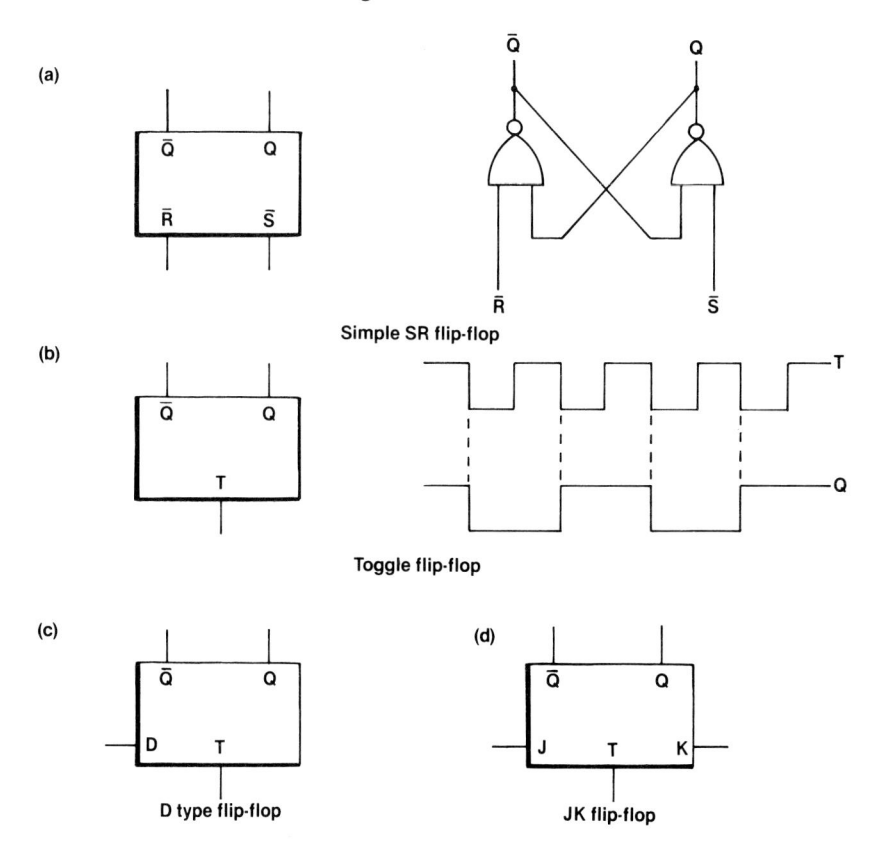

Fig. A.4 Types of flip-flop.

The SR flip-flop. The logic symbol shows it to be a four-terminal black box. The output state is available at the 'Q' terminal which is set or reset by a negative-going pulse on S or R respectively. The term negative-going means a sudden drop in voltage from HIGH to LOW. It is important to realise that, although a transition from HIGH to LOW is required, it is not necessary to maintain the LOW state. In fact, the easiest way to try it out would be momentarily to touch the S terminal with a grounded wire. If it is already in the set state, nothing will happen. If it is in the reset state, the Q terminal will go from 0 to 1 and remain in the new state until you flick the R terminal. The action is similar to the push-on/push-off switch found on table lights – it memorises the last order.

When a RS flip-flop is needed, it is customary to 'make' one from two cross-strapped NANDs (this only takes half a 7400). As a 'free gift', the Q terminal is always in the opposite state to $\overline{Q}$. Knowledge of this can often save an inverter.

The T flip-flop. This is often called a 'toggle' because every negative-going edge of a pulse on T will change the state at Q – it toggles the state backwards and forwards. The waveforms shown on Fig. A.4(b) indicate that a continuous pulse of frequency f applied to T causes an output frequency of $f/2$, illustrating its primary use as a frequency divide-by-two stage. The Q output will be at the same half-frequency as $\overline{Q}$ but in the opposite phase. Direct set and reset terminals, which override T, may also be present in some types.

The D flip-flop. The D stands for 'Data'. The state at Q is oblivious to the D state until a trigger pulse arrives at T. When the negative going edge of the trigger arrives, the state of D (at that time) is passed (latched) into the flip-flop. In other words, the Q state is always the state which D was, prior to the arrival of the trigger. The 7475 is a quad D-type latch, containing four identical D flip-flops. Two of these can be used to latch in a byte of data.

The JK flip-flop. This is a versatile breed of flip-flop, shown in Fig. A.4(d). The logic state on the J,K terminals decide the eventual state of Q after the next trigger pulse on T. The action is best described with the aid of the following truth table:

J	K	State of Q after next trigger
0	0	No change
0	1	Reset (Q=0)
1	0	Set (Q=0)
1	1	Change

Note that when J and K are both 0, the flip-flop is paralysed, unable to respond to any triggers.

If J and K are both held at 1, a trigger will always change the state. In other words, this perm of J,K transforms it to a T flip-flop.

If J is joined to K by an inverter, it is transformed to a D flip-flop, the J terminal acting as a D.

From this, it is easy to see why the JK flip-flop was described as versatile.

Finally, it should be mentioned that some diagrams will choose different labels for the trigger terminal. The terminal we have marked T may, in some diagrams, be marked clock or just C.

Wired-OR and tristate outputs

A microprocessor system is based on the common bus. The output data from RAM, ROM, etc., are all wired in parallel across the same wires. It is important that such devices in the disabled state are effectively disconnected from the common bus. Normal TTL logic allows inputs to be connected together but under no circumstances must outputs be connected together unless they are of the class known as open-collector. Figure A.5(a) shows the idea behind wired-OR connections.

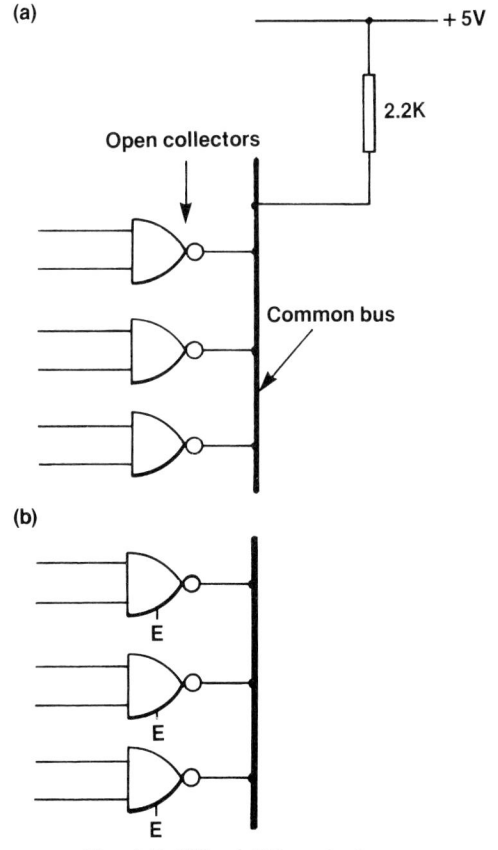

Fig. A.5. Wired-OR and tristate.

The output stage of normal TTL consists of two transistors in series across the 5 V supply (known as totem pole) with the gate output emerging from the centre point. The top transistor is missing in open-collector types and the feed to the 5 V line must come from an external pull-up resistor. This allows several outputs to be connected together, providing they all share the same pull-up resistor. Many of the popular chips in the TTL family are available in both standard and open-collector version.

Although wired-OR connections are useful in odd places, the solution is too messy for computer bus work. The alternative, and cleaner, solution is to provide chips with tristate outputs as shown in Fig. A.5(b). An extra transistor is built in to each output line, acting as a series switch and turned on or off by the enable terminal. When the chip is disabled, the outputs are effectively removed from the bus. The TTL chips offering tristate outputs are normally more complex than simple gates. RAM and ROM chips are almost always tristate.

Mechanical switches

Some disconcerting effects can occur if logic voltages are applied by means of an ordinary mechanical switch, particularly if the terminal supplied expects a single pulse. Due to the natural resonance of the operating spring, switches bounce backwards and forwards several times before coming to rest in the final position. The evil is called switch-bounce and can be overcome by either of the following two methods:

(1) Using an SR flip-flop and a single pole two-way switch as shown in Fig. A.6. The flip-flop can be fashioned from the two strapped-NANDs previously described.

(2) Using software, incorporating a few milliseconds delay before 'reading' the state of the switch.

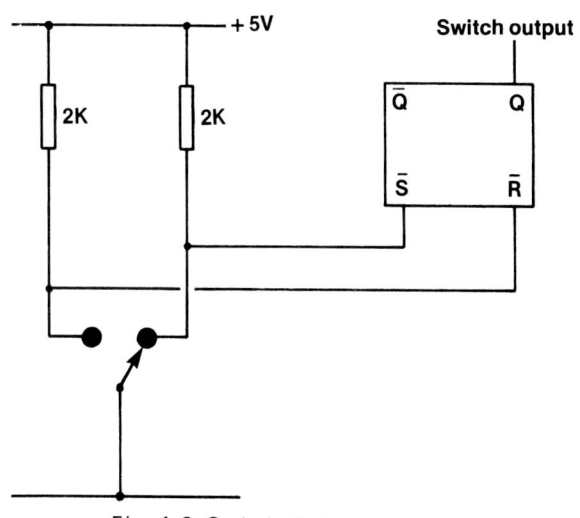

Fig. A.6. Switch de-bounce circuit.

Driving lamps and relays

Small lamps are popular for displaying logic states. All lamps take current which can be ill afforded in logic work. Incandescent filament lamps are sluggish and take 50 mA or more. Neons take negligible current but require about 80 volts before they emit the characteristic red glow. This leaves the light-emitting diode (LED) as the only serious contender. They give a reasonable light with about 5 mA and only drop about 1.2 volts. They must always be fed via a series resistor somewhere in the chain in order to ensure current, rather than voltage, drive. They are best driven from the output of an inverter as shown in Fig. A.7.

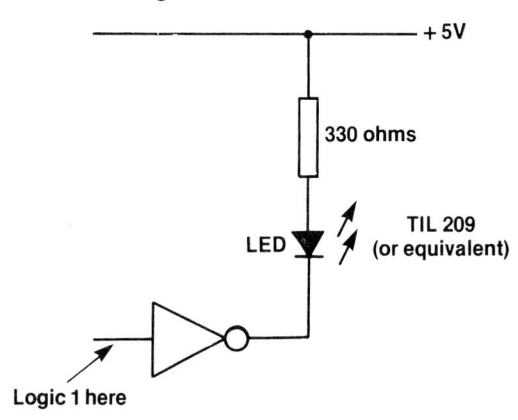

Fig. A.7. Feeding a LED.

The LED lights when a 1 is applied to the inverter input. The inverter output then drops to near ground, completing the circuit through the LED. The output of the inverter is said to be sinking the LED current to ground.

Devices which require current in excess of 20 mA or voltages in excess of 5 V cannot be driven from logic circuits without help. This help can be supplied by the familiar electromagnetic relay, the opto-isolator or a combination of both. Figure A.8 shows some arrangements.

In spite of the glamour associated with the semiconductor age, there are still uses for the traditional electromagnetic relay. Design methods have improved and the modern forms are efficient, physically small and take relatively low currents. Although no different in principle, the variant known as the reed relay, shown in Fig. A.8(c), is common-place in modern interface circuitry. The operating contacts are enclosed within a glass tube filled with inert gas, which prevents the build-up of oxidation products. Because of this, the contact life is much higher than in the traditional open-contact relay. The operating coil is a separate component slipped over the tube and therefore can cater for a variety of current and impedance requirements.

Relays fulfil two primary requirements of the power interface:

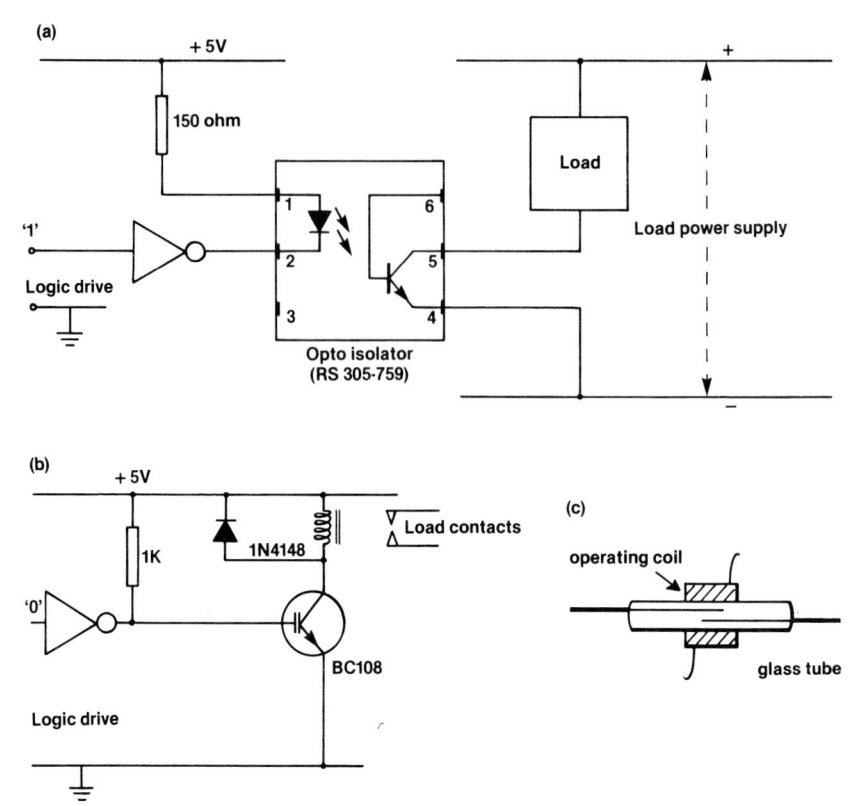

228 *Advanced Machine Code Techniques for The BBC Micro*

Fig. A.8. Relays and opto-isolator drives.

(a) They allow the weak logic output from the computer to control high power.

(b) They electrically isolate the computer from high voltage circuits.

They must never be used without a reverse diode across the operating coil. The diode safeguards the logic circuits from induced voltages which appear when the current is interrupted. Figure A.8(b) shows a typical drive arrangement, using a common npn transistor as a current amplifier. The transistor conducts through the operating coil of the relay. The 1K resistor supplying the requisite base current. The presence of the inverter gate means that the transistor conducts on a logic 0 input and switches off on a logic 1. This is a case of an active-low drive causing a back-to-front action. If this is undesirable, the remedy is to insert an extra series inverter to bring it right again or substitute a non-inverting buffer gate. In either case, some form of logic gate is desirable in home constructed projects rather than a direct raw feed from the computer output port. Gates are cheap, computers aren't!

The opto-isolator is another popular component in interface work. Like the electromagnetic relay, the objective is to isolate electrically the computer from any high power/voltage/current components. In fact, the only connection is via the light emitted from a small LED falling on the base of a light-sensitive transistor. They are available singly as 6-pin chips, with the diode and transistor buried within the silicon. A typical circuit using a single opto-isolator is shown in Fig. A.8(a). The RS 305759 is only one of the many types available in the catalogues.

The box marked 'load' is a blanket term covering any contraption driven by the isolator. In all probability, this will include yet another transistor because the opto-isolator introduces a power 'gain' of less than unity (typically 0.2). To convert the loss into a gain, some opto-isolators incorporate two transistors and are classified as Darlington-connected. Some chips are available which contain four independent opto-isolators so two of these could handle the output from an 8-bit port.

Schmitt triggers

When the logic state changes from 0 to 1, or vice versa, logic chips expect the change to be rapid. In other words, the wave form should display, as far as possible, straight-sided pulses. If the input changes are sluggish, the behaviour could be impaired, particularly for clock-type inputs. If the input is obtained from the output of another logic circuit and the wiring between the two is not too long, there is no problem. However, if the input is obtained from an analogue, or 'home-made' source, the waveform is probably suspect and must be cleaned up before qualifying as a legitimate gate input. The 74 logic series has the answer in the form of the schmitt trigger, a standard circuit which accepts a poor pulse shape and transforms it into a steep-sided version. Figure A9 shows the gate symbol with typical input and output waveforms. The 7414 is a hex schmitt inverter, performing in the same way as a normal inverter but accepts poor waveforms. The schmitt does not protect against voltages which are out of range. It offers waveform but not voltage protection.

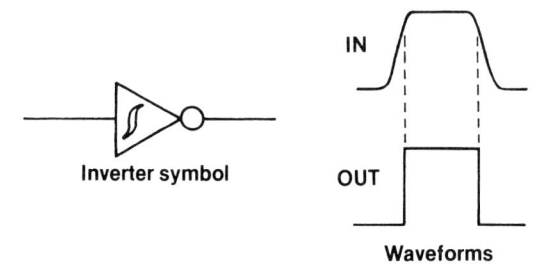

Fig. A.9. The schmitt trigger.

With reference to the mention of 'long' wires, it is worth pointing out that distributed capacity across wires, or between wires and ground, is often a cause of weird faults. It is sometimes a source of complaint that manufacturers of peripheral equipment appear to be miserly in the length of connecting cable supplied. In all fairness, this is not always due to cost penny-pinching. It is simply a wise precaution to avoid complaints of erratic behaviour which might arise if the cable length were increased. Apart from distributed capacity, the longer the wire, the more chance of picking up stray induced voltages.

Timer chips

It must be admitted that discussion of these chips is a little out of place here. The 555 timer chip is not strictly a logic circuit although, if operated from a +5V supply, it accepts and delivers reasonable TTL voltage states. It is versatile, very low-priced, and easy to use. We are concerned here only with its use as a hardware timer. That is to say, a device which, on receipt of a single narrow pulse, delivers an output HIGH state for a certain time before reverting to the quiescent LOW state automatically. Figure A10 (a) shows the pin connections, wiring and waveforms.

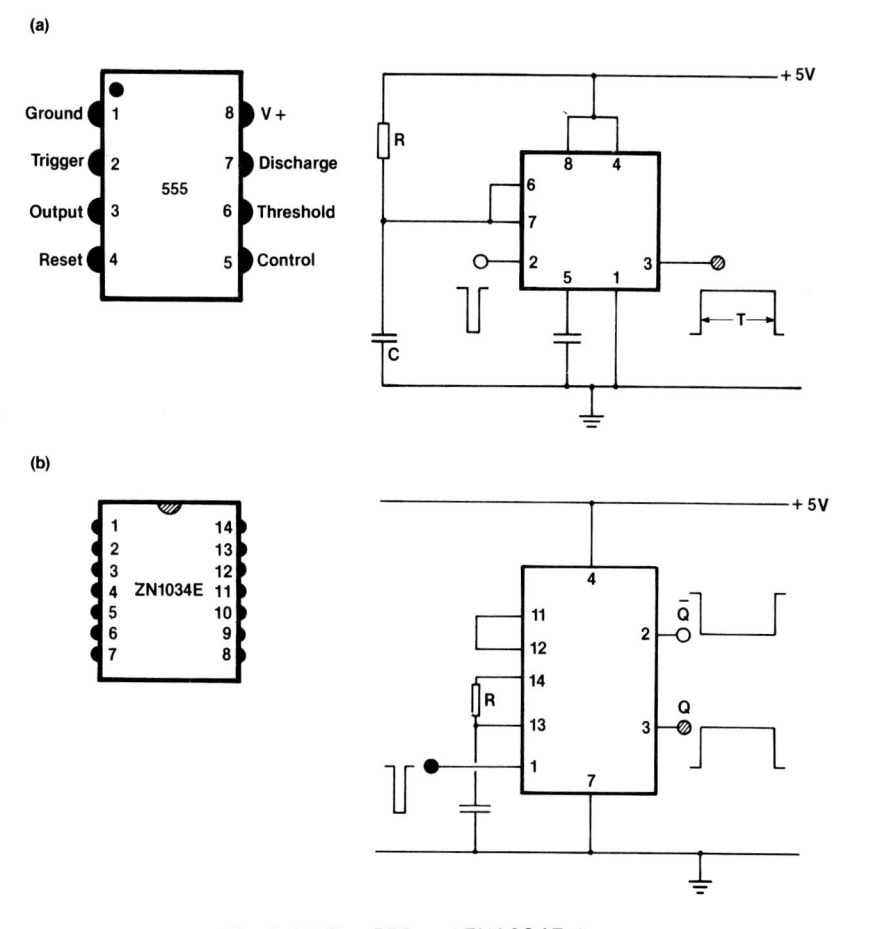

Fig. A.10. The 555 and ZN1034E timers.

Binary and Logic **231**

The 555 is ideal for cases where a single pulse from the computer can turn on a device (electric motor, perhaps) but is not required to stop under computer control. It is realised, of course, that the BBC machine includes programmable timer facilities so the job could have been entirely software-controlled without a 555. However, it is good to be aware of alternative possibilities.

The output pulse-width, which determines the ON time of the device, is dependent on the value of C and R according to the following formula:

T = 1.1 CR (where C is in μF and R is in megohms)

For example, if C = 0.1 μF and R = 100K, the ON time will be 0.011 seconds. The figures illustrate that the 555 is not generally suitable for long time periods. It is not recommended to use R values greater than 1M, and capacities of the order of some microfarads means using electrolytics with wide tolerances. For periods over several seconds up to minutes, it is better to use one of the more sophisticated timers such as the ZN1034E shown in Fig. A.10(b). The timing formula is:

T = 2736 CR (where C is in μF and R in megohms)

The multiplication factor 2736 is achieved by an internal 12-bit binary counter allowing time periods up to an hour or more. A useful feature is the provision of two complementary outputs, marked Q and $\overline{Q}$ in the diagram. It is a complex 14-pin chip with some of the pins allocated to external calibration resistors but only the simplified wiring is shown. To utilise the full potential, it is worth sending for detailed data sheets.

Decoders
A decoder will have several outputs but only one selected output can be activated at a time. The particular output depends on the specific combination applied to the selection input. Three select terminals can provide only eight different combinations of binary digits, the rule being:

Number of combinations of n bits = 2n

For example, to select any one of sixteen outputs requires four select inputs. There is a wide range of decoders in the TTL series. In addition to the select inputs, there will be one or more enabling inputs, allowing decoders to be linked together. Some of these may be active-high and some active-low. It is important to realise that all enable inputs must be activated before the chip becomes 'live'.

Demultiplexers
A demultiplexer routes serial input data to one particular output line and is the logic equivalent to a single pole multiway switch. Like the decoder, the particular output selected depends on the combination supplied to the select

terminals. In fact, a decoder with enable inputs can be used as a demultiplexer by feeding the data to one which is active-high.

Multiplexers

These are mirror images of demultiplexers. They route any one of many input data sources to a single output line. The particular input source depends on the combination applied to the select inputs. The usual enable terminals will be present in most TTL chips.

Encoders

An encoder delivers a particular binary pattern on the output terminals. depending on which of the many input lines is activated. For example, there could be ten inputs, each capable of producing a unique four-bit pattern on the outputs and acting as a decimal to binary encoder. Most microcomputer keyboards are decoded by scanning software but some of the more expensive types are hardware encoded.

Counters

A counter is essentially a device which delivers an output binary pattern which changes on receipt of each input pulse. The TTL range offers a wide variety of counters. They may be classified as follows:

Binary counters. The input pulses cause the four-bit output to progress from 0000 to 1111 in a simple binary sequence. The pulse starts the count again at 0000.

BCD counters. The input pulses cause the four-bit output to progress from 0000 to 1001 (0 to 9 decimal). The tenth pulse starts the count again at 0000.

All counters will be supplied with a reset-to-zero input and most supply a terminal which emits a pulse when the count goes over the top to 0000. This is useful for cascading the output of one counter to the input of another. Two binary counters in cascade would then handle counts up to 1111 1111 (255 decimal) and two BCD counters up to 1001 1001 (99 decimal). There is another classification according to the direction of count. For example, those described above are up-counters but some varieties can be persuaded to down-count. For example, a four-bit binary down-counter has 1111 as the 'reset' state and decreases on each input pulse towards 0000. Down-counters are not supplied as such but some of the more sophisticated varieties have a control terminal which can be maintained HIGH for up-count and LOW for down-count. It is worth mentioning that an ordinary up-counter can be turned into a down-counter by inverting the outputs.

Shift-registers

It is self-evident that a shift-register shifts but, as with counters, there are generic variants depending on the direction of shift (left or right) and whether the initialised data is applied serially or in parallel. They will all have a 'shift' terminal (marked T or Clock). Every pulse on T shifts the contents one place, bits being pushed out at one end.

Parallel-in-parallel-outs, known as *PIPOs*, accept parallel data on the four inputs, and data is available on the four output lines after the shift pulses have ended. The new input data is only let in to the register when an enabling level is applied to the appropriate terminal.

Parallel-in-serial-outs, known as *PISOs*, are similar to above but the output data can only be obtained a bit at a time on the serial output line.

Whatever other facilities they posses, shift-registers will always have serial-in and serial-out terminals. Many varieties exist in the TTL range. Some handle 8-bits and some can shift left or right depending on the state of a control terminal. The most obvious use for shift-registers is for parallel to serial or serial to parallel conversion.

Buffer registers

A buffer is a temporary holding register for data, the contents of which are subject to a latching pulse. Typically, there will be four data inputs, four data outputs and a terminal which is used to latch in the new data. Data variations at the input are 'unseen' until a latching pulse is applied when the current data overwrites the old. Some buffers have tristate outputs and are bi-directional.

Appendix B
Operating System Calls

Subroutine (name)	Address (hex)	Vector (hex)	Function	Register/s involved
OSWRCH	FFEE	20E	Write character	A
OSRDCH	FFE0	210	Read character	A
OSNEWL	FFE7	—	LF and CR to screen	A
OSASCI	FFE3	—	Write character (NL if A=0D)	A
OSCLI	FFF7	208	Interprets command line	X,Y
OSBYTE	FFF4	20A	All OSBYTE calls and *FX	A,X,Y
OSWORD	FFF1	20C	All OSWORD calls	A,X,Y
OSFILE	FFDD	212	Load and save file	A,X,Y
OSBGET	FFD7	216	Load and save data file	A,X,Y
OSBPUT	FFD4	218	Put byte in file	A,Y
OSFIND	FFCE	21C	Open or close file	A,X,Y
OSGBPB	FFD1	21A	Multiple OSBPUT and OSBGET	A,X,Y
NVRDCH	FFCB	—	Non-vectored read character	
NVWRCH	FFC8	—	Non-vectored write character	
GSREAD	FFC5	—	Read string character	
OSEVEN	FFBF	—	Activate event	
GSINIT	FFC2	—	Initialise string input	
OSRDRM	FFB9	—	Read paged ROM byte	

Appendix C
6502 Complete Instruction Set

Appendix C1
6502 Complete Instruction Set

ADC	Add with carry	A+M+C→A	NZCV

Address mode	Op-code	Bytes	Cycles
Immediate	&69	2	2
Zero-page	&65	2	3
Zero-page,X	&75	2	4
Absolute	&6D	3	4
Absolute,X	&7D	3	4 or 5
Absolute,Y	&79	3	4 or 5
(Indirect,X)	&61	2	6
(Indirect),Y	&71	2	5

AND	And with A	A and M→A	NZ

Address mode	Op-code	Bytes	Cycles
Immediate	&29	2	2
Zero-page	&25	2	3
Zero-page,X	&35	2	4
Absolute	&2D	3	4
Absolute,X	&3D	3	4 or 5
Absolute,Y	&39	3	4 or 5
(Indirect,X)	&21	2	6
(Indirect),Y	&31	2	5

| **ASL** | Shift left | C←(7...0)←0 | NZC |

Address mode	Op-code	Bytes	Cycles
Accumulator	&0A	1	2
Zero-page	&06	2	5
Zero-page,X	&16	2	6
Absolute	&0E	3	6
Absolute,X	&1E	3	7

| **BCC** | Branch if C=0 | Flags unaltered |

Address mode	Op-code	Bytes	Cycles
Relative	&90	2	3 or 2

| **BCS** | Branch if C=1 | Flags unaltered |

Address mode	Op-code	Bytes	Cycles
Relative	&B0	2	3 or 2

| **BEQ** | Branch if Z=1 | Flags unaltered |

Address mode	Op-code	Bytes	Cycles
Relative	&F0	2	3 or 2

| **BIT** | A and M, M7→N, M6→V | Z,N,V |

Address mode	Op-code	Bytes	Cycles
Zero-page	&24	2	3
Absolute	&2C	3	4

| **BMI** | Branch if N=1 | Flags unaltered |

Address mode	Op-code	Bytes	Cycles
Relative	&30	2	3 or 2

6502 Complete Instruction Set

BNE	Branch if Z=0	Flags unaltered

Address mode	Op-code	Bytes	Cycles
Relative	&D0	2	3 or 2

BPL	Branch if N=0	Flags unaltered

Address mode	Op-code	Bytes	Cycles
Relative	&10	2	3 or 2

BRK	Break	PC+2	I flag=1

Address mode	Op-code	Bytes	Cycles
Implied	&00	1	7

BVC	Branch if V=0	Flags unaltered

Address mode	Op-code	Bytes	Cycles
Relative	&50	2	3 or 2

BVS	Branch if V=1	Flags unaltered

Address mode	Op-code	Bytes	Cycles
Relative	&70	2	3 or 2

CLC	Clear Carry	C flag=0

Address mode	Op-code	Bytes	Cycles
Implied	&18	1	2

CLD	Clear Decimal	D flag=0

Address mode	Op-code	Bytes	Cycles
Implied	&D8	1	2

| CLI | Clear I mask | I flag=0 |

Address mode	Op-code	Bytes	Cycles
Implied	&58	1	2

| CLV | Clear overflow | V flag=0 |

Address mode	Op-code	Bytes	Cycles
Implied	&B8	1	2

| CMP | Compare A | A-M | NZC |

Address mode	Op-code	Bytes	Cycles
Immediate	&C9	2	2
Zero-page	&C5	2	3
Zero-page,X	&D5	2	4
Absolute	&CD	3	4
Absolute,X	&DD	3	4 or 5
Absolute,Y	&D9	3	4 or 5
(Indirect,X)	&C1	2	6
(Indirect),Y	&D1	2	5 or 6

| CPX | Compare X | X-M | NZC |

Address mode	Op-code	Bytes	Cycles
Immediate	&E0	2	2
Zero-page	&E4	2	3
Absolute	&EC	3	4

| CPY | Compare Y | Y-M | NZC |

Address mode	Op-code	Bytes	Cycles
Immediate	&C0	2	2
Zero-page	&C4	2	3
Absolute	&CC	3	4

6502 Complete Instruction Set

| **DEC** | Decrement M | M−1→M | | NZ |

Address mode	Op-code	Bytes	Cycles
Zero-page	&C6	2	5
Zero-page,X	&D6	2	6
Absolute	&CE	3	6
Absolute,X	&DE	3	7

| **DEX** | Decrement X | X−1→X | | NZ |

Address mode	Op-code	Bytes	Cycles
Implied	&CA	1	2

| **DEY** | Decrement Y | Y−1→Y | | NZ |

Address mode	Op-code	Bytes	Cycles
Implied	&88	1	2

| **EOR** | Exclusive-OR | A exc M→A | | NZ |

Address mode	Op-code	Bytes	Cycles
Immediate	&49	2	2
Zero-page	&45	2	3
Zero-page,X	&55	2	4
Absolute	&4D	3	4
Absolute,X	&5D	3	4 or 5
Absolute,Y	&59	3	4 or 5
(Indirect,X)	&41	2	6
(Indirect),Y	&51	2	5

| **INC** | Increment M | M+1→M | | NZ |

Address mode	Op-code	Bytes	Cycles
Zero-page	&E6	2	5
Zero-page,X	&F6	2	6
Absolute	&EE	3	6
Absolute,X	&FE	3	7

INX	Increment X	X+1→X	NZ

Address mode	Op-code	Bytes	Cycles
Implied	&E8	1	2

INY	Increment Y	Y+1→Y	NZ

Address mode	Op-code	Bytes	Cycles
Implied	&C8	1	2

JMP	Jump	Flags unaltered	

Address mode	Op-code	Bytes	Cycles
Absolute	&4C	3	3
Indirect	&6C	3	5

JSR	Jump to SR	Flags unaltered	

Address mode	Op-code	Bytes	Cycles
Absolute	&20	3	6

LDA	Load A	M→A	NZ

Address mode	Op-code	Bytes	Cycles
Immediate	&A9	2	2
Zero-page	&A5	2	3
Zero-page,X	&B5	2	4
Absolute	&AD	3	4
Absolute,X	&BD	3	4 or 5
Absolute,Y	&B9	3	4 or 5
(Indirect,X)	&A1	2	6
(Indirect),Y	&B1	2	5 or 6

LDX	Load X	M→X	NZ

Address mode	Op-code	Bytes	Cycles
Immediate	&A2	2	2
Zero-page	&A6	2	3
Zero-page,Y	&B6	2	4
Absolute	&AE	3	4
Absolute,Y	&BE	3	4 or 5

LDY	Load Y	M→Y	NZ

Address mode	Op-code	Bytes	Cycles
Immediate	&A0	2	2
Zero-page	&A4	2	3
Zero-page,X	&B4	2	4
Absolute	&AC	3	4
Absolute,X	&BC	3	4 or 5

LSR	Logical SR	0→(7...0)→C	N−0,ZC

Address mode	Op-code	Bytes	Cycles
Accumulator	&4A	1	2
Zero-page	&46	2	5
Zero-page,X	&56	2	6
Absolute	&4E	3	6
Absolute,X	&5E	3	7

NOP	No operation	Flags unaltered

Address mode	Op-code	Bytes	Cycles
Implied	&EA	1	2

ORA	Inclusive OR	A or M→A	NZ

Address mode	Op-code	Bytes	Cycles
Immediate	&09	2	2
Zero-page	&05	2	3
Zero-page,X	&15	2	4
Absolute	&0D	3	4
Absolute,X	&1D	3	4 or 5
Absolute,Y	&19	3	4 or 5
(Indirect,X)	&01	2	6
(Indirect),Y	&11	2	5

PHA	Push A	Flags unaltered

Address mode	Op-code	Bytes	Cycles
Implied	&48	1	3

PHP	Push status	Flags unaltered

Address mode	Op-code	Bytes	Cycles
Implied	&08	1	3

PLA	Pull A	NZ

Address mode	Op-code	Bytes	Cycles
Immediate	&68	1	4

PLP	Pull status	Flags as status

Address mode	Op-code	Bytes	Cycles
Implied	&28	1	4

| **ROL** | Rotate L | ←(7...0)←C← | NZC |

Address mode	Op-code	Bytes	Cycles
Accumulator	&2A	1	2
Zero-page	&26	2	5
Zero-page,X	&36	2	6
Absolute	&2E	3	6
Absolute,X	&3E	3	7

| **ROR** | Rotate R | →C→(7...0)→ | NZC |

Address mode	Op-code	Bytes	Cycles
Accumulator	&6A	1	2
Zero-page	&66	2	5
Zero-page,X	&76	2	6
Absolute	&6E	3	6
Absolute,X	&7E	3	7

| **RTI** | Return from I | Flags as pulled |

Address mode	Op-code	Bytes	Cycles
Implied	&40	1	6

| **RTS** | Return from SR | Flags unaltered |

Address mode	Op-code	Bytes	Cycles
Implied	&60	1	6

| **SBC** | Subtract | A−M−C→A | NZCV |

Address mode	Op-code	Bytes	Cycles
Immediate	&E9	2	2
Zero-page	&E5	2	3
Zero-page,X	&F5	2	4
Absolute	&ED	3	4
Absolute,X	&FD	3	4 or 5
Absolute,Y	&F9	3	4 or 5
(Indirect,X)	&E1	2	6
(Indirect),Y	&F1	2	5 or 6

SEC	Set carry	C=1

Address mode	Op-code	Bytes	Cycles
Implied	&38	1	2

SED	Set decimal	D=1

Address mode	Op-code	Bytes	Cycles
Implied	&F8	1	2

SEI	Set I mask	I=1

Address mode	Op-code	Bytes	Cycles
Implied	&78	1	2

STA	Store A	A→M	Flags unaltered

Address mode	Op-code	Bytes	Cycles
Zero-page	&85	2	3
Zero-page,X	&95	2	4
Absolute	&8D	3	4
Absolute,X	&9D	3	5
Absolute,Y	&99	3	5
(Indirect,X)	&81	2	6
(Indirect),Y	&91	2	6

STX	Store X	X→M	Flags unaltered

Address mode	Op-code	Bytes	Cycles
Zero-page	&86	2	3
Zero-page,Y	&96	2	4
Absolute	&8E	3	4

| STY | Store Y | Y→M | Flags unaltered |

Address mode	Op-code	Bytes	Cycles
Zero-page	&84	2	3
Zero-page,X	&94	2	4
Absolute	&8C	3	4

| TAX | Transfer | A→X | NZ |

Address mode	Op-code	Bytes	Cycles
Implied	&AA	1	2

| TAY | Transfer | A→Y | NZ |

Address mode	Op-code	Bytes	Cycles
Implied	&A8	1	2

| TYA | Transfer | Y→A | NZ |

Address mode	Op-code	Bytes	Cycles
Implied	&98	1	2

| TSX | Transfer | SP→X | NZ |

Address mode	Op-code	Bytes	Cycles
Implied	&BA	1	2

| TXA | Transfer | X→A | NZ |

Address mode	Op-code	Bytes	Cycles
Implied	&8A	1	2

246 *Advanced Machine Code Techniques for The BBC Micro*

TXS	Transfer	X→SP	Flags unaltered

Address mode	Op-code	Bytes	Cycles
Implied	&9A	1	2

Appendix C2
6502 Instruction Set: Classification by processor flag

Updates N, Z and C flags:
ADC,ASL,CMP,CPX,CPY,ROL,ROR,SBC.

Updates N and Z flags:
AND,DEC,DEX,DEY,EOR,INC,INX,INY,LDA,
LDX,LDY,ORA,PLA,TAX,TAY,TYA,TSX,TXA.

Updates N, Z, C and V flags:
ADC,SBC.

Updates N, C and clears N:
LSR.

Op-codes not mentioned above either: (a) have no effect on processor flags or
(b) set or reset certain flags by direct programming
(CLC,CLD,CLI,CLV,SEC,SED,SEI).

Appendix C3
6502 Instruction Set: Classification by addressing modes

Immediate:
ADC,AND,CMP,CPX,CPY,EOR,LDA,LDX,LDY,ORA,SBC

Zero-page:
ADC,AND,ASL,BIT,CMP,CPX,CPY,DEC,EOR,INC,LDA,LDX,
LDY,LSR,ORA,ROL,ROR,SBC,STA,STX,STY

Zero-page, X:
ADC,AND,ASL,CMP,DEC,EOR,INC,LDA,LDY,LSR,ORA,ROL,
ROR,SBC,STA,STY

Absolute:
ADC,AND,ASL,BIT,CMP,CPX,CPY,DEC,EOR,INC,JMP,JSR,
LDA,LDX,LDY,LSR,ORA,ROL,SBC,STA,STX,STY

Absolute,X:
ADC,AND,ASL,CMP,DEC,EOR,INC,LDA,LSR,ORA,ROL,ROR,
SBC,STA

Absolute, Y:
ADC,AND,CMP,EOR,LDA,LDX,ORA,SBC,STA

(Indirect,X):
ADC,AND,CMP,EOR,LDA,ORA,SBC,STA

(Indirect),Y:
ADC,AND,CMP,EOR,LDA,ORA,SBC,STA

Accumulator:
ASL,LSR,ROL,ROR

Implied:
BRK,CLC,CLD,CLI,CLV,DEX,DEY,INX,INY,NOP,PHA,PHP,PLA,
PLP,RTI,RTS,SEC,SED,SEI,TAX,TAY,TSX,TXA,TXS,TYA

Relative:
BCC,BCS,BEQ,BMI,BNE,BPL,BVC,BVS

The following instructions have no effect on status flags:
BCC,BCS,BEQ,BMI,BNE,BPL,BVC,BVS,JMP,JSR,NOP,PHA,PHP,
RTS,STA,STX,STY,TXS

Appendix C4
6502 Instructions in order of common usage

In common use:
ADC BCC BCS BNE CLC CMP CPX CPY DEX DEY INX
INY LDA LDX LDY RTS
SBC SEC STA STX STY TAX TAY TYA TXA

Often used:
BEQ ASL BMI BPL DEC INC JMP JSR LSR PLA
PHA ROL ROR

Sometimes used:
AND BIT BRK BVC BVS CLV EOR NOP ORA

Seldom used:
CLD PHP PLP RTI SED SEI TSX TXS

The above classification must not be taken too seriously. It is very much a question of personal preference and programming style. It is doubtful if two writers would ever agree. However, it may still be useful, particularly if you are in the initial learning phase.

Appendix D
Glossary of Terms

absolute address: the numerical number identifying an address.

accumulator: the main register within the microprocessor and the only one equipped for arithmetic.

ACR: abbreviation for Auxiliary Control Register. One of the VIA registers.

active high: any input which requires a logic 1 to turn it on.

active low: any input which requires a logic 0 to turn it on.

address bus: the 16 lines from the microprocessor which activate the selected memory location or device.

address: a number which is associated with a particular memory location. This number can be in decimal or hexadecimal.

and gate: a gate which delivers a logic 1 out only if all inputs are logic 1.

anding: using a mask to ensure selected bits become or remain 0.

assembler mnemonics: a three-letter group uniquely defining an op code.

assembler: a program which converts a program written in assembly code to the equivalent machine code.

base address: the operand address of an indexed instruction.

base: the number of different characters used in a counting system. Decimal is base 10, binary is base 2 and hex is base 16.

bit: one of the two possible states of a binary counting system, 1 or 0.

block diagram: a simplified diagram of an electrical system using interconnected labelled boxes.

Boolean algebra: an algebraic notation, introduced by George Boole, for manipulating two-state logic.

bubble sort: sorting an array by pairs at a time until all data is in order.

bus: a collection of wires having some common purpose such as data bus, address bus and control bus.

byte: a group of 8 bits.

Centronics: trademark for a standardised parallel interface for printers.

chip: accepted slang for an integrated circuit.

compiler: system software which translates a program written in high level language into a machine code equivalent. The entire program is translated before it is run.

conditional assembly: when parts or all of the assembled code can vary depending on test conditions.

Darlington: a two-transistor configuration used to multiply the current gain.

data bus: the 8 lines from the microprocessor which carry the data to and from memory or external devices.

DDRB: abbreviation for Data Direction Register B. One of the VIA registers.

decimal: the normal counting system using the ten characters 0,1, ...9.

decoder: a logic device with many possible outputs, only one of which can be activated at a time. This depends on the logic pattern applied to the 'select' inputs.

direct addressing: the operand is a two-byte address as distinct from zero page addressing which is a single byte address. Also called absolute addressing.

disassembler: a program which will display a machine code program in assembly language. The opposite process to assembly.

effective address: the sum of the base and relative address.

exclusive or gate: a gate which delivers a logic 1 only if the inputs are at different logic states.

exclusive oring: using a mask to ensure that selected bits assume the opposite state.

firmware: programs already in ROM.

flag: a single bit used to indicate whether something has happened or not (see program status register).

handshaking: a term used to describe the method of synchronising an external device to the computer.

hardware: all the bits and pieces of a computer such as the chips, circuit board, keys, etc. That which you can see, feel and break.

hex: see *hexadecimal*.

hexadecimal: a counting system using sixteen characters 0,1,...9,A,B,C, D,E,F.

high byte: the most significant half of a two-byte number.

high-level language: a language written in the form of statements, each statement being equivalent to many machine code instructions. BASIC is a high level language.

IER: abbreviation for Interrupt Enable Register. One of the VIA registers.

IFR: abbreviation for Interrupt Flag Register. One of the VIA registers.

immediate addressing: the operand is the data itself rather than an address.

implicit address: see *implied address*.

implied address: an address which is inherent in the op-code, therefore requiring no following operand.

index register: either the X or Y register when used to modify an address.

indexed address: an address which has been formed by the addition of an index register's contents.

indexed indirect addressing: the indirect address is the sum of the operand and contents of Y.
indirect addressing: the operand refers to an address in page zero which is the address of the wanted data.
indirect indexed addressing: the indirect address is modified by the addition of Y.
instruction register: a register within the microprocessor holding the op-code during instruction decoding.
integer: a whole number without a fraction.
integrated circuit: a chip containing a number of interconnected circuits.
interpreter: system software which translates and executes each high level language statement separately. BASIC is normally interpreted although compiler versions exist.
IRB: abbreviation for Input Register B. One of the VIA registers.
latch: a buffer register which retains old data until new data is enabled.
logic gates: electrical circuits which behave as switches. The input conditions determine whether the switch is 'open' or 'closed'.
low byte: the least significant half of a two-byte number.
low-level language: a series of codes rather than a language, each line resulting in one order to the microprocessor.
lsb: the least significant bit in the byte (the right-most bit).
LSI: large scale integration. Normally taken to mean in the order of tens of thousands of circuits on a single chip. The 6502 microprocessor is LSI.
machine code: strictly, this term should be used for instructions written in binary; now used loosely to include hex coding and assembly language.
macro: a routine assembled in line each time it is called.
mask: a bit pattern used in conjunction with either AND, EOR or ORA to act on selected bits within a byte.
merge sort: similar to bubble sort but faster due to progressive halving of the array before sorting into pairs.
microprocessor: the integrated circuit which is the central processor or 'brain' of the computer. The BBC machine uses the 6502 species.
microprogram: a program inside the microprocessor which informs it how to carry out each machine code instruction.
mnemonics: code groups chosen so we can memorise them easily.
MOB: abbreviation for Moving OBject. Any screen object which is destined to be moved.
msb: the most significant bit in the byte (the leftmost bit).
msi: medium scale integration. Normally taken to mean up to a few hundred circuits on a single chip.
nibble: a group of 4 bits.
nybble: see *nibble*.
object code: the translated version of the source code.
one's complement: a number formed by changing the state of all bits in a register.

op-code: abbreviation for operational code. It is that part of a machine code instruction which tells the computer what kind of action is required.

operand: that part of a machine code instruction which gives the data or where to find the data.

operating system: the software already in ROM which is designed to help you use the computer.

or gate: a gate which delivers a logic out if any one or more inputs are logic 1.

ORB: abbreviation for Output Register B. One of the VIA registers.

oring: using a mask to ensure selected bits become or remain 1.

OSBYTE: keyword for Operating System Byte. Allows machine code calls to the operating system.

OSRDCH: keyword for Operating System Read Character. A subroutine for reading a character from selected input systems.

OSWORD: keyword for Operating System Word. Similar to OSBYTE but allows more parameters to be passed.

OSWRCH: keyword for Operating System Write Character. Passes character to selected output system.

page one address: any address within the range 256 to 511 decimal or 0100 to 01FF hex.

PC: see *program counter.*

PCR: abbreviation for Peripheral Control Register. One of the VIA registers.

PIA: abbreviation for the 6820 Peripheral Interface Adaptor.

pixel: a small picture element.

program counter: the only 16-bit register in the 6502. Contains the address of the next instruction byte.

program status register: a register containing flag bits which indicate if overflow, carries, etc. have been caused by the previous instruction.

PSR: see *program status register.*

read: to examine the existing data in a register or memory location, usually by means of LDA,LDX or LDY.

relative address: the contents of the index register.

resident assembler: an assembler which is already in ROM when you purchase the machine.

resident subroutines: those in ROM which you can use, providing you know their starting address.

ROM: abbreviation for Read Only Memory. Information stored is permanent even when the power supply is off.

rotate: similar to shift but any bit pushed out from the carry is reinserted at the other end.

rpn: abbreviation for 'reverse Polish notation', which is concerned with the order in which numeric variables are processed by a machine.

RS423: a standardised interface which passes data serially along a single line.

Glossary of Terms 253

scrolling: movement of the screen vertically or horizontally in order to bring fresh data into view.

shift: to move the bit pattern, one place to the left or right.

signed binary: the binary system which uses the msb as a sign bit.

silicon chip: most chips are fabricated from a silicon base although some of the super-fast modern varieties may be using a mixture of gallium and arsenic.

software: general term for all programs.

source code: the program in its high level form.

sprite: a screen object destined to be moved, together with accompanying coordinate data. Similar to MOB.

SR: abbreviation for Shift Register.

ssi: small scale integration. Normally taken to mean a few circuits, often simple logic gates, on a single chip.

subroutine: a program segment which will normally have general-purpose use and which can be used in other programs.

supply rail: a wire, feeding several components with a specific voltage.

symbolic address: an arbitrarily chosen name used in place of the numerical address. It is only recognised if it has been previously assigned to this number.

tristate: logic devices which can be either in the HIGH, LOW or open circuit state. When in the open circuit state, the output of the device is transparent to a common bus line.

TTL: abbreviation for Transistor Transistor Logic, a family of compatible logic chips operating on 5 volts. First launched by Texas Instruments but soon second-sourced by other manufacturers.

two-pass assembly: passing the source code twice through the assembler. Essential if branches are to forward addresses.

two's complement: a number formed by adding 1 to the one's complement. Used for negative number representation.

unsigned integer: a binary number without using the msb as a sign bit.

user port: one of the output sockets which can be used to control your own special devices.

user subroutines: subroutines which you can make for yourself.

vector: a word in memory containing the address of an operating system routine.

VIA: abbreviation for the 6522 Versatile Interface Adaptor chip.

volatile memory: one which loses all data when power is interrupted.

write: to place new data into a register or memory location, usually by means of STA,STX or STY. The old data is overwritten by the new.

X register: a general-purpose register which can be used in indexed addressing.

Y register: similar to X register.

zero page address: any address within the range 0 to 255 decimal or 00 to FF hex.

Answers to Self Test Questions

Chapter One

1.1 FF.
1.2 Because the delay caused by the electronics, even when using serial transmission, is negligible in relation to the printer mechanics.
1.3 The transmission cable can be much longer.
1.4 General term is 'transducer'.
1.5 1.8 volts.
1.6 FF.
1.7 FC=FRED.FD=JIM.FE=SHEILA.
1.8 The 'B' side.
1.9 Key *HELP.
1.10 SEI.
1.11 8 for ASCII and 2 for START/STOP.
1.12 0.6 volts.
1.13 Any address within the range FC03 to FCE3.
1.14 0.63 volts.
1.15 Same as before, 4F. It doesn't change until the next clock pulse arrives.
1.16 The bar negates the logic. For example, NOT A can be written as $\overline{A}$.
1.17 Chip enable.
1.18 63.
1.19 FCFF is the paging register in the FRED band, used for supplying the JIM page address.
1.20 Resident peripheral interfaces.
1.21 The 1 MHz bus.
1.22 Primarily reserved for extra ROM/RAM.

Chapter Two

2.1 Dynamic (DRAMs).
2.2 Expensive and lower packing density.

Answers to Self Test Questions 255

- **2.3** Each peripheral is activated by a specific address (or addresses), rather than by a special op-code.
- **2.4** By special op-code in the instruction set.
- **2.5** It supports the true arithmetical operations, addition and subtraction. Many of the instructions only perform on the accumulator.
- **2.6** &2D03.
- **2.7** Each bit is an independent flag.
- **2.8** D,I and C.
- **2.9** D,I.
- **2.10** N,V,B and Z.
- **2.11** When working in unsigned binary.
- **2.12** It is activated by bit 6 of the data during the BIT test.
- **2.13** The last instruction left non-zero data.
- **2.14** The C bit.
- **2.15** Page 1 or RAM.
- **2.16** Via the X register, using TXS.
- **2.17** Before.
- **2.18** C.
- **2.19** High-byte.
- **2.20** The program counter.
- **2.21** The next higher address.
- **2.22** R/W (sometimes written R/NW).
- **2.23** Fixed by the microprocessor designers.
- **2.24** The Instruction Register, IR.
- **2.25** If by software BRK, the B bit is set in the status register.
- **2.26** The 8080.

Chapter Three

- **3.1** STA memory.
  ASL A.
  ADC memory.
- **3.2** AND #&DF.
- **3.3** EOR #&48.
- **3.4** ORA #&04.
- **3.5** &EE.
- **3.6** Double-byte operand not allowed in immediate addressing.
- **3.7** Program counter.
- **3.8** 112 to 143 inclusive.
- **3.9** &11.
- **3.10** JMP.
- **3.11** X register.
- **3.12** Indirect indexed.
- **3.13** &74.

256 *Advanced Machine Code Techniques for The BBC Micro*

3.14 &79.
3.15 Post-indexed indirect.

Chapter Four

4.1 Full-stop between BNE and Label is wrong.
4.2 OPT.
4.3 3.
4.4 No, because &83 is a negative relative address.
4.5 (a) 02 (b) 04 (c) 05.
4.6 (a) 56 (b) 12.
4.7 PRINT ~!34587.

Chapter Five

5.1 0000 0011.
5.2 0000 1001.
5.3 &FF.
5.4 2000 million.
5.5 No.

Chapter Six

6.1 Wordlength, clock frequency, instruction repertoire, operating system and language interpreter.

No formal answers are applicable to tests 6.2 to 6.5, 7.1 to 7.5 and 8.1 to 8.4.

Chapter Nine

9.1 &FE6D.
9.2 &FE69.
9.3 &DF.
9.4 CB1.
9.5 Bit 4 and bit 7 in the IER must be set and the I-bit in the process status register must be reset.
9.6 Set bit 1 in the ACR.

Index

6502 microprocessor 33
6502 vectors 44
a/d conversion 11
absolute addressing 63
absolute indexed addressing 66
accumulator 37
active levels 221
address bus 19
address coordinates 179
address decoding 23
address modification 38
address pointer 69
address register 45
addressing modes 62
ALU 47
application note 1, 22
arithmetic instructions 56
array variable storage 114
ASIA 11
assembler 77

bank switching 6
benchmarks 33
binary 215
binary coded decimal 217
branch labels 79
bubble 21
bubble sorts 114
buffer registers 233

calling 84
chip enable 19
clearing registers 57
clock 20
code efficiency 218
comparisons 61
composite video 5
conditional assembly 89
control lines 19
current page 28

data bus 19
data transfers 37
decode matrix 47
decoders 231
demultiplexers 231
direct screen 173
direction register 197
double-byte working 101

encoders 232
execute phase 44
external interrupts 212

fetch phase 44
fixed-length records 144
fixed locations 82
flip flops 223
floating point array storage 139
floating point merge sorts 138
forward branching 85
four-byte addition 103
four-byte subtraction 105
Fred address 16

generations 2
glossary 249

hardware scrolling 185
hex op-code 54
hexadecimal 216

immediate addressing 62
implied addressing 62
indexed addressing 66
indexed indirect addressing 72
indexing 38
indirect addressing 68
indirect indexed addressing 70
indirection operators 97
instruction register 44

Index 258

instruction set 235
instructions 52
integer array addition 108
internal interrupts 210
interrupt 8
interrupt enable register 204
interrupt flag register 202
interrupt mask 9

Jim 28

LEDs 227
logic gates 219
logic levels 218
lsi 2

macros 87
memory mapping 14
merge sorts 126
microprograms 45
mnemonic op-codes 78
moving objects 169
multi-byte counting 106
multi-colour MOBs 177
multifield sorts 143
multiplexers 232

nibble 173

one's complement 59
operand 52
operand variables 78
operating system calls 234
operation symbols 54
opto-isolator 228

page boundary 29
paging register 30
parameter passing 90
pixel 173
power pack 5
process status register 39
program counter 42
PROM programmers 7
pseudo-variables 82

read/write 20

refreshing 34
relative addressing 65
relays 227
remarks 80
reset line 20
Reverse Polish 37
ROM chips 6
RS423 10

saving code 98
schmitt trigger 229
screen output 5
second processor 3
Sheila addresses 14
shift registers 232
sideways scrolling 185
Silicon Valley 2
software interrupt 48
sorting times 154
stack pointer 41
static RAM 35
storing code 80
string bubble sort 120
switch bounce 226

timers 205
tristate 225
TTL 2
two's complement 59
two-dimensional sorts 148

UHF 5
UHF modulator 5
up/down counting 57
user port 7

VDU codes 162
vectors 158
vertical scrolling 190
VIA 7
VIA registers 195

wired-OR 225
word length 3

zero-page addressing 64